Frommer's®

P9-AFL-633

Edinburgh & Glasgow
day BY day™
1st Edition

by Barry Shelby

WILEY

Wiley Publishing, Inc.

Contents

Published by:

Wiley Publishing, Inc.

111 River St.
Hoboken, NJ 07030-5774

ISBN 978-0-470-24762-4

Editor: Naomi P. Kraus
Production Editor: Jonathan Scott
Photo Editor: Richard Fox, with Photo Affairs, Inc.
Cartographer: Andrew Murphy
Production by Wiley Indianapolis Composition Services

For information on our other products and services or to obtain technical support, please contact our Customer Care Department within the U.S. at 800/762-2974, outside the U.S. at 317/572-3993 or fax 317/572-4002.

Wiley also publishes its books in a variety of electronic formats. Some content that appears in print may not be available in electronic formats.

Manufactured in China

5   4   3   2   1

A Note from the Publisher

Organizing your time. That's what this guide is all about.

Other guides give you long lists of things to see and do and then expect you to fit the pieces together. The Day by Day guides are different. These guides tell you the best of everything, and then they show you how to see it *in the smartest, most time-efficient way*. Our authors have designed detailed itineraries organized by time, neighborhood, or special interest. And each tour comes with a bulleted map that takes you from stop to stop.

Hoping to see the architectural legacy left behind by Robert Adam and Charles Rennie Mackintosh, tee off on the Old Course at St. Andrews, or tour Edinburgh's many free museums? Planning a drive through The Borders, or a tour of the Trossachs and Loch Lomond? Whatever your interest or schedule, the Day by Days give you the smartest routes to follow. Not only do we take you to the top attractions, hotels, and restaurants, but we also help you access those special moments that locals get to experience—those "finds" that turn tourists into travelers.

The Day by Days are also your top choice if you're looking for one complete guide for all your travel needs. The best hotels and restaurants for every budget, the greatest shopping values, the wildest nightlife—it's all here.

Why should you trust our judgment? Because our authors personally visit each place they write about. They're an independent lot who say what they think and would never include places they wouldn't recommend to their best friends. They're also open to suggestions from readers. If you'd like to contact them, please send your comments my way at mspring@wiley.com, and I'll pass them on.

Enjoy your Day by Day guide—the most helpful travel companion you can buy. And have the trip of a lifetime.

Warm regards,

Michael Spring,
Publisher
Frommer's Travel Guides

About the Author

Barry Shelby is a freelance writer, editor, and aspiring *flaneur*. Born in Berkeley, California (and later graduating from the University of California, Berkeley), he earned a master's degree at Northwestern University in the 1980s. For 13 years, he was a journalist at *World Press Review* magazine in New York City. Since moving to Scotland in 1997, he has written numerous articles and reviews for publications such as the *Guardian*, *The List*, and Glasgow's *Herald*. He is also the author of *100 Classic Cocktails* and *Frommer's Edinburgh & Glasgow*, as well as *Scotland For Dummies*. He resides in Glasgow with his wife, a dog, one cat, and two hens.

Acknowledgments

Thanks to my editor, Naomi Kraus, for her forbearance and encouragement.

An Additional Note

Please be advised that travel information is subject to change at any time—and this is especially true of prices. We therefore suggest that you write or call ahead for confirmation when making your travel plans. The authors, editors, and publisher cannot be held responsible for the experiences of readers while traveling. Your safety is important to us, however, so we encourage you to stay alert and be aware of your surroundings.

Star Ratings, Icons & Abbreviations

Every hotel, restaurant, and attraction listing in this guide has been ranked for quality, value, service, amenities, and special features using a **star-rating system.** Hotels, restaurants, attractions, shopping, and nightlife are rated on a scale of zero stars (recommended) to three stars (exceptional). In addition to the star-rating system, we also use a **kids icon** to point out the best bets for families. Within each tour, we recommend cafes, bars, or restaurants where you can take a break. Each of these stops appears in a shaded box marked with a coffee-cup-shaped bullet 💭 .

The following **abbreviations** are used for credit cards:

AE	American Express	DISC	Discover	V	Visa
DC	Diners Club	MC	MasterCard		

Frommers.com

Now that you have this guidebook to help you plan a great trip, visit our website at **www.frommers.com** for additional travel information on more than 4,000 destinations. We update features regularly to give you instant access to the most current trip-planning information available. At Frommers.com, you'll find scoops on the best airfares, lodging rates, and car rental bargains. You can even book your travel online through our reliable travel booking partners. Other popular features include:

A Note on Prices

In the "Take a Break" and "Best Bets" sections of this book, we have used a system of dollar signs to show a range of costs for 1 night in a hotel (the price of a double-occupancy room) or the cost of an entree at a restaurant. Use the following table to decipher the dollar signs:

Cost	Hotels	Restaurants
$	under $125	under $15
$$	$125–$300	$15–$30
$$$	$300–$450	$30–$45
$$$$	$450–$600	$45–$60
$$$$$	over $600	over $60

An Invitation to the Reader

In researching this book, we discovered many wonderful places—hotels, restaurants, shops, and more. We're sure you'll find others. Please tell us about them, so we can share the information with your fellow travelers in upcoming editions. If you were disappointed with a recommendation, we'd love to know that, too. Please write to:

Frommer's Edinburgh & Glasgow Day by Day, 1st Edition
Wiley Publishing, Inc. • 111 River St. • Hoboken, NJ 07030-5774

16 Favorite
Moments

16 Favorite **Moments**

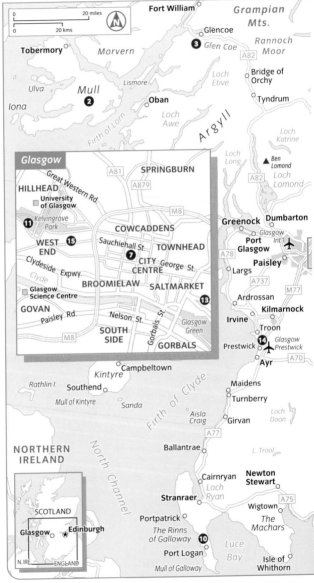

| 0 | 20 miles |
| 0 | 20 kms |

Fort William

Grampian Mts.

Glencoe
3 *Glen Coe*
Rannoch Moor
A82

Tobermory
Morvern
Bridge of Orchy

Ulva
Lismore
Tyndrum

Iona
Mull
2
Oban
Loch Etive

Firth of Lorn
Loch Awe
A r g y l l

Loch Katrine

Loch Long
▲ Ben Lomond

Glasgow

Great Western Rd.
A81
SPRINGBURN
A879
Loch Lomond
A82

HILLHEAD
University of Glasgow
M8

Kelvingrove Park
11
COWCADDENS
Greenock **Dumbarton**

WEST END
15
Sauchiehall St.
TOWNHEAD
○ *Glasgow Int'l*

Clydeside Expwy.
7
CITY CENTRE
George St.
Port Glasgow
A78
Paisley

Clyde
Glasgow Science Centre
BROOMIELAW
SALTMARKET
○ Largs
A737
M77

GOVAN
Paisley Rd.
13
Ardrossan
Kilmarnock

M8
Nelson St.
Gorbals St.
Glasgow Green
Irvine
○ Troon

SOUTH SIDE
GORBALS
Prestwick ○
14
✈ *Glasgow Prestwick*

○ **Campbeltown**
Ayr
A70

Kintyre
Maidens
○

Rathlin I.
Southend ○
○ Turnberry

Mull of Kintyre
Sanda
Aisla Craig
○ Girvan
Loch Doon

A77

NORTHERN IRELAND
Ballantrae ○
L. Trool

North Channel
Cairnryan
Newton Stewart
○

Loch Ryan
Stranraer ○
Wigtown
○
A75

Portpatrick ○
The Machars

SCOTLAND
The Rinns of Galloway
10
Luce Bay

Glasgow ○
★ **Edinburgh**
Port Logan ○
Isle of Whithorn
○

N. IRE.
ENGLAND
Mull of Galloway

Previous Page: Scenic lochs, like this one in the Trossachs, are just some of the examples of breathtaking natural beauty you'll find in Scotland.

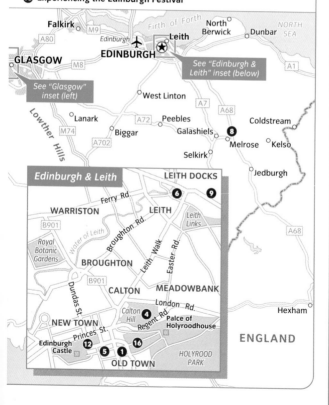

Edinburgh's Old Town, with its dramatic castle perched high on a hill, and the city's 18th-century New Town are highlights of any trip to Scotland. But while the capital of Scotland offers memorable tourist destinations, there is more to the country than one city. Much more—from the cosmopolitan city of Glasgow less than 50 miles (80km) west of Edinburgh, to the majestic ruins of abbeys and castles in the south, to Scotland's dramatic coastlines, charming villages, and unspoilt islands. Here are some of my favorite experiences.

1 Strolling through the Old Town in Edinburgh. The historic core of this ancient city is a UNESCO World Heritage site, with intriguing alleys and passageways (lose yourself in them!) branching off it, like ribs from a spine. It's probably the most visited place in Scotland—and with good reason. Be sure to take in the Royal Mile, Scotland's most famous road, which lies at the heart of Edinburgh, linking Edinburgh castle to the Palace of Holyroodhouse. *See p 9,* **3**.

2 Setting sail to an island. Scotland offers literally hundreds of islands to explore. One of my all-time favorite islands is Mull, a gem that's home to historic attractions, wildlife, and some excellent natural scenery. The ferry rides to Mull and the other Scottish islands are half the fun, and island visits are always relaxing and quiet, and offer loads of local color, too. *See p 195,* **5**.

3 Seeing a bit of the Highlands. I could devote an entire guide to the delights of the Scottish Highlands, and it can take weeks to see the entire region. Luckily, sampling a mere taste of the Highlands will enrich your vacation. If you're time-limited, head for Glencoe, a lovely valley with lots of natural beauty—and some rather violent history. *See p 196,* **8**.

4 Climbing one of Edinburgh's hills. Calton Hill, on the edge of Edinburgh's New Town, was author Robert Louis Stevenson's favorite vantage point for overlooking the city. You'll probably agree if you make the climb yourself. For the best (and highest) views, scale Arthur's Seat. *See p 9,* **2***, and p 56.*

5 Sampling a dram of whisky. Don't leave Scotland without sampling the local "water of life." Royal

Glencoe's natural beauty belies a bloody history.

The Nelson Monument on Edinburgh's Calton Hill.

Mile Whiskies on Edinburgh's Royal Mile is the best shop for Scotland's classic single malt whiskies, while in Glasgow the best pub for downing a dram (shot) or two is the Pot Still. *See p 54 and p 149.*

6 **Feasting on fine foods.** Scotland's natural larder includes some world-class food, including wild salmon, hand-dived scallops, Aberdeen Angus, blackface lamb, and heather honey. And the country's best restaurants, such as Restaurant Martin Wishart in Leith, know how to prepare it, too. *See p 72.*

7 **Marveling at Glasgow's architecture.** Home to some of the best Victorian buildings in the world, Glasgow arguably deserves to be a UNESCO-approved city of architecture and design. Two of its most prolific architects were the great Charles Rennie Mackintosh and his lesser-known but no less talented precursor, Alexander "Greek" Thomson. *See p 118.*

8 **Exploring castles and abbeys.** The ruins of grand abbeys and stout castles, particularly in the Borders and Galloway regions, remain impressive sights, as well as poignant reminders of the proud, turbulent history of Scotland. The Gothic design of Melrose Abbey, the final resting place of several Scottish kings, so moved Sir Walter Scott, he wrote of it, "If thou would'st view fair Melrose alright, go visit in the pale moonlight." *See p 162,* **2**.

9 **Going to the pub.** What better way to see and meet Scottish folk than to raise a pint or sip a dram with them at a local pub? None that I know of. Try a real hand-pulled Scottish ale, such as Deuchars IPA. At some spots, such as the Shore in Leith, you might be treated to a bit of live music, too. *See p 83.*

10 **Visiting magnificent gardens.** Thanks to the mild influences of the Gulf Stream and North Atlantic drift washing over Scotland's western shores, the country is home to a wealth of plants. Logan Botanic Garden in the Galloway is the best for seeing the range of flora that grows here. *See p 165,* **11**.

11 **Admiring the art.** Edinburgh is home to the Scottish National Gallery, whose collection ranges from Renaissance paintings to pop

MIld weather on the Galloway's western shore allows palm trees to grow in the Logan Botanic Garden.

St. Andrews is arguably the sport of golf's most hallowed ground.

art sculpture. Glasgow has one of the best municipal collections in Europe; the Burrell Collection is the overwhelming critical favorite, though the Kelvingrove Art Gallery & Museum is arguably the soul of the city's collection. Best of all, admission to all these options is free. *See p 18; p 111,* ❶; *and p 109* ❽.

⓬ **Digging into Scottish history.** Scotland is one of the oldest recognized countries in northern Europe and much of its rich history is exemplified in its capital, Edinburgh. To hit all of the significant spots, try my historic tour of the city. *See p 22.*

⓭ **Hearing live rock and roll.** Scotland has a host of burgeoning bands and live acts. Try catching the next KT Tunstall or Franz Ferdinand show at one of the hot venues in Glasgow. The best place in town is Barrowland, a rough-and-ready old ballroom. *See p 151.*

⓮ **Driving a golf ball.** Scotland is the unofficial home of the sport, so why not take a swing at one of the many links-style golf courses? Unless you're an expert (and ready for the hallowed courses of St. Andrews), try the Royal Troon Golf Club in Ayrshire. *See p 172,* ❺.

⓯ **Sauntering through Glasgow's West End.** Home to the city's oldest university, leafy avenues, and hilly Kelvingrove Park, this district is Glasgow's most desirable. To see all the area has to offer, try my West End Hike. *See p 124.*

⓰ **Experiencing the Edinburgh Festival.** The most popular entertainment at Scotland's biggest festival is found at the Fringe, which draws top comics and performance artists from around the world. During the day, the Royal Mile is full of free performances. *See p 91.* ●

You'll find many zany performances at the Edinburgh Festival Fringe.

1 The Best **Full-Day Tours**

The Best in **One Day**

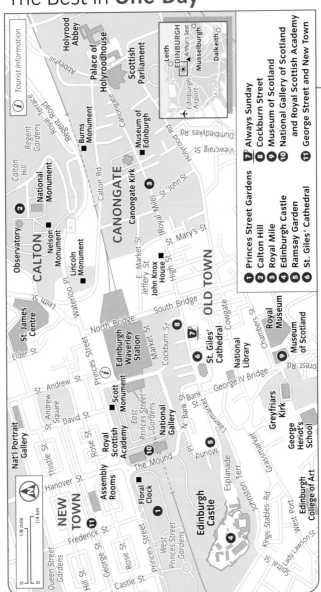

ⓘ *Tourist Information*

1 Princes Street Gardens
2 Calton Hill
3 Royal Mile
4 Edinburgh Castle
5 Ramsay Garden
6 St. Giles' Cathedral
7 Always Sunday
8 Cockburn Street
9 Museum of Scotland
10 National Gallery of Scotland and Royal Scottish Academy
11 George Street and New Town

Previous Page: A guard in ceremonial uniform patrols the grounds at Edinburgh Castle.

With only 1 day to spend in Scotland's capital city, you will have to be quite selective about the places you visit. This tour is packed with intriguing sites, and concentrates primarily on the historic heart of Edinburgh, the Old Town (where the city first began)—though it will introduce you to a bit of the New Town, the largest historical conservation area in Great Britain. START: **Princes St., at Waverley Bridge. Bus: 3, 10, 12, 17, 25, or 44.**

Iconic Edinburgh Castle offers some of the best views in the city.

❶ ★★ Princes Street Gardens. With Edinburgh Castle looming above, this is one of the most picturesque parks in Europe. In the early 19th century, this was a nasty sewage-filled loch. How times have changed. Today, the 15-hectare (37-acre) park is a great spot for a picnic . . . or you can join the locals and lounge on its grassy slopes on a nice day. ⏱ *45 min. Princes St. (at Waverley Bridge.)* ☎ *0131/529-4068. www.cac.org.uk. Admission free. Daily dawn–dusk.*

❷ ★★★ Calton Hill. Get an overview of the city, literally. Rising 106m (348 ft.), Calton Hill offers perhaps the best panoramic views of Edinburgh, and was Robert Louis Stevenson's favorite spot for gazing at the city. The hill also boasts a pair of noteworthy monuments. The first is the so-called National Monument, an unfinished replica of the Parthenon—meant to honor war

dead—that helped earn Edinburgh the name "Athens of the North." The Nelson Monument, in honor of Admiral Horatio Nelson, was built in the shape of an inverted telescope and visitors can climb to the top of it. Americans should find the Lincoln Memorial in the old Calton Burial Ground off Waterloo Place. ⏱ *1 hr. Waterloo Place., at the Royal High School. Nelson Monument open Mon–Sat. Tickets £3. Bus: x25.*

❸ ★★★ Royal Mile. This is the most famous street in Scotland; it runs east for about 1.6km (1 mile) from Edinburgh Castle down to the new Scottish Parliament building and the ancient Palace of Holyroodhouse. Walking is best way to experience this truly ancient road, which follows the crest of one of Edinburgh's many hills. Also take time to explore some of the narrow alleys that jut off the street, like ribs off a spine. Do note that the Royal Mile takes different names along its length: Castlehill, Lawnmarket, High Street, and finally Canongate. ⏱ *1–2 hr. High St., at North Bridge. Bus: 28.*

❹ ★ Edinburgh Castle. I'm not completely sold on the tour of this castle's interiors, the oldest bit of which (St. Margaret's Chapel) dates back to the 12th century. But even if you don't go inside, you should at least take a look at its ramparts and esplanade, located at the head of the Royal Mile. You'll get views in practically all directions, so have your camera ready. ⏱ *30 min. Castlehill. See p 23. Bus: 28.*

5 ★★ **Ramsay Garden.** While you're at the top end of the Royal Mile, I strongly encourage you to take time to admire the set of picturesque late-19th-century buildings known as Ramsay Garden (in honor of the poet Allan Ramsay, whose 18th-c. home was incorporated into the project). They are one of the landmarks perched on the edge of the ridge above Princes Street Gardens. The brainchild of Sir Patrick Geddes (1854–1932), a city planner and general polymath whose efforts helped to preserve the Old Town you see today, the complex is still used for private residences and, alas, tourists cannot get inside. ⏲ *15 min. Castlehill (northeast corner of the castle esplanade). Bus: 28.*

6 ★ **St. Giles' Cathedral.** The English burned this church, originally constructed in the 12th century and named for the patron saint of cripples, when they overran the city in 1385; most of the current

You'll be hard-pressed to see all of the Museum of Scotland's numerous historical exhibits in a single visit.

exterior of the church, also known as the High Kirk of St. Giles or St. Giles' parish church, is the result of Victorian renovations. On the sidewalk near the main entrance, make sure to note the heart-shaped arrangement of cobbles, which marks the site of the Old Tolbooth and a city jail—the latter referenced in Sir Walter Scott's history-filled novel *The Heart of Midlothian.* Spitting into it supposedly brings good luck. ⏲ *30 min. High St., at Parliament Sq. See p 24. Bus: 35.*

Ramsay Garden is a photogenic mix of Scottish baronial and English cottage architecture.

7 **Always Sunday** is a welcome break from the sometimes overly touristy competition on the Royal Mile. Come to this cafe for good and fresh home cooking in modern surroundings. *170 High St.* ☎ *0131/ 622-0667. www.alwayssunday.co.uk. $. Bus: 35.*

8 **Cockburn Street.** This "recent" addition to the Old Town cityscape was built in 1856. Curvy Cockburn Street cuts across older, extremely steep steps (such as those of the macabre-sounding Fleshmarket Close) that descend precipitously down the hill toward Waverley train station. There are some interesting shops (CDs, art books, gifts), as well as some pubs and restaurants on this winding road, originally designed to make it easier to get from Waverley railway station to Old Town. ⏱ *20 min. Between High St. & Market St. Bus: 35.*

⑨ ★★ Museum of Scotland. Opened in 1998, this impressive sandstone building contains exhibits outlining the story of Scotland, from its geology and ancient archaeology to royalty, technology, and science. On display are around 12,000 items, which range from 2.9-billion-year-old stones to a cute Hillman Imp, one of the last 500 automobiles manufactured in Scotland. The roof garden has more excellent views, while the Royal Museum, which has been incorporated into the newer building, includes a well-preserved and airy Victorian-era Main Hall and some 36 more galleries. ⏱ *2 hr. Chambers St.* ☎ *0131/247-4422. www.nms.ac.uk. Free admission. Daily 10am–5pm. Bus: 2, 7, 23, 31, 35, 41, or 42.*

⑩ ★★ National Gallery of Scotland and Royal Scottish Academy. Located on the Mound, a hump of earth that divides the valley of Princes Street Gardens (and which also forms a land bridge between the Old and New Towns), this complex of Victorian exhibition halls is home to the National Galleries of Scotland's core collection of art. It includes Renaissance, Impressionist, and key Scottish art. The National Gallery building, designed in 1850 by architect William Playfair (1790–1857), is today connected internally to the Royal Scottish Academy building, also by Playfair in 1825. They are classic examples of the Victorian

love affair with classical architecture. ⏱ *30 min.; more to view the art. The Mound. See p 27. Bus: 3, 10, 12, 17, 25, 28, 41, or 44.*

⑪ ★★ George Street and New Town. This broad boulevard is the central street of Edinburgh's New Town, devised during the reign of George III and constructed between 1766 and 1840. However "new" it was, that means this district is still older than the formation of the United States and is now a World Heritage Site. Notice how all the names of the main streets refer in some way to Hanoverian royalty, whether it be Frederick Street (George III's son) or Charlotte Street (George III's wife). Once the home of bankers and finance, George Street is now one of the hottest shopping strips in Edinburgh, as well as the avenue with the city's trendiest bars, flashy restaurants, and dressy nightclubs. ⏱ *1 hr. George St., at Frederick St. Bus: 13, 24, 36, 41, or 42.*

The National Gallery is home to a well-chosen collection that includes Old Masters, Impressionists, and key Scottish artists.

The Best in **Two Days**

1. Edinburgh Bus Tours
2. John Knox House
3. Palace of Holyroodhouse
4. Scottish Parliament
5. Our Dynamic Earth
6. Scottish National Portrait Gallery
7. Charlotte Square
8. Northern New Town
9. Anima
10. Stockbridge
11. Royal Botanic Garden
12. Leith

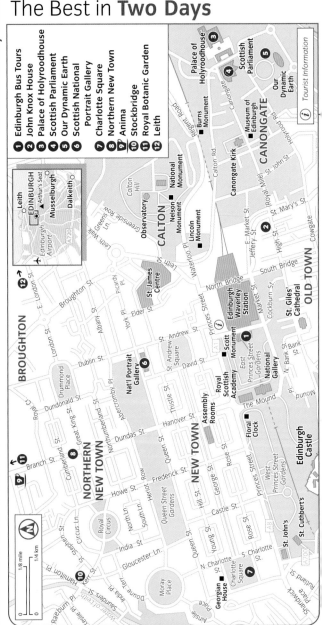

i Tourist Information

In 2 days, you can dig a bit deeper and see more of the nuances of Edinburgh, which is usually stuffed with tourists from Easter right through to end of September. With this tour you'll get a fuller picture of central Edinburgh, which is in fact fairly compact. Use buses to get across Old Town and New Town, but when the weather is fine (when there is only a drizzly rain or less), I suggest that you walk to many of the attractions on this tour and get a feel for the city. START: **Waverley Bridge. Bus: 10, 12, 17, 25, or 44.**

❶ ★ Edinburgh Bus Tours. For entertaining and informative tours that offer an overview of the city's principal attractions, these open-top buses cannot be beat. During the trip, you will see most of the major sights along the Royal Mile, and also get a gander at the Grassmarket, Princes Street, George Street, and more. The Majestic Tour buses—the ones that are blue and orange—don't take any longer, but deviate from the others' route, by seeing fewer central Edinburgh landmarks while including the port of Leith on its tour. ⏱ 1½ hr. *Waverley Bridge.* ☎ *0131/220-0770.* www.edinburgh tour.com. *Tickets £9 adults, £3 kids. Daily May–Oct every 15–20 min. 9:30am–5:30pm; Nov–Apr every 30 min. 9:45am–4pm.*

❷ John Knox House. This Royal Mile landmark (built in 1490) is difficult to miss, jutting out into the sidewalk on High Street. There is some doubt that Scotland's most famous reformation preacher, who was key to removing the Catholic Church as Scotland's official religious authority in the 16th century, ever actually lived here. But the photogenic building impresses nonetheless; especially noteworthy is its hand-painted ceiling. ⏱ *20 min. 43 High St. For visitor information see p 24.* Bus: 35 or 36.

❸ ★ Palace of Holyrood-house. "Rood" is the Scots word for cross, and King David I established the now ruined abbey at Holyrood in 1128. In the 16th century, James IV (1473–1513) started construction on a palatial residence for royalty off one side of the abbey, though what you see today dates more from the 17th century. A critical episode in the fraught reign of Mary Queen of Scots (1542–87) was played out at Holyrood: the assassination of her loyal assistant David Rizzio in 1566. The grounds include landscaped gardens and the Queen's Gallery, which exhibits bits of the royal art collection. ⏱ *1 hr. Canongate, bottom of the Royal Mile. See p 25, ❽.* Bus: 35.

The King's Bed Chamber in the Palace of Holyroodhouse.

The very modern garden lobby inside the Scottish Parliament.

❹ Scottish Parliament. After a right brouhaha over its cost (almost £500 million) and delays in construction, the new Scottish Parliament complex finally opened in autumn of 2004, 5 years after the first Scottish Parliament in 300 years was convened. Designed by the late Barcelona-based architect Enric Miralles, it's a remarkable, though controversial, bit of modern design. Take the tour if you're really interested in Scottish government and want to see more of the modern interiors. ⏱ *1 hr. Holyrood Rd., across from the Queen's Gallery.* ☎ *0131/348-5000. www.scottish.parliament. uk. Admission: guided tour £3.50 adult; £1.75 seniors, students & kids over 5. Open Tues–Thurs 9am–7pm (when Parliament is in session); Mon–Fri (when Parliament is in recess) Apr–Oct 10am–6pm, Nov–Mar (& Sat–Sun year-round) 10am–4pm. Bus: 35.*

❺ kids Our Dynamic Earth. Under a tentlike canopy, Our Dynamic Earth celebrates the evolution and diversity of the planet, with an emphasis on seismic and biological activity. Simulated earthquakes, meteor showers, and views of outer space are part of the display. Skies in a tropical rainforest darken every 15 minutes, offering torrents of rain

and creepy-crawlies underfoot. ⏱ *2 hr. Holyrood Rd.* ☎ *0131/550-7800. www.dynamicearth.co.uk. Admission £8.95 adults, £5.45 seniors & kids 5–15, £1.50 kids under 5. Daily July–Aug 10am–6pm; Apr–June & Sept–Oct 10am–5pm; Wed–Sun Nov–Mar 10am–5pm. Bus 35.*

❻ ★ Scottish National Portrait Gallery. Part of the National Galleries of Scotland (the Scottish national collection of art), this handsome red-stone Gothic-style museum was designed by architect Sir Robert Rowand Anderson (1834–1921). Inside you'll find many of the country's historic and current luminaries in portraiture—from Mary Queen of Scots to the 21st-century composer James MacMillan—done by everyone from Kokoschka to Raeburn. ⏱ *1 hr. 1 Queen St. See p 28,* ❻. *Bus: 4, 10, 12, 16, or 26.*

❼ ★ Charlotte Square. With a charming park at its core, this square—designed by Robert Adam—epitomizes the urbane grace of Edinburgh's New Town. You can almost imagine 18th-century horse-drawn carriages circumnavigating the place, with gaslights illuminating the sidewalks. You can tour the interiors of two properties on the square: no. 28 on the south side (home of the Scottish National Trust); and the so-called Georgian House on the

Our Dynamic Earth is home to a number of climate simulations, including one of a polar region.

opposite side of the square (see p 39). ⏱ *30 min. George St., at S. Charlotte St. National Trust drawing room Mon–Fri 11am–3pm. Free admission. Bus: 19, 36, or 41.*

❽ ★ Northern New Town.

Once Edinburgh's first New Town development was finished, proving exceptionally popular, work began north of Queen Street Gardens on a second model city. Architects William Sibbald (d. 1809) and Robert Reid (1775–1856) were the key designers in 1801, and used a grid pattern of streets, punctuated by "circuses"— round arcs of handsome town houses. At the northern edge of the development is Canonmills, so named for the milling community that served the abbey at Holyrood. ⏱ *45 min. Between Dublin St. & Royal Circus. Bus: 13, 24, 27, or 42.*

❾ Anima is a pizza parlor and cafe (everything's available to go) that aims to offer "Italian soul food." However humble this operation looks, it offers an extensive wine list to complement the cuisine. *11 Henderson Row. ☎ 0131/558-2918. www. anima-online.co.uk. $. Bus: 23 or 27.*

❿ ★★ Stockbridge.

No matter how bustling Edinburgh gets during the tourist high season, this neighborhood just northwest of the city center almost always offers a slower, calmer pace. Once a hippie enclave, and still possessing bohemian vibes, Stockbridge is now one of the more affluent and desirable districts in which to live and play. When I visit, I like simply to stroll around, look at the shops, and perhaps visit a cafe or pub, such as the Bailie Bar (see p 39). ⏱ *45 min. Kerr St., at Hamilton Place. Bus: 24, 29, or 42.*

⓫ ★★ Royal Botanic Garden.

This is one of the grandest parks in all

The city's first botanical garden, the Royal Botanic Garden, is one of the best in all the U.K.

of Great Britain—and that's no modest boast given all the impressive gardens in the U.K. Sprawling across some 28 hectares (69 acres), Edinburgh's first botanic was inaugurated in the late 17th century as a place for studying plants with medical uses. In spring, the various rhododendrons are almost reason alone to visit here, but the plantings in all areas ensure year-round interest. *20A Inverleith Row. ☎ 0131/552-7171. www.rbge. org.uk. Free admission (donations accepted). Daily Apr–Sept 10am–7pm; Mar & Oct–Dec 10am–6pm; Jan–Feb 10am–4pm. Bus: 8, 17, 23, or 27.*

⓬ ★ Leith.

The Port of Leith is only a few kilometers north of the city center. The area is rapidly gentrifying, losing some of its historic character as a rough-and-tumble maritime community. Still, you can use a bit of your imagination while wandering about the old docks near the Shore, the street that follows the Water of Leith as it spills into the harbor. One big attraction of Leith is its pubs—and its restaurants, three of which have Michelin stars. ⏱ *1–2 hr. The Shore, at Bernard St. For a walking tour, see p 42. Bus: 7, 10, 16, 22, 35, or 36.*

The Best in **Three Days**

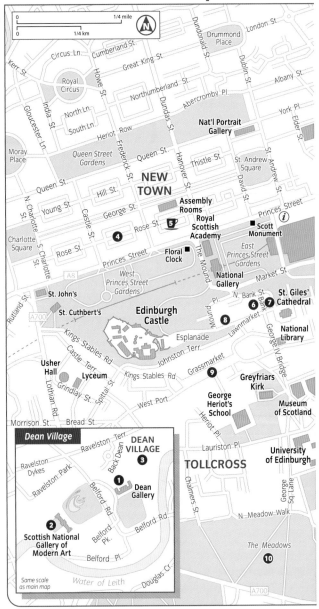

0   1/4 mile
0   1/4 km

Circus Ln.   Cumberland St.   Dundonald St.   Drummond Place   London St.

Kerr St.   Great King St.   Dublin St.   Albany St.

Royal Circus   Howe St.   Northumberland St.   York Pl.

India St.   North Ln.   Abercromby Pl.   Elder St.

Gloucester Ln.   South Ln.   Heriot Row   Nat'l Portrait Gallery

Moray Place   Queen Street Gardens   Queen St.   Thistle St.   St. Andrew Square

N. Charlotte St.   Queen St.   Hill St.   **NEW TOWN**

Young St.   George St.   David St.

Charlotte Square   Castle St.   Rose St.   ❺   Assembly Rooms   Royal Scottish Academy   Princes Street   ℹ

S. Charlotte St.   ❹   Rose St.   Scott Monument

Princes Street   Floral Clock ■   East Princes Street Gardens

Rutland St.   West Princes Street Gardens   National Gallery   Market St.   St. Giles' Cathedral

St. John's   N. Bank St.   ❻❼

St. Cuthbert's   Edinburgh Castle   Mound   ❽   National Library

Kings Stables Rd   Esplanade   Lawnmarket   George IV Bridge

Castle Terr.   Johnston Terr.

Usher Hall   Lyceum   Kings Stables Rd.   Grassmarket   ❾   Greyfriars Kirk

Grindlay St.   Spittal St.   West Port   George Heriot's School   Museum of Scotland

Lothian Rd.   Morrison St.   Bread St.   Heriot Pl.

Lauriston Pl.   University of Edinburgh

Dean Village

Ravelston Terr.   **DEAN VILLAGE**   ❸   **TOLLCROSS**

Ravelston Dykes   Back Dean   Chalmers St.   George Sq. Lane

Ravelston Park   Belford Rd.   ❶   Dean Gallery

❷   Belford Pk.   Belford Rd.   N. Meadow Walk

Scottish National Gallery of Modern Art   Belford Pl.

Same scale as main map   Water of Leith   Douglas Cr.   The Meadows   ❿

A700

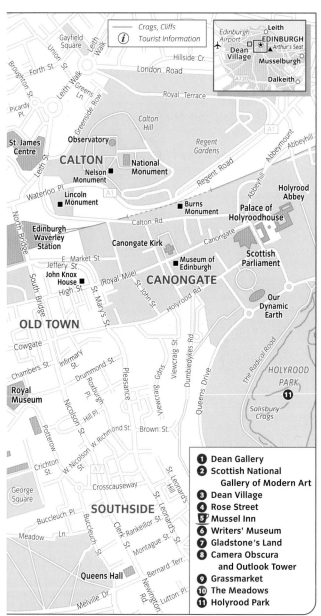

1 Dean Gallery
2 Scottish National
   Gallery of Modern Art
3 Dean Village
4 Rose Street
5 Mussel Inn
6 Writers' Museum
7 Gladstone's Land
8 Camera Obscura
   and Outlook Tower
9 Grassmarket
10 The Meadows
11 Holyrood Park

Although you may feel like you've seen a lot in 2 days, Edinburgh attractions whether more branches of its National Galleries of Scotland, classic New Town streetscapes, or the historic buildings of Old Town, offer a greater feast for visitors than can be sampled in a couple of days. On day three, you'll traverse the city center from west to east. This tour also offers spots for you to reflect on your visit to Scotland's capital. START: **Belford Rd., northwest of the city center. Bus: 13.**

1 ★ Dean Gallery. The most recent addition to the National Galleries of Scotland, the Dean hosts the best temporary exhibits of modern art and design in Edinburgh, ranging from paintings by Picasso to the architectural plans and detailed drawings of Sir Basil Spence (1907–76). You'll also find permanent exhibits of surrealist art and the re-created studio of pop artist Eduardo Paolozzi (1924–2005). ⏱ *1 hr. 73 Belford Rd. See p 27,* **3**. *Bus: 13.*

Head to the Camera Obscura and Outlook Tower for a neat 360-degree view of the city. See p 20.

An international collection of 20th century works tempts visitors to the Scottish National Gallery of Modern Art.

2 ★ Scottish National Gallery of Modern Art. Yet another branch of the Scottish National Galleries. Highlights of the collection, which occupies two floors of a Neo-Classical building that once functioned as a school, include works by French post-impressionists Bonnard and Matisse; European expressionists, such as Kirchner and Nolde; and recent acquisitions from such contemporary Scottish artists as Christine Borland. ⏱ *1 hr. 75 Belford Rd. See p 28,* **5**. *Bus: 13.*

3 ★★ Dean Village. Like Stockbridge, this tiny enclave offers a break from the buzz of the bigger city. A milling village stood here probably as early as the days of King David I in the 12th century. While nothing nearly that old survives today, there are historic buildings that were in a terrible state of disrepair until the middle of the 20th century, when conservation helped preserve their picturesque charm along the Water of Leith. See my walking tour of the area (p 60) for more details. ⏱ *30 min. Just west of the intersection of Queensferry & Belford rds. Bus: 13 or 41.*

❹ ★ **Rose Street.** I fondly remember shopping on this pedestrian-only lane in Edinburgh's New Town on my very first visit to the city in the mid-1980s. Designed originally to provide homes and workshops for artisans, the road offers lots of shopping, though it's probably best known as the place in the city center to have a nice, compact pub crawl, which can include the Abbotsford (p 80). ⏱ *1 hr. Between Princes St. & George St. Bus: 19, 23, 27, or 42.*

Owned by shellfish farmers on Scotland's West Coast, the casual 🄻 **Mussel Inn** serves great steaming bowls of fresh mussels and broth, grilled queen scallops, and other seafood options. *61–65 Rose St.* 📞 *0131/225-5979. www. mussel-inn.com. $$.*

The 400-year-plus Gladstone's Land is home to displays on 17th-century life in Edinburgh.

Pedestrian-only Rose Street is home to a host of shops, pubs, and cafes.

❻ ★ **Writers' Museum.** Devoted to Scotland's three greatest (so far) authors—Burns, Scott, and Stevenson—this museum displays its vast amount of memorabilia in a notable 17th-century town house. My favorite items are the front-page London newspaper notice of Robert Burns's death in 1796, and the basement exhibit filled with various possessions that the great traveler Robert Louis Stevenson had in Polynesia, such as his riding boots and fishing rod. A small shop sells editions of their best works. ⏱ *1 hr. See p 31. Lady Stair's Close, Lawnmarket. Bus: 28 or 41.*

❼ ★ **Gladstone's Land.** This is probably my favorite historic house (that allows visitors inside) in Edinburgh. But first some explanation of a "land" is necessary: Lands are basically the individual plots on which the buildings that face the Royal Mile have been constructed. A land is often quite narrow, but the property is usually deep, running down the hill away from the street.

The Meadows has been a popular place for recreation since the 1700s.

A merchant named Gladstone (then spelled Gladstane) took over this 16th-century property in 1617, adding on a new floor and also expanding the property toward the street. Upstairs you can see the original external facade with friezes depicting classical columns and arches. ⏱ 45 min. 477 Lawnmarket. See p 23. Bus: 28 or 41.

8 kids **Camera Obscura and Outlook Tower.** Because the camera obscura was added to this 17th-century building in the 1890s by Patrick Geddes, whom I hold in great regard for his work to prevent the wholesale demolition of Edinburgh's Old Town, I'll admit I'm always peeved that this attraction doesn't do more to publicly celebrate its creator. Still, the camera obscura (set atop the tower) is a neat trick: projecting a 360-degree view of the city on a table using a 150-year-old periscope-type lens. To magnify the image, you just need a bit of cardboard. ⏱ 45 min. Castlehill. ☎ 0131/226-3709.

www.camera-obscura.co.uk. Admission: £7.50 adults; £5 kids. Daily 9:30am–6pm Apr–Oct (later July–Aug); 10am–5pm Nov–Mar. Bus: 28 or 41.

9 ★ **Grassmarket.** In a city rich with history, the Grassmarket (shaped like a rectangle with a short street and a small city park running along it) certainly has more than its share. Convicted criminals were once famously hung here until the 1780s, although the area was first intended as the best place for a weekly market at the base of Castle-hill. Robert Burns records staying at the Grassmarket's White Hart Inn. Indeed, today, the area still has lots of pubs, hotels, and restaurants. ⏱ 45 min. Between West Port & West Bow. Bus: 2.

10 ★★ **The Meadows.** This sprawling public park, popular for ballgames of all sorts (from golf to cricket), dates back to the 1700s. Tree-lined paths crisscross the playing fields, and during the Edinburgh Festival there are often big tents erected in the park with loud live performances heard for nearly miles around. During the rest of the year, though, it's quite an excellent place for relaxing and quiet reflection, or perhaps even a bit of kite flying. ⏱ 1 hr. Melville Dr., at Lonsdale Terrace. Bus: 24 or 41.

11 ★★ **Holyrood Park.** Holyrood Park is a bit of the great outdoors set right in the middle of the city. It's another super escape, abounding with hiking trails and wildlife. At its center is a long-dormant volcano, the hill known as Arthur's Seat. You don't need to hike to the top to enjoy the surroundings, but if you're up for it see my preferred route on p 56. ⏱ 30 min–2 hr. ☎ 0131/652-8150. Free admission. Daily dawn–dusk. Bus: 2 or 35. ●

Historic Edinburgh

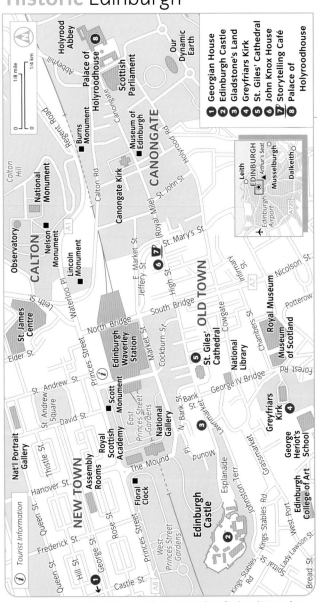

1 Georgian House
2 Edinburgh Castle
3 Gladstone's Land
4 Greyfriars Kirk
5 St. Giles' Cathedral
6 John Knox House
7 Storytelling Café
8 Palace of Holyroodhouse

Previous Page: Queen Elizabeth II stays in the imposing Palace of Holyrood House when she's in Edinburgh, though it's most often associated with Mary Queen of Scots.

From Old Town to New Town, there are bucket loads of history in Edinburgh. Thankfully, the city has done a pretty excellent job preserving it for the benefit of visitors. The name of the Scottish capital probably stems from the Gaelic *Din Eidyn,* meaning "fort on a hill slope." Not counting any prehistoric villages that are believed to have sprouted on the city's several knolls, the settlement of Edinburgh can be traced to the site of Edinburgh castle, atop a sloping rocky outcropping where a 6th-century hall is thought to have stood.

START: **Charlotte Sq. Bus: 19, 36, or 41.**

1 Georgian House. This historic town house on the north side of the square displays the furnishings of upper-class 18th-century Edinburgh, including classic Chippendale chairs, a dining table set with fine Wedgwood china, and the piss pot that the men passed around once their womenfolk retired. ⏱ *1 hr. 7 Charlotte Sq.* ☎ *0131/226-3318. www. nts.org.uk. Admission £5 adults, £4 kids, £14 family. Daily July–Aug 10am–7pm; Apr–Jun, Sept–Oct 10am–5pm; Mar, Nov 11am–3pm.*

Historic Greyfriars Kirk was named for the Franciscan order that founded it, but later became the first "reformed" church in Edinburgh. See p 24.

2 Edinburgh Castle. Its earliest history is a bit vague, but in the 11th century, Malcolm III and his Saxon queen, later venerated as St. Margaret, founded a castle on this spot. In 1542, the castle ceased being a

One of the many antiques-filled rooms inside the historic Gladstone's Land.

dedicated royal residence, having already begun to be used as an ordinance factory. (Instead, the monarchs favored Holyroodhouse when staying in Edinburgh.) For my taste, the focus of this attraction's exhibits is too heavily weighted toward the military (the castle still barracks soldiers). Still, visitors can see the Great Hall (where Scottish Parliaments used to convene) and the Scottish Crown Jewels. ⏱ *1¾ hr. to tour the interior. Castlehill.* ☎ *0131/ 225-9846. www.historic-scotland. gov.uk. Admission £10 adults, £4.50 kids. Daily Apr–Sept 9:30am–6pm; Oct–Mar 9:30am–5pm. Bus: 23 or 41.*

3 ★ Gladstone's Land. This 17th-century merchant's house gives a clear impression of how confined living conditions were some 400 years ago, even for those who were quite well-off. On the second level is a sensitively restored timber

The brooding, Victorian-influenced exterior of St. Giles' Cathedral.

ceiling, looking suitably weathered and aged, but still bearing colorful paintings of flowers and fruit. ⏱ *45 min. 477B Lawnmarket.* ☎ *0131/ 226-5856. www.nts.org.uk. Admission £5 adults, £4 kids, £14 family. Daily Apr–June, Sept–Oct 10am–5pm; July–Aug 10am–7pm. Bus: 23 or 41.*

④ ★ Greyfriars Kirk. Dedicated in 1620, this was the first "reformed" church in Edinburgh, where the National Covenant, favoring Scottish Presbyterianism over the English Episcopacy, was signed in 1638 (you can see an original copy here). Among many restorations, one in the 1930s used California redwood to create the current ceiling. For details on the kirkyard see p 35, ②. ⏱ *45 min. Greyfriars Place.* ☎ *0131/225-1900. www. greyfriarskirk.com. Free admission. Apr–Oct Mon–Fri 10:30am–4:30pm, Sat 10:30am–2:30pm; Nov–Mar Thurs 1:30–3:30pm. Bus: 2, 23, 27, 41, 42, or 45.*

⑤ ★ St. Giles' Cathedral. Its steeple is a key city landmark, visible across central Edinburgh, and this is where Scotland's Martin Luther, John Knox, preached about reform. Also called the High Kirk of St. Giles (which is the correct post-Reformation

name), the building combines a dark and brooding stone exterior (the result of a Victorian-era restoration) with surprisingly graceful buttresses. ⏱ *45 min. High St.* ☎ *0131/225-9442. www.stgilescathedral.org.uk. £2 donation suggested. May–Sept Mon–Fri 9am–7pm, Sat 9am–5pm, Sun 1–5pm; Oct–Apr Mon–Sat 9am–5pm, Sun 1–5pm. Bus: 35.*

⑥ John Knox House. Knox (1510–72), the acknowledged father of the Presbyterian Church of Scotland, lived during the Reformation, a time of great religious and political upheaval. While some regard him as a prototypical Puritan, he actually proposed progressive changes and apparently had a sharp wit. Even if you're not interested in the firebrand reformer (who may have never lived here anyway), you should visit this late-15th-century house, which is characteristic of the homes of its time. ⏱ *45 min. 43–45 High St.* ☎ *0131/556-9579. www. scottishstorytellingcentre.co.uk. Admission £3.50 adults, £1 kids. Daily July–Aug 10am–6pm; Sept–June Mon–Sat. Bus: 35.*

A stained glass window from the John Knox House, the former home of the father of the Scottish Reformation.

8 ★ **Palace of Holyrood-house.** Most of the palace's current structure was built at the behest of King Charles II in the 1670s, although he ironically never stayed here. The reigning monarch, Queen Elizabeth, however, does whenever she's in town, and you can see the reception rooms that she uses, such as the Throne Room. The real highlight of the tour, however, is in the oldest surviving section of the palace (constructed ca. 1530), where Mary Queen of Scots lived on the second floor. Be sure to check out some of the queen's needlework, which depicts her cousin (and the woman who had her beheaded), England's Elizabeth I, as a cat, and herself as a mouse. The audio tour is good, and the staff is knowledgeable, so don't hesitate to ask questions. ⏱ *1½ hr.* ☎ *0131/ 556-5100. www.royal.gov.uk. Admission £9.50 adults, £5.50 kids, £25 families. Daily Mar–Oct 9:30am–5pm; Nov–Feb 9:30am–3:30pm (closed when Royal Family in residence, 2 weeks in May–June). Bus: 35.*

Scotland's history, from costume to furniture to technology, is on display at the Museum of Edinburgh.

Next to John Knox House, in the Storytelling Centre, is the **7** **Storytelling Café**, run by the same good folk who run Spoon (see p 73). They serve light, creative sandwiches and soups until 6pm daily. *43–45 High St.* ☎ *0131/556-9579. www.scottish storytellingcentre.co.uk. $.*

History in a Local Landmark

Across from the Canongate Kirk, and housed in part of historic Huntly House, is the **Museum of Edinburgh,** 142 Canongate (☎ 0131/529-4143; www.cac.org.uk). It concentrates on the capital's history with a set of rooms on different levels featuring reproductions and original items to represent the city and its traditional industries, such as glassmaking, pottery, wool processing, and cabinetry. One notable piece in the collection is the collar of Greyfriars Bobby (p 35, **2**). Huntly House is actually three small 16th-century houses joined as one; it gets its name from a Duchess of the Gordons of Huntly, who kept an apartment here in the 1700s. The museum is open Monday to Saturday from 10am to 5pm, and on Sunday (Aug only) from noon to 5pm. Admission is free.

Edinburgh for Art Lovers

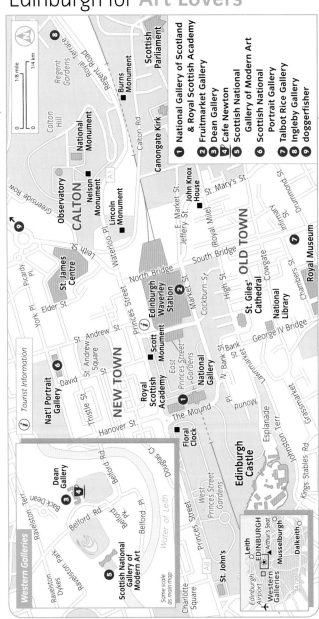

1. National Gallery of Scotland & Royal Scottish Academy
2. Fruitmarket Gallery
3. Dean Gallery
4. Cafe Newton
5. Scottish National Gallery of Modern Art
6. Scottish National Portrait Gallery
7. Talbot Rice Gallery
8. Ingleby Gallery
9. doggerfisher

Edinburgh is home to the country's national collection of art, sculpture, and design—all of it housed in the various branches of the National Galleries of Scotland. But these art museums, from the main National Gallery with its classic masterpieces to the surrealist art in the Dean Gallery, are just the beginning for art lovers. Contemporary 21st-century art in Scotland is booming and there are several independent art galleries as well. The result is a range of artistic works, ranging from ancient to modern conceptual.
START: **The Mound. Bus: 23, 27, 41, 42, or 45.**

Titian's The Three Ages of Man is just one of many masterpieces hanging in the National Gallery of Scotland.

① ★★ National Gallery of Scotland & Royal Scottish Academy. While the displayed collection is relatively small, there is only enough space in these galleries to show part of the total holdings, which include classics by Titian, El Greco, and Rembrandt—plus some French impressionist and post-impressionist artwork. In the basement wing, Scottish art is highlighted. I love the pastoral scenes and square, chunky brushstrokes of the notable 19th-century "Glasgow Boys," such as James Guthrie. The gallery takes particular pride in Sir Henry Raeburn's 1790s portrait, *The Reverend Robert Walker Skating on Duddingston Loch.* Next door, and connected by a basement interior hall with cafes and shops, the RSA hosts major exhibitions, such as paintings by Monet or the late Joan Eardley. ⏱ *2 hr. The Mound.*

☎ *0131/624-6200. www.national galleries.org. Free admission, except for temporary exhibits. Daily 10am–5pm (Thurs to 7pm).*

② ★ Fruitmarket Gallery. The city's leading contemporary art gallery is housed in an old fruit market (built in 1938) that's been updated and modernized. It hosts exhibits of both local and internationally renowned modern artists, from Yoko Ono to Nathan Coley. The bookshop and cafe are equally appealing. ⏱ *45 min. 45 Market St.* ☎ *0131/225-2383. www.fruitmarket. co.uk. Free admission. Mon–Sat 11am–6pm; Sun noon–5pm. Bus: 36.*

③ ★ Dean Gallery. Opened in 1999, the Dean Gallery is the permanent home for the Scottish National Galleries' Surrealist art, including works by Dali, Miró, and Picasso. It's also home to a replication of the

The Fruitmarket Gallery hosts both local and international shows by respected modern artists.

studio of Leith-born pop-art pioneer Eduardo Paolozzi. The gallery hosts traveling and special exhibitions of 20th-century art. ⏱ *1 hr. 73 Belford Rd.* ☎ *0131/624-6200. www.national galleries.org. Free admission, except for some temporary exhibits. Daily 10am–5pm. Bus: 13 or National Galleries shuttle.*

4 **Cafe Newton** in the Dean Gallery offers a slightly more sophisticated dining experience than the museum norm: table service for hot dishes, or cakes and coffee. *Dean Gallery, 73 Belford Rd.* ☎ *0131/624-6273. $.*

5 ★ **Scottish National Gallery of Modern Art.** Scotland's collection of late-19th- and 20th-century art opened in 1960 in a building in the Royal Botanic Garden until it moved to these premises in 1980. The collection is international in scope and quality, with works ranging from Matisse and Picasso to Balthus and

A modern art sculpture by Sir Eduardo Paolozzi at the Scottish National Gallery of Modern Art.

If you're a fan of Surrealist and pop art, the Dean Gallery is the place to visit in Edinburgh.

Hockney. ⏱ *1 hr. 75 Belford Rd.* ☎ *0131/624-6200. www.national galleries.org. Free admission, except for some temporary exhibits. Daily 10am–5pm. Bus: 13 or National Galleries shuttle.*

Free National Galleries Bus

If you plan to visit the various branches of the Scottish National Galleries, from the Dean to the Portrait, a good way to get around is by using the free shuttle bus service that stops near or right at the entrances of them all. The buses run at 45-minute intervals from about 11am to 5pm daily, although you should check with gallery staff at each branch to confirm they're running on their regular schedule.

6 ★ **Scottish National Portrait Gallery.** Opened in 1889, the country's portrait gallery gives you a chance to see many Scots, from Robert Burns and Sir Walter Scott to early golfers or Sean Connery, as well as Enlightenment thinkers and some famous sports personalities, too. Some of the artists whose

works you'll see here include Rodin, Ramsay, and Nasmyth. Highlights of the gallery's handsome central hall are its ground-floor statues and the second-floor mural—and a "pageant frieze"—that covers the walls with many noteworthy and historic Scottish folk, from St. Ninian to Adam Smith. The beautiful Venetian Gothic building (quite similar to Mount Stuart on the Isle of Bute; see p 172, 6) was a gift to the country from the principal owner of the *Scotsman* newspaper, J. R. Findlay, who paid for its construction from 1885 to 1890. ⏱ *1½ hr. 1 Queen St.* ☎ *0131/624-6200. www.nationalgalleries.org. Free admission, except for some temporary exhibits. Daily 10am–5pm. Bus: 4, 10, 12, 16, 26, or National Galleries shuttle.*

7 Talbot Rice Gallery. Part of the University of Edinburgh and housed in the handsome Old College, the Talbot Rice displays the university's permanent art collection of Old Masters (in the William Playfair–designed Georgian Gallery) and puts on temporary shows by significant contemporary artists from around the world (in the White Gallery and round room). The gallery is named after fine art professor David Talbot Rice, who taught at the university from 1934 to 1972. ⏱ *45 min. Old College, South Bridge.* ☎ *0131/650-2211. www.trg.ed.ac.uk. Free*

The doggerfisher gallery is known for shows that push the boundaries of modern art.

admission. Tues–Sat 10am–5pm. Bus: 3, 8, 29, or 49.

8 Ingleby Gallery. Small but almost perfectly formed on the ground floor of a Georgian townhouse (the owner and his family live upstairs), this is a well-regarded place for viewing contemporary works by British and international artists. ⏱ *45 min. 6 Calton Terr.* ☎ *0131/556-4441. www.inglebygallery.com. Free admission. Mon–Sat 10am–5pm. 10 min. walk from bus x25 stop on Waterloo Place.*

9 doggerfisher. If you like cutting edge, this gallery (as you might judge from its name) pushes the boundaries. You'll find installations, videos—and even some paintings now and again. It's the one that London aesthetes look to for the latest in contemporary and conceptual Scottish art. ⏱ *45 min. 11 Gayfield Sq.* ☎ *0131/558-7110. www.doggerfisher.com. Free admission. Tues–Fri 11am–6pm; Sat noon–5pm, or by appointment. Bus: 10, 12, 14, or 22.*

A bust of Nobel-prize-winning politician John Hume inside the National Portrait Gallery.

Literary Edinburgh

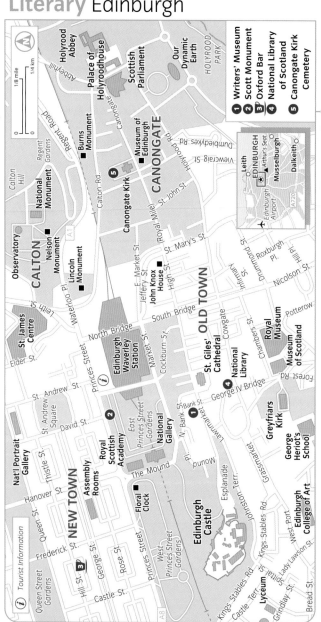

1 Writers' Museum
2 Scott Monument
3 Oxford Bar
4 National Library
   of Scotland
5 Canongate Kirk
   Cemetery

From the virtual inventor of the historic novel in the 1800s, Sir Walter Scott, to today's master of crime mysteries, Ian Rankin, Edinburgh has been linked to many famous writers. In the 18th century, Burns made regular visits to the city, and even the first edition of the Encyclopaedia Britannica was printed here in the 1760s. In recognition of its rich literary history, it recently became UNESCO's first International City of Literature (www.cityofliterature.com). START: **The Royal Mile, Lady Stair's Close. Bus: 23 or 41.**

The Writers' Museum salutes the talents of many of Scotland's best-known scribes.

1 ★ Writers' Museum. This 17th-century house contains a treasure-trove of portraits, relics, and manuscripts relating to Scotland's greatest men of letters: Robert Burns (1759–96), Sir Walter Scott (1771–1832), and Robert Louis Stevenson (1850–94). The museum building, Lady Stair's House, with its narrow passages and low clearances, was originally built in 1622. ⏱ *1 hr. Lady Stair's Close, off the Lawnmarket.* ☎ *0131/529-4901. Free admission. Mon–Sat 10am–5pm & Sun noon–5pm in Aug. Bus: 28 or 41.*

2 Scott Monument. In the center of this 60-plus-meter (200-ft.) tower's Gothic spire (it opened in 1846) is a marble statue of Sir Walter Scott and his dog, Maida, with Scott's fictional heroes carved as small figures in many niches throughout the steeple-like structure. Climb the 287 stairs to the top

for worthwhile views: Look east and you can clearly see the Burns Monument, designed by Thomas Hamilton in 1830, on the side of Calton Hill. ⏱ *45 min. East Princes St. Gardens, near Waverley Station.* ☎ *0131/529-4068. www.cac.org.uk. Admission £3. Daily Apr–Sept 10am–6pm; Oct–Mar 10am–3pm. Bus: 3, 12, 25, 33, or 45.*

Why not stop at the **3 ★ Oxford Bar**? This classic pub is the occasional hangout in real life of leading crime author Ian Rankin—and it's the regular dive for his main fictional character, the world-weary Inspector Rebus. A great place for a pint, but squeeze past the people at the small bar and into a side room,

This statue of Sir Walter Scott is part of the immense Gothic tower that makes up the Scott Monument.

where there's more space and usually a gas fire burning. Food is limited to snacks. *8 Young St.* ☎ *0131/ 539-7119. www.oxfordbar.com. Daily noon–midnight. Bus: 13, 19, or 41. $.*

❹ National Library of Scotland. Formed in 1925, the country's central library hosts readings and activities throughout the year, plus summer exhibitions. Apparently each and every book published in the U.K. and Ireland is on the shelves here; one of its most important holdings is a complete copy of the Gutenberg Bible (1455). ⏱ *1 hr. George IV Bridge.* ☎ *0131/623-3700. www. nls.uk. Free admission. Exhibitions June–Oct Mon–Sat 10am–5pm, Sun 2–5pm. Bus: 2, 23, 27, 41, 42, or 45.*

❺ ★ Canongate Kirk Cemetery. Several literary connections are found here, from the grave of Adam Smith, who wrote *The Wealth of Nations,* to that of Robert Burns's paramour Agnes McLehose (his beloved Clarinda). Burns also arranged for the kirkyard's 1789 monument to poet Robert Fergusson,

A grave at historic Canongate Kirk Cemetery, the final resting place of several noteworthy Scots, including economist Adam Smith.

which bears an inscription by Burns: "This simple Stone directs Pale Scotia's way/To pour her sorrows o'er her Poet's dust." ⏱ *1 hr. Canongate, the Royal Mile. Free admission. Daily dawn–dusk. Bus: 35.* ●

Following in Authors' Footsteps

The Literary Pub Tour retraces the footsteps of Burns, Stevenson, and Scott via the city's more atmospheric taverns, highlighting the tales of Jekyll and Hyde, or the erotic love poetry of Burns. The walking tour costs £7 and departs nightly at 7:30pm (June–Sept) from the Beehive Inn on the Grassmarket (☎ 0131/226-6665; www. edinburghliterarypubtour.co.uk).

Complete with readings and dramatizations, the **Edinburgh Book Lovers' Tour** (☎ 01573/223-888; www.edinburghbooklovers tour.com) departs from the Writers' Museum (see ❶). Its guide is Allan Foster, the author of *The Literary Traveller in Edinburgh,* a compendium of writers' observations and quips about their stays and visits to Edinburgh. Described as an odyssey around Old Town, this walking tour costs £10 and departs at 10:30am and 1:30pm Saturday and Sunday throughout the year, and daily during the Edinburgh Festival.

The Southside

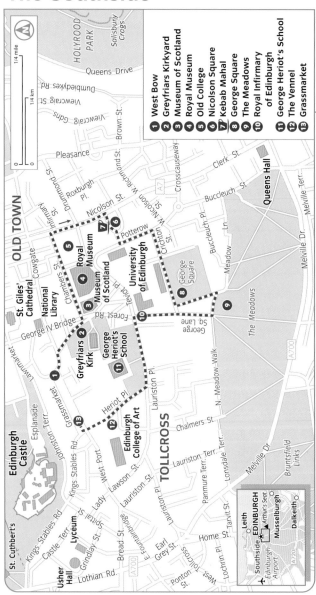

1 West Bow
2 Greyfriars Kirkyard
3 Museum of Scotland
4 Royal Museum
5 Old College
6 Nicolson Square
7 Kebab Mahal
8 George Square
9 The Meadows
10 Royal Infirmary of Edinburgh
11 George Heriot's School
12 The Vennel
13 Grassmarket

Previous Page: The Southside is home to many outdoor cafes, shops, and pedestrian-friendly zones.

This walk combines parts of Old Town with the historic settlements south of the original burgh, an area now dominated by the University of Edinburgh. The walls that once surrounded the medieval city of Edinburgh, such as the Flodden Wall, were generally expanded each time the fortifications needed improving, after attack either by English armies or by medieval thieves and general trouble-makers. Eventually, they extended past the original Old Town boundaries to include districts such as the Grassmarket and ancient streets such as the Cowgate. START: **West Bow and the Grassmarket.**

Charming West Bow arcs out of the Royal Mile and is home to lots of bars and restaurants.

① ★ **West Bow.** Initially this street zigzagged right up the steep slope from the Grassmarket to Castlehill. Combined with Victoria Street (added in the 19th c.), it now forms a charming arc to the Royal Mile via the George IV Bridge, and is filled with unpretentious shops, bars, and restaurants. At the base of the street is West Bow Well, which was built in 1674. *East end of the Grassmarket.*

② ★★ **Greyfriars Kirkyard.** Completed in 1620, the church (see p 24, ④) was built amid a cemetery (or kirkyard) that Queen Mary proposed in 1562 because burial space at St. Giles' Cathedral (p 10, ⑥) was exhausted. The kirkyard has a bit of the Flodden Wall, built after the Scots' disastrous defeat at Flodden in the early 16th century. It is full of 17th-century monuments, but its most celebrated grave is that of a

19th-century policeman whose faithful dog, Bobby, reputedly stood watch over the plot for 14 years. Bobby's statue is at the top of Candlemaker Row, just outside the pub named in his honor. *Candlemaker Row, at Chambers St.* ☎ *0131/225-1900. www.greyfriarskirk.com.*

③ ★★ **Museum of Scotland.** This striking contemporary edifice was designed by architects Benson and Forsyth and built mostly of beige sandstone from the northeast of Scotland. Opened in 1998, it was purpose-built for exhibitions that chart the history of Scotland. *George IV Bridge, at Chambers St. See p 11,* ⑨.

The grave of Bobby, the famously faithful dog with the most celebrated tombstone in Greyfriars Kirkyard.

The majestic Great Hall of the Royal Museum.

❹ The Royal Museum. This Victorian-era museum is one of the architectural highlights on Chambers Street, a broad but short boulevard named after a 19th-century lord provost (the equivalent of a mayor). The museum was designed by the same architects responsible for London's Royal Albert Hall. As I write, it is undergoing some massive refurbishment that will hopefully modernize the pile without ruining its historic charms, such as the atrium of the Great Hall. *Chamber St.*

❺ ★★ Old College. The 1781 exteriors of the University of Edinburgh Old College have been called the greatest public work of neoclassical architect Robert Adam (1728–92). This "Old College" actually replaced an earlier Old College that dated to the 1500s. Construction of the quadrangle of buildings was suspended during the Napoleonic wars, and William Playfair designed the Quad's interiors in 1819. The Old College is also home to the Talbot Rice Gallery (p 28, **❼**). *Chambers St., at South Bridge. www.ed.ac.uk.*

❻ Nicolson Square. This small plaza dates to 1756, and the buildings along its north fringe were apparently the first to be built in this area. In the square's park is the Brassfounders' Column, designed in 1886 for the International Exhibition in Edinburgh by esteemed architect and city planner Sir James Gowans (1822–90).

Along the north side of the square, **❼ Kebab Mahal** serves up inexpensive but tasty and generous portions of Indian food. Its simple and unpretentious surroundings draw a real cross-section of Edinburgh: professors, students, construction workers, and visitors to the nearby central mosque. *7 Nicolson Sq.* ☎ *0131/622-5214. $.*

❽ ★ George Square. Almost entirely redeveloped (and architecturally ruined) by the University of Edinburgh in the 20th century, George Square originally had uniform mid-18th-century town houses. You can see the few that remain on the west end of the square, which remains historically important in Edinburgh because the buildings here actually predated the city's New Town developments, usually seen as the first expansion of the city beyond the Old Town. Sir Walter Scott played in the park as a child. (By the way, the square was named after the brother of its designer, James Brown, and not a king.) *Crichton St., at Charles St.*

❾ ★★ The Meadows. This large public park was once a loch (the South Loch, to be exact), but today it is a green expanse crisscrossed by tree-lined paths. At the western end of the park is Bruntsfield Links, which some speculate entertained golfers in the 17th century and still has a pitch-and-putt course today. *Golf can be played May–Sept, dawn–dusk for free. No rental clubs or balls.*

❿ Royal Infirmary of Edinburgh. The expansive grounds of the Royal Infirmary of Edinburgh include George Watson's Hospital, which dates to the 1740s. The wards in the hospital's grand Victorian-era baronial buildings built later were among the first to incorporate the open-plan layouts of Florence Nightingale, who approved the designs. To the east is the University of Edinburgh Medical School. It faces Teviot Place, a hotbed of university life, filled with popular cafes and bars, seemingly open and bustling at all hours of the day and well into the night. *Forrest Rd., at Bristo Place.*

⓫ George Heriot's School. Heriot (1563–1624) was nicknamed the Jinglin' Geordie. As jeweler to King James VI, he exemplified the royal hangers-on who left Scotland and made their fortunes in London when James was made king of England as well. Heriot, at least, bequeathed several thousand pounds to build this facility for disadvantaged boys, which opened in

George Heriot's School is notable for its Renaissance architecture.

Weekly markets were held in the Grassmarket for nearly 400 years, but today the district is home to a number of cafes and pubs.

1659. Of the 200-odd windows in the Renaissance pile, only two are exactly alike. Today, it is a private school for young men and women. *Lauriston Place.*

⓬ The Vennel. Near the top of the steep steps on this footpath ("vennel" is a Scots word that translates as alley) is a good hunk of the Flodden Wall (marked with a sign), indicating how areas well below the castle's rocky perch, such as the Grassmarket, were enclosed within a fortified city by the 16th century. *Heriot Place, at Keir St.*

⓭ ★ Grassmarket. This was once a market square and a place for executions. One of the most infamous was of Margaret Dickson. Poor Maggie was convicted for having a baby out of wedlock. After she was duly hung in 1724, her body was en route to burial when her escorts heard a banging in the coffin. Maggie was alive and according to one version of the tale lived another 40 years. A bar in the Grassmarket is named in her honor.

New Town

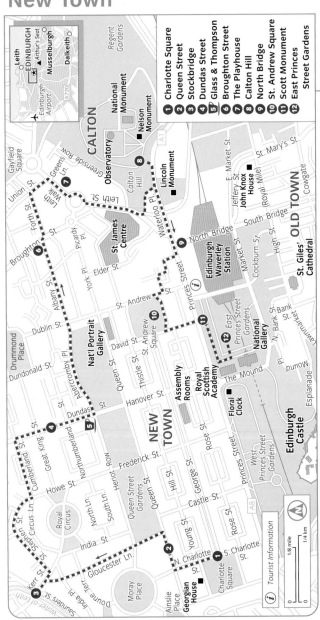

1. Charlotte Square
2. Queen Street
3. Stockbridge
4. Dundas Street
5. Glass & Thompson
6. Broughton Street
7. The Playhouse
8. Calton Hill
9. North Bridge
10. St. Andrew Square
11. Scott Monument
12. East Princes Street Gardens

In 1767, the city fathers realized that the best way to relieve the increasingly cramped and unhygienic Old Town was to create a New Town. It is perhaps the definitive example of rational Georgian town planning, with new roads laid out in a strict grid. With subsequent additions, Edinburgh's New Town became a new city center with fine housing, offices, and commercial space. START: **West end of George St.**

The central park at Charlotte Square during the Edinburgh Book Festival.

1 ★ Charlotte Square. This is actually the final bit of the first New Town, designed by the preeminent Georgian-era architect Robert Adam in 1791, just before his death. The central park was subsequently expanded from a circle to form an octagon in 1873, and a statue of Prince Albert was added. On the south side of the square, at No. 28, the National Trust for Scotland has offices, a cafe, a shop, and exhibition space (see p 14). Recent work on the building's foundations uncovered a cannonball presumably shot in defense of the castle long before anything was built here. Across the square on the north side is Bute House, the official residence of the Scottish First Minister. *George St., at Charlotte St.*

2 Queen Street. This northernmost street of the original New Town development has the area's largest number of original buildings. As on Princes Street, townhouses were built only on one side of what is today a very busy boulevard, with the private Queen Street Gardens running opposite. On a clear day, you can see right across northern Edinburgh to Leith, the Firth of Forth, and Fife in the distance. *Queen St., at N. Castle St.*

3 ★★ Stockbridge. This charming neighborhood's name comes from the Stock Bridge (p 61, 1), which crosses the Water of Leith. It was a hippy enclave in the '60s and '70s, but is now a refuge of the well-heeled. Deanhaugh Street serves as the local main street. St. Stephen Street has a variety of places to shop and eat.

The Playhouse is an opulent venue for theatrical productions.

4 ★ **Dundas Street.** The heart of Northern New Town was planned in the first years of the 19th century by architects Robert Reid and William Sibbald. Dundas Street is at its core, and if you like antiques, it's worth doing a bit of window-shopping here. The layout of Northern New Town is similar to Edinburgh's first New Town development, set on an east–west axis, but running along the slope of a hill this time rather than along its crest. Northern New Town wasn't built in a day, however. Land for the development was first acquired around the 1790s, but buildings were still being added as late as the 1850s. *Dundas St., at Great King St.*

5 **Glass & Thompson** is a classic, upscale cafe that feels part and parcel of Edinburgh's rather posh New Town. Platters feature a mix of local and Continental ingredients, cheese, seafood, cold meats, and salad. Open until late afternoon. *2 Dundas St.* ☎ *0131/557-0909.* $.

6 **Broughton Street.** This is one of the key places for nightlife in Edinburgh today, home to traditional pubs, stylish bars, and some restaurants. Broughton Street is also central to the city's gay scene. At the top of the road, at the large and busy roundabout, is the short street called Picardy Place. Picardy is what this area was once called, the land being acquired in 1730 for some silk weavers who had fled France. Their attempts to grow mulberry trees for the silkworms, however, didn't work. *Broughton St., at Picardy Place.*

7 **The Playhouse.** Here at what all locals simply call the Top of Leith Walk, this opulent theater was designed (1927–29) by Glasgow architect John Fairweather (1867–1942) for films and theater productions (see p 91). While it appears to be only two stories high from the front, the land behind the facade drops off and the interior space fills four floors. Fairweather was inspired by a trip to the U.S. and the auditorium was designed to hold more than 3,000 people—huge in its day. He also wanted to build similar Playhouses in Glasgow and Dundee. It didn't happen. They no longer screen films at the Playhouse, but the glass Omni Centre just up the road has a multiplex cinema. *18–22 Greenside Place.*

8 ★★★ **Calton Hill.** See p 9, **2**.

9 **North Bridge.** This is an excellent vantage point for viewing Edinburgh Castle (bring your camera!). Curiously, like this elevated crossing, few of the city's many bridges actually cross water; they link hills instead. The first North Bridge took some 9 years to complete from 1763 to 1772. The current broad span was built from1894 to 1897, soaring over railway lines and Waverley Station. *At Princes St.*

10 **St. Andrew Square.** Named for the patron saint of Scotland, this square is the eastern bookend to George Street (p 11, **11**). Unlike Charlotte Square at the street's

The Scottish War Memorial at North Bridge.

western terminus, it doesn't carry the same Georgian character. Atop the 38m (125-ft.) column (modeled on Trajan's Column in Rome) in the middle of the square's gated garden stands Lord Melville (1742–1811), once one of Scotland's most powerful politicians. *George St., at St. David St.*

⓫ Scott Monument. Victorian critic John Ruskin hated this monument to Scotland's greatest novelist, describing it as the top of a church spire plunked on the ground. He might have been peeved that its designer, George Meikle Kemp (1795–1844), a carpenter by trade, was actually third in the competition to create the tribute to Scott. After prolonged discussions by the committee formed to commission the monument, Kemp eventually rose to the top. Never mind the critique or the slightly dodgy process—the Gothic shrine remains one of the most notable landmarks in the city. *Princes St., at Waverley Bridge. See p 31,* ❷.

⓬ ★★ East Princes Street Gardens. It took many years to completely drain the old Nor' Loch that once covered this area, and the 3.4-hectare (8.5-acre) park that now fills the valley was begun in 1830. The original designs for the park, however, had to be altered in the wake of the construction of the railway lines into Waverley Station. The panoramic views of Old Town rising to Ramsay Gardens and Edinburgh Castle are quite fine from here. *The southern end of Princes Street, running from The Mound to Waverley Station.*

East Princes Street Gardens is especially lovely in spring, when its flowers are in full bloom.

Leith

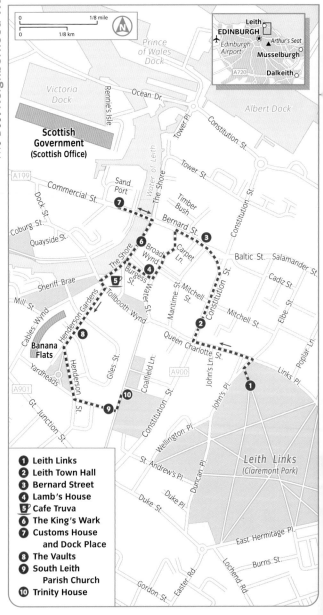

1 Leith Links
2 Leith Town Hall
3 Bernard Street
4 Lamb's House
5 Cafe Truva
6 The King's Wark
7 Customs House
   and Dock Place
8 The Vaults
9 South Leith
   Parish Church
10 Trinity House

Edinburgh's long-standing port at Leith was established here because a natural harbor had formed where the little Water of Leith river fed into the massive Firth of Forth estuary. Though it was properly incorporated into Edinburgh's city limits in the 20th century, Leith has long had its own identity and it was effectively Scotland's capital during the interim rule of Mary of Guise in the 16th century. Her daughter, Mary Queen of Scots, made a celebrated arrival here in 1561. START: **John's Place. Bus: 12, 16, or 35.**

1 ★ **Leith Links.** Older than Bruntsfield Links golf course in Edinburgh's Southside park, the Meadows, Leith Links is by some accounts the birthplace of golf. A version of the sport was first played here in the 1400s. In 1744, the first rules of the game were laid down at Leith Links. Today, no one plays golf here: It's just a pleasant public park, but running adjacent to John's Place was the fairway of this ancient course's first hole. *East of John's Place, between Duke St. & Links Gardens. Free admission. Daily dawn–dusk. Bus: 12, 16, or 35.*

2 **Leith Town Hall.** This neoclassical building was originally constructed as the Leith Sheriff Court in 1828. The designers' firm is emblazoned on the Queen Charlotte Street frontage: "R. & R. Dickson." The adjoining property was incorporated later after the town became a parliamentary burgh in 1833. *75–81 Constitution St. & 29–41 Queen Charlotte St.*

The 17th-cenurty Lamb's House is an architectural gem that's the finest of its kind in Edinburgh.

Golf's rules were first codified at Leith Links, but today it's just a public park.

3 ★ **Bernard Street.** Bernard Street has been termed Leith's "most formal" architectural space. It's quite short and almost feels more like a square than a street, with a mix of Georgian and 19th-century commercial buildings, such as the former Leith Bank. At its eastern end, where it meets Constitution Street, is another of Scotland's many monuments to poet Robert Burns. This bronze statue was erected in 1898. At this corner, as well, is the **Leith Assembly Rooms (37–43 Constitution St.).** The building includes a merchant's meeting place built in the 1780s and a two-story ballroom.

4 ★★ **Lamb's House.** A detour up Carpet Lane takes you to this handsome, four-story red-tile roofed building. The first thing you might notice is the odd window built into the corner of the facade. Originally a large early-17th-century merchant's house (the finest example of its type in Edinburgh), it is a masterpiece of architecture, with crow-stepped gables and corbels. I know people who once worked here (it's been converted into offices) and they're convinced that a ghost or two haunt the place. *Burgess & Water sts.*

5 Cafe Truva is a Mediterranean/Turkish-influenced cafe with good strong coffee to go with its mezze platters, sandwiches, and eggs Florentine. The selection of sweet things is tempting, too. *77 The Shore.* ☎ *0131/554-5502. $.*

6 ★ The King's Wark. This building dates to the beginning of the 1700s, but its history is richer. The original King's Wark on this site (c. 1434) was believed to be a palace and arsenal that King James VI had rebuilt during his reign in the 17th century, and which was later given to a tavern-keeping buddy of his, Bernard Lindsay. It now houses a pub, one of many welcoming options on The Shore, Leith's first main street. *36 The Shore.*

7 ★ Customs House and Dock Place. Designed by Robert Reid in 1810, the Customs House is quite a monumental (if somewhat harsh) building, with sturdy fluted columns. Look out for the royal arms of King George III in the triangular pediment that rests on the columns. Nearby is the original entrance to the Old East Dock (established at the start of the 19th c. and today redeveloped into modern Leith), the Commercial Quay. This area also skirts the walls of a citadel built for Oliver Cromwell, with fragments apparently still part of Dock Street. *Commercial St., at Dock Place.*

8 ★ The Vaults. This handsome and broad stone warehouse dates to 1682, but the vaulted passage and wine cellar underneath may be 100 years older. There is more to Scotland's Auld Alliance with France

than simply plotting wars against England. Leith is where bottles and bottles of French wine were shipped. Indeed, the word "claret" is believed by some to be one that Scots gave to red wine from Bordeaux. A link to that history is maintained by the Vintners Rooms restaurant (see p 74). The Scotch Malt Whisky Society is located on the second floor. *87 Giles St.*

9 South Leith Parish Church. A church has been standing at this site since about 1480. The one that is here today was built in 1848, thanks to an Act of Parliament. A plaque in the kirkyard details the intervening history, which includes some very heavy bombardment in 1560 by English troops and Oliver Cromwell's later decision to use the poor, ravaged church as a munitions hold. *6 Henderson St.*

10 Trinity House. Trinity House is an early-1800s survivor amid the urban renewal and tall apartment buildings of central Leith. Owned by Historic Scotland, it is home to the Incorporation of Shipmasters, an organization that dates to the 14th century. *99 Kirkgate.* ☎ *0131/554-3289. Group tours by reservation.* ●

The members room at The Scotch Malt Whisky Society, which is headquartered in The Vaults.

4 Edinburgh: The Best **Shopping**

Shopping in Edinburgh

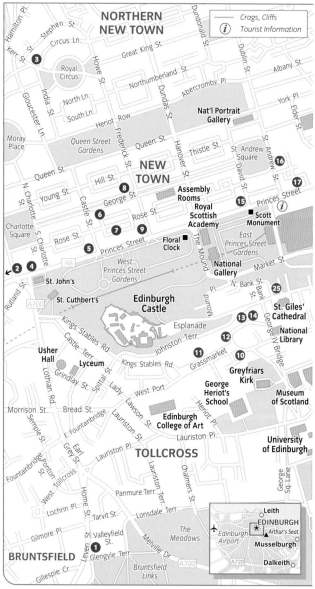

Crags, Cliffs

(i) Tourist Information

NORTHERN
NEW TOWN

Hamilton Pl.
Stephen St.
Circus Ln.
Kerr St.
Great King St.
Dundonald St.
3
Royal
Circus
Howe St.
Northumberland St.
Dublin St.
India St.
Gloucester Ln.
North Ln.
South Ln.
Abercromby Pl.
Albany St.
Heriot Row
Queen St.
Dundas St.
York Pl.
Elder St.
Moray
Place
Queen Street
Gardens
Nat'l Portrait
Gallery
Frederick St.
Hanover St.
Thistle St.
St. Andrew
Square
16
Queen St.
Hill St.
NEW
TOWN
David St.
St. Andrew St.
17
Young St.
George St.
8
Assembly
Rooms
15
Princes Street
(i)
N. Charlotte St.
Castle St.
6
Rose St.
Royal
Scottish
Academy
Scott
Monument
Charlotte
Square
S. Charlotte St.
Rose St.
7
9
Floral
Clock
East
Princes Street
Gardens
2 **4**
5
Princes Street
A8
West
Princes Street
Gardens
National
Gallery
Market St.
Rutland St.
A700
St. John's
St. Cuthbert's
Edinburgh
Castle
The Mound
N. Bank St.
S. Bank St.
25
St. Giles'
Cathedral
Esplanade
13 **14**
George IV Bridge
National
Library
Kings Stables Rd.
Castle Terr.
Johnston Terr.
12
Usher
Hall
Lyceum
Grindlay St.
Spittal St.
Lady Lawson St.
Kings Stables Rd.
West Port
Grassmarket
11
10
Greyfriars
Kirk
Lothian Rd.
Morrison St.
Bread St.
George
Heriot's
School
Heriot Pl.
Museum
of Scotland
E. Fountainbridge
Lauriston St.
Edinburgh
College of Art
Lauriston Pl.
University
of Edinburgh
Semple St.
Earl Grey St.
Lauriston Pl.
Chalmers St.
Fountainbridge
Ponton St.
Home St.
West Tollcross
Panmure Terr.
Lauriston Terr.
George Sq. Lane
Lochrin Pl.
Tarvit St.
Lonsdale Terr.
TOLLCROSS
Gilmore Pl.
Valleyfield St.
Melville Dr.
The
Meadows
Leven St.
Bruntsfield
Links
Glengyle Terr.
1
BRUNTSFIELD
Gillespie Cr.

Leith
Edinburgh
Airport
EDINBURGH
Arthur's Seat
Musselburgh
A720
Dalkeith

Previous Page: James Pringle Weavers sells a host of wool products and tartans.

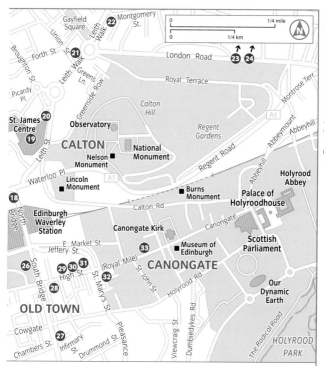

Shopping **Best Bets**

Best **Italian Deli**
★★ Valvona & Crolla, *19 Elm Row*
(p 74)

Best **Cheese Monger**
★★★ IJ Mellis Cheesemongers,
Bakers Place (Kerr St., p 51)

Best **Kilts**
★ Geoffrey (Tailor) Kiltmakers,
57–59 High St. (p 52)

Best **Wooly Jumpers**
★ Ragamuffin, *276 Canongate*
(p 53)

Best **Gifts to Take Home**
Jenners, *48 Princes St. (p 50)*

Best **Foot Forward**
Schuh, *6 Frederick St. (p 54)*

Best **Men's Fashions**
★★ Walker Slater, *20 Victoria St.*
(p 50)

Best for **Designer Labels**
arkangel, *4 William St. (p 49)*

Best for **Women's Fashions**
★ Corniche, *2 Jeffrey St. (p 49)*

Best for **Urban Chic**
★ Cruise, *94 George St. (p 50)*

Best for **Knickknacks**
Tartan Gift Shop, *54 High St. (p 52)*

Best **Fashion Jewelry**
Hamilton & Inches, *87 George St.*
(p 52)

Best for **Antiquarian Books**
★★ McNaughton's Bookshop,
3a Haddington Place (p 49)

Best **Book Selection**
★ Waterstones, *128 Princes St.*
(p 49)

Best **Department Store**
★★ John Lewis, *St. James Centre*
(p 51)

Best for **Keeping Your Head
Warm**
★★ Fabhatrix, *13 Cowgatehead*
(p 52)

Best for **New Tunes**
★ Avalanche, *63 Cockburn St.*
(p 53)

Best for **Scottish Crafts**
★ Ness Scotland, *336 Lawnmarket*
(p 52)

Best **Whisky Shop**
★★★ Royal Mile Whiskies, *379
High St. (p 54)*

There's no better place to pick up cheese in Edinburgh than IJ Mellis Cheesemongers.
See p 51.

Edinburgh **Shopping A to Z**

Bookworms will delight in the secondhand selection at McNaughtan's Bookshop.

Bring That Passport!

Take along your passport when you go shopping in case you make a purchase that entitles you to a VAT (value-added tax) refund. For details, see "Taxes," on p 209.

Books

Blackwells OLD TOWN   Near the Royal Mile, this outlet of a chain of booksellers has a knowledgeable staff and wide-ranging shelves of fiction and nonfiction. *53 S. Bridge.* ☎ *0131/622-8222. www.blackwells. com. AE, MC, V. Bus: 3, 7, 30, or 37. Map p 46.*

★★ **McNaughtan's Bookshop**
NEW TOWN   In business since 1957, this is one of the city's best antiquarian and secondhand book purveyors. A must stop for book lovers. *3a Haddington Place (Leith Walk, near Gayfield Sq.).* ☎ *0131/ 556-5897. www.mcnaughtansbook shop.com. MC, V. Bus: 7, 12, 16, or 22. Map p 46.*

★ **Waterstones** NEW TOWN   A giant Barnes-and-Noble–like operation, with plenty of reading options and soft seats. This is the most prominent and best-stocked book retailer in the city center. *128 Princes St. (across from Waverley Station).* ☎ *0131/226-2666. AE, MC, V. Bus: 8, 22, 25, 33. Map p 46.*

Clothing & Fashions

arkangel WEST END   William Street, in the city's affluent West End, is home to a host of boutique shops. This one specializes in designer labels exclusive to Scotland. *4 William St.* ☎ *0131/226-4466. www.arkangelfashion.co.uk. MC, V. Bus: 4 or 25. Map p 46.*

★ **Corniche** OLD TOWN   One of the more sophisticated boutiques in Edinburgh; if it's the latest in Scottish fashion, expect to find it here. *2 Jeffrey St. (near the Royal Mile).* ☎ *0131/556-3707. www.corniche. org.uk. AE, MC, V. Bus: 35. Map p 46.*

For boutique Scottish labels, head straight for arkangel.

Avante-garde fashion is the name of the game at Cruise.

★ **Cruise** NEW TOWN This home-grown fashion outlet began in Edinburgh's Old Town—not generally considered fertile ground for the avant-garde. There is still a branch off the Royal Mile, but the New Town outlet is the focus for couture. *94 George St.* ☎ *0131/226-3524. www.cruiseclothing.co.uk. MC, V. Bus: 19, 37, or 41. Map p 46.*

★★ **Walker Slater** OLD TOWN Well-made and contemporary (if understated) men's clothes, usually made of cotton and dyed in rich, earthy hues. My moleskin suit from here has served me well for years. Also carries Mackintosh overcoats and accessories. *20 Victoria St.* *(near George IV Bridge).* ☎ *0131/ 220-2636. www.walkerslater.com. MC, V. Bus: 35, 41, or 42. Map p 46.*

Department Stores

★ **Harvey Nichols** NEW TOWN Initially, locals were not quite prepared for this store's multiple floors of expensive labels and goods by designers such as Jimmy Choo and Alexander McQueen. But they've learned. *30–34 St. Andrew Sq.* ☎ *0131/524-8388. www.harvey nichols.com. AE, MC, V. Bus: 8, 12, 17, or 45. Map p 46.*

Jenners NEW TOWN This neo-gothic landmark opened in 1838

The Shopping Scene

For visitors from abroad, prices in the U.K. could seem high. In recent years, the British pound sterling has been strong relative to other currencies, especially the U.S. dollar. Many items carry the same numerical price in pounds as they would in dollars. For example, a pair of hiking shoes that cost $100 in New York might well be priced £100 in Edinburgh, making it twice as expensive. Shopping hours in central Edinburgh are generally from 9 or 10am to 6pm Monday through Wednesday, and on Friday and Saturday. On Thursday, many shops remain open until 8pm. On Sunday, shops open at 11am or noon and close around 5pm.

and sells a variety of local and international merchandise. The food hall offers a wide array of gift-oriented Scottish products. *48 Princes St.* ☎ *0870/607-2841. AE, MC, V. Bus: 8, 22, 25, or 33. Map p 46.*

★★ John Lewis NEW TOWN   The largest department store in Scotland, this branch of John Lewis is many people's first choice when it comes to shopping for clothes, appliances, furniture, toys, and more. *St. James Centre (at the top of Leith Walk).* ☎ *0131/556-9121. www.johnlewis.com. AE, MC, V. Bus: 7, 14, 22, or 25. Map p 46.*

Food & Wine
★★★ IJ Mellis Cheesemongers STOCKBRIDGE   This shop sells award-winning British and Irish cheeses, and the staff really know their stuff. There are similar shops in Old Town on Victoria Street (convenient to the Royal Mile), as well as on Morningside Road on the Southside. *Bakers Place (Kerr St.).* ☎ *0131/225-6566. www.ijmellischeesemonger.com. MC, V. Bus: 24, 29, or 42. Map p 46.*

★ Lupe Pintos WEST END   This wee shop in the Tollcross neighborhood specializes in Mexican food, but also stocks U.S. goods, as well as exotic treats from the Far East.

A city landmark, Jenners sells a wide range of Scottish and international goods.

24 Leven St. (near the King's Theatre). ☎ *0131/228-6241. www.lupepintos.com. MC, V. Bus: 11, 15, or 45. Map p 46.*

★★ Valvona & Crolla NEW TOWN   This Italian deli has an excellent reputation across the U.K. thanks to a wonderful range of cheeses and cured meats, fresh fruit and vegetables, plus baked goods from rolls to sourdough loaves. *19 Elm Row (Leith Walk).* ☎ *0131/556-6066. www.valvonacrolla.co.uk. MC, V. Bus: 7, 14, 22, or 25. Map p 46.*

The very reputable Valvona & Crolla is a great source for all the fixings you'd need for a picnic.

Gifts

kids Geraldine's of Edinburgh
OLD TOWN   Also known as the Doll
Hospital, this doll and teddy bear
factory has more than 100 heirloom-
quality options on display. *133–135
Canongate.* ☎ *0131/556-4295.
www.dollsandteddies.com. MC, V.
Bus: 35. Map p 46.*

★ **Ness Scotland** OLD TOWN   A
shop full of knitwear, skirts, T-shirts,
and whimsical accessories scoured
from around the country—from the
Orkney Islands to the Borders. *336
Lawnmarket.* ☎ *0131/225-8155.
www.nessbypost.com. MC, V. Bus:
28. Map p 46.*

Tartan Gift Shop OLD TOWN   A
bewildering array of hunt and dress
tartans for men and women, sold by
the yard. There's also a line of lamb's
wool and cashmere sweaters and all
the proper kilt accessories, such as
sporrans. *54 High St.* ☎ *0131/558-
3187. MC, V. Bus 35. Map p 46.*

Hats

★★ **Fabhatrix** OLD TOWN   I'm
partial to hats and this shop has
hundreds of handmade ones: practical and attractive options, as well as

*The stylish hats at Fabhatrix range from
super fine to fun and frivolous.*

a few that are downright frivolous
but extremely fun. *13 Cowgatehead
(off Grassmarket).* ☎ *0131/225-
9222. www.fabhatrix.com. MC, V.
Bus: 2. Map p 46.*

Jewelry

Alistir Wood Tait NEW TOWN   It
has a reputation for Scottish gems
and precious metals, and this shop
also sells Victorian "Scottish Pebble"
brooches and contemporary
designs. *116A Rose St.* ☎ *0131/
225-4105. www.alistirtaitgem.co.uk.
MC, V. Bus: 19. Map p 46.*

Hamilton & Inches NEW TOWN
Since 1866, the prestigious Hamilton & Inches has sold gold and silver
jewelry, porcelain, silver, and gift
items. *87 George St.* ☎ *0131/225-
4898. www.hamiltonandinches.com.
AE, MC, V. Bus: 19 or 41. Map p 46.*

Kilts & Tartans

Anta OLD TOWN   Shop here for
some of the most stylish tartans,
especially cool mini-kilts and silk
earasaids (oversize scarves) for
women. *Crocket's Land, 91–93 West
Bow.* ☎ *0131/225-4616. www.anta.
co.uk. MC, V. Bus: 35, 41, or 42. Map
p 46.*

★ **Geoffrey (Tailor) Kiltmakers**
OLD TOWN   Its customers have
included Dr. Ruth Westheimer and
Mel Gibson (who apparently favors
the "Hunting Buchanan" tartan), and
it stocks 200 of Scotland's best-
known clan patterns. *57–59 High St.*
☎ *0131/557-0256. www.geoffrey
kilts.co.uk. MC, V. Bus: 35. Map
p 46.*

Hector Russell OLD TOWN
Bespoke—that is, made to order—
clothes made from tartan can be
ordered from this well-known High-
land-based kilt maker, with shops on
the Royal Mile and Princes Street.
137–141 High St. ☎ *0131/558-1254.*

modernized adaptations of traditional Scottish patterns for both men and women. *66 Grassmarket.* ☎ *0131/225-3249. www.billbaber. com. MC, V. Bus: 2. Map p 46.*

Edinburgh Woollen Mill Shop

NEW TOWN   There are several outlets of this chain in the capital and about 280 throughout the United Kingdom. All of them sell practical Scottish woolens. *139 Princes St.* ☎ *0131/226-3840. www.ewm.co.uk. AE, MC, V. Bus: 8, 22, 25, or 33. Map p 46.*

★ **Ragamuffin** OLD TOWN   The apparel here is unique: "wearable art" created by some 150 designers from all over the U.K. Ragamuffin also has a shop on the Isle of Skye. *276 Canongate.* ☎ *0131/557-6007. www.ragamuffinonline.co.uk. MC, V. Bus: 35. Map p 46.*

Music

★ **Avalanche** OLD TOWN   This excellent indie music CD shop is good for finding new releases of Scottish and U.K. bands and secondhand CDs. Another branch is on West Nicolson Street. *63 Cockburn St.* ☎ *0131/225-3939. MC, V. Bus: 35. Map p 46.*

Zavvi NEW TOWN   Formerly the Virgin Megastore, here you'll find

Alistir Wood Tait is known for its Victorian-style brooches.

www.hector-russell.com. MC, V. Bus: 35. Map p 46.

James Pringle Weavers LEITH

This Leith mill produces a large variety of wool items for sale and also boasts a clan ancestry center with a database containing more than 50,000 family names. *70–74 Bangor Rd.* ☎ *0131/553-5161. MC, V. Bus: 36. Map p 46.*

Knits & Woolens

Bill Baber OLD TOWN   This workshop and store turns out artfully

Geoffrey (Tailor) Kiltmakers stocks 200 of Scotland's best-known tartans.

Harvey Nichols stocks the latest in designer couture. See p 50.

one of the biggest selections of DVDs and CDs in Scotland. *125 Princes St.* ☎ *0131/220-2230. www.zavvi.co.uk. AE, MC, V. Bus: 8, 22, 25, or 33. Map p 46.*

Shoes

Schuh NEW TOWN   Schuh (pronounced "shoe") has the latest in footwear: Expect fierce, funky finds as well as name brands. *6 Frederick St.* ☎ *0131/220-0290. Bus: 19, 29, or 42. Map p 46.*

Shopping Centers

Ocean Terminal LEITH   Ultimately just another modern indoor shopping mall, albeit one with the royal yacht *Britannia* moored at its side. *Ocean Dr.* ☎ *0131-555-8888. www.oceanterminal.com. Bus: 22 or 35. Map p 46.*

Princes Mall NEW TOWN   There's practically something for everyone (except a leading department store)

at this tri-level shopping center next to Waverley Station. *Princes St.* ☎ *0131/557-3759. www.princes mall-edinburgh.co.uk. Bus: 8, 22, 25, or 33. Map p 46.*

St. James Centre NEW TOWN Slightly more upmarket than the Princes Mall, this shopping center is anchored by the John Lewis department store (p 51). *Leith St. (at Princes St.).* ☎ *0131/557-0050. www.stjamesshopping.com. MC, V. Bus: 7, 14, 22, or 25. Map p 46.*

Whisky

★★★ Royal Mile Whiskies OLD TOWN   The stock at this rather small shop on the Royal Mile is huge: Some 1,000 different Scotch and other nations' whiskies are available. The staff is very knowledgeable, so don't hesitate to ask for advice. *379 High St.* ☎ *0131/622-6255. www. royalmilewhiskies.com. AE, MC, V. Bus: 35. Map p 46.* ●

Royal Mile Whiskies carries almost 1,000 different varieties of the beloved spirit.

5 The **Great Outdoors**

Arthur's Seat

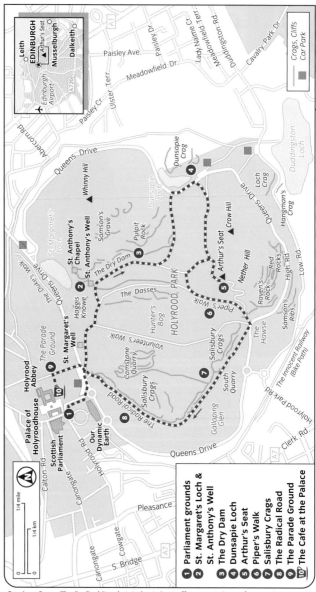

Crags, Cliffs
Car Park

1 Parliament grounds
2 St. Margaret's Loch &
St. Anthony's Well
3 The Dry Dam
4 Dunsapie Loch
5 Arthur's Seat
6 Piper's Walk
7 Salisbury Crags
8 The Radical Road
9 The Parade Ground
10 The Cafe at the Palace

Previous Page: The Radical Road at Arthur's Seat offers great views of many city landmarks.

The most invigorating of Edinburgh's outdoor escapes lies quite literally at the doorstep of Old Town. Holyrood Park (263 hectares/650 acres) is home to Arthur's Seat, and a climb to the top of this landmark hill provides some of the best views in the region. Though the park and hill have lots of paths for rambling about and you don't have to climb all the way to the summit, I recommend it. Allow about 2 hours to get to the top and back using this tour, which is my preferred route. START: **Take Bus 35 or 36 to Holyrood Lodge Information Centre.**

The Parliament grounds are a fine example of modern park design.

1 Parliament grounds. One of the final parts of the new Parliament complex to be finished, this pleasant if slightly exposed urban park uses modern landscape design, with reflecting pools and tiers of concrete benches and bedding planted with low-maintenance grasses and wildflowers in summer. Look up toward Arthur's Seat and you will glimpse ant-size people walking about the peak. ⏱ *20 min. Adjacent to Scottish Parliament, on the bottom of Royal Mile, opposite the Palace of Holyroodhouse.*

2 ★ St. Margaret's Loch & St. Anthony's Well. Named for St. Margaret (1045–93), a pious queen consort of Scotland, this pleasant large pond teems with bird life. If you're lucky, you might see a weasel nip by on the hillside. Near the ruins of St. Anthony's Chapel (whose history is somewhat fuzzy, though it definitely dates back to the 15th c.) on the stony bluff above the loch, the path runs past a boulder and smaller rock basin marking St. Anthony's Well. ⏱ *10 min. Just south of Queens Dr.*

3 ★ The Dry Dam. This rutted trail (along a glacial cirque, or valley) takes you straight toward Arthur's Seat, clearly the highest peak amid the other hilltops and ridgelines. Take a rest and catch your breath. Be sure to look behind you for views of Calton Hill to the left and Hiberian football park in the direction of Leith and the River Forth. Not a bad spot for a photo or two. ⏱ *10 min.*

A statue inside the Parliament grounds.

What's in a Name?

Many presume that Arthur's Seat is a reference to the mythical king of Camelot. Not so. There are various theories behind the name. The moniker may have come from a 6th-century prince of Strathclyde named Arthur, or it could be a corruption of "archer," given the hill's defensive position. My pick is that it's a bastardization of Gaelic for the height of Thor, or "Ard Thor."

4 ★★ **Dunsapie Loch.** From the ridge above this man-made loch (created in 1844), you'll get a good panorama looking north across the firth to Fife—and east to the coastal towns of East Lothian. On a sunny day, the eastern horizon reveals the dark cone of North Berwick Law, some 30km (19 miles) away, as well as shimmering silvery Bass Rock, the famous bird sanctuary in the sea. Just below the loch is terrain believed to be ancient farmlands. ⏱ *15 min. Where Dry Dam joins Piper's Walk.*

5 ★★★ **Arthur's Seat.** Congrats! You are now standing atop a long-dormant volcano, some 250m (820 ft.) above sea level. Don't be surprised if there's a howling gale blowing—my eyes water on every visit. Take time to soak in the breathtaking 360-degree vistas from this peak. There is a landmark indicator to help you identify the sights. Facing due north, Bass Rock is at 2 o'clock from your position. On the clearest day you can see as far as Ben Lomond in the northwest (at about 10 o'clock), some 95km (59 miles) away. Take care as the rocks (nearly polished by the soles of frequent visitors) can be slippery. ⏱ *30–45 min.*

6 ★★ **Piper's Walk.** The Piper's Walk (the name commemorates a successful protest staged by the Highland troops—and their pipers—atop Arthur's Seat in 1778) is a narrow path below the summit, with prickly gorse bushes growing to your left amid rocky outcrops. The route offers a good view below of the Hunter's Bog (a haven for butterflies and moths) and another valley path called the Volunteer's Walk. ⏱ *20 min.*

7 ★★ **Salisbury Crags.** As the southern part of Edinburgh comes into view (note the charming baronial-style stone buildings of the Pollok Hall student residences), you'll head under Salisbury Crags. Years of stone quarrying have revealed this bare but geologically significant facade of igneous rock. Climbing the 122m (400-ft.) edifice is discouraged. ⏱ *15 min. West side of Holyrood Park.*

The peak of Arthur's Seat has some of the best vistas in the entire region.

If the weather cooperates, stand on the ridge above Dunsapie Loch and you'll be rewarded with views as far as Fife.

❽ ★ The Radical Road. This trail offers good views of the Pentlands Hills in the distance and several city landmarks, including Edinburgh Castle. As you round the final bend, you'll get a good look at the gigantic white tent of Our Dynamic Earth and the arresting abstract geometry of the Scottish Parliament buildings. The name for the path allegedly stems from those who built it in the 1820s—unemployed artisans who fomented revolutionary ideas. Their political efforts failed, but they were given the task of constructing this road and the name's stuck ever since. ⏱ *15 min.*

❾ The Parade Ground. This vast stretch of lawn is perfect for Frisbee or a ballgame. In the mid–19th century, it was filled every August by scores of regiments on view for Queen Victoria (as well as 100,000 spectators) as part of the Royal Scottish Volunteer Review. ⏱ *15 min. North of Queen's Dr., east of Palace of Holyroodhouse.*

After this hike, you deserve a break. **🔟 The Cafe at the Palace** offers drinks (hot and cold) and snacks, as well as a selection of soup, salads, and a couple of entrees. Order at the counter and sit outside if the sun shines. *On the grounds of Holyrood Palace.* ☎ *0131/524-1032. $.*

Wordsworth on the Rock

The famous English poet William Wordsworth, along with his younger sister Dorothy and fellow writer Samuel Coleridge, toured Scotland at the beginning of the 19th century. Dorothy's memoirs were published as *Recollections of a Tour Made in Scotland, AD 1803*. The trio climbed Arthur's Seat on Friday, September 6, and Dorothy notes: "We set out on our walk . . . to the hill called Arthur's Seat, a high hill, very rocky at the top, and below covered with smooth turf. . . . We came to St. Anthony's Well and Chapel, as it is called, but it is more like a hermitage than a chapel—a small ruin, which from its situation is exceedingly interesting, though in itself not remarkable. We sate [sic] down on a stone not far from the chapel, overlooking a pastoral hollow as wild and solitary as any in the heart of the Highland mountains."

Water of Leith

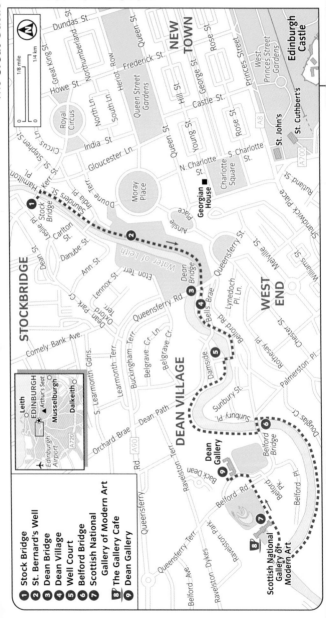

1 Stock Bridge
2 St. Bernard's Well
3 Dean Bridge
4 Dean Village
5 Well Court
6 Belford Bridge
7 Scottish National
  Gallery of Modern Art
8 The Gallery Cafe
9 Dean Gallery

This relatively easy walk (a bit more than a hour long) follows the small river—called the Water of Leith—that flows northeast on a meandering line through Edinburgh to the port of Leith. The trail includes the lovely Dean Village. The name Dene is posted once or twice along the route. It is the older spelling of Dean, which means "deep valley." START: **Water of Leith Walkway sign at the corner of Stockbridge and Saunders sts.**

1 Stock Bridge. This crossing is the focus of the neighborhood/village known as Stockbridge. The bridge was first constructed in 1773 and later renovated in 1827 and 1901. As you follow the path southwest from the bridge (with the river on your right), you'll next come to St. Bernard's Bridge (c. 1824) and its massive stone flight of stairs. ⏱ *10 min. Corner of Stockbridge & Saunders sts.*

2 ★ St. Bernard's Well. Commissioned in 1788 to replace an earlier structure, this Romanesque domed temple contains a statue of Hygeia, the Greek goddess of good health. What you cannot see behind locked doors, alas, is the beautifully decorated interiors of the pump room. Some wooden decking takes you around the riverside of the well. ⏱ *10 min. At the banks of the Water of Leith.*

Be sure to admire the stonework (some of it dating back many centuries) you'll pass as you stroll through Dean Village.

3 ★★ Dean Bridge. One of the landmark engineering and design triumphs of the great engineer Thomas Telford (1757–1834). The four arches of this stone crossing rise magnificently from the ravine, ultimately soaring some 30m (almost 100 ft.) above the gently cascading riverbed below. It was constructed from 1831 to 1832, and was paid for by a former lord provost (mayor) who was redeveloping the lands of the former Dean estate. ⏱ *15 min. 200m/656 ft. past St. Bernard's Well; Queensferry Rd. (500m/1,640 ft. from city center).*

4 ★★★ Dean Village. Originally Water of Leith Village, this was a milling settlement that may date back to the 12th century. The picturesque buildings of Bell's Brae and Hawthornbank Lane are considerably younger, but no less attractive. Admire the stonework on the yellow facade of the building at Bell's Brae, with its 17th-century panel of cherubs, scales, and more milling imagery—as well as a well-eroded inscription blessing the Baxters (bakers) of Edinburgh. The exposed half-timber construction of the Hawthorn Buildings dates to 1895. Wander to the middle of the low stone bridge (called the Old Bridge) that crosses the Water of Leith in the middle of the village for good river views. ⏱ *30 min. 1km/⅔-mile northwest of the city center, off Belford Rd.*

5 Well Court. This impressive baronial-style building, which

The massive stone flight of stairs that lead to St. Bernard's Bridge. See p 61.

housed apartments and a public hall, was built from 1883 to 1886 for the benefit of the community (whose milling business was going elsewhere). But the primary benefactor, newspaper owner Sir John Findlay, had an ulterior motive: The building made an attractive focal point from his home on the bluff above. ⏲ *10 min.*

⑥ **Belford Bridge.** Before you reach this single-arch stone bridge, you'll get a real sense of the depth of the gorge that the Water of Leith passes through as you walk along the wooded banks. Belford Bridge was completed in 1887 and has panels featuring the Edinburgh city coat of arms. ⏲ *15 min.*

⑦ **Scottish National Gallery of Modern Art.** The neoclassical building housing Scotland's National Gallery of Modern Art was formerly John Watson's School and dates to 1825. At the front of the grounds is a 2002 addition called *Landform*. Its spiraling banks of lawns, set around calm ponds, were designed by American landscape architect Charles Jencks. ⏲ *20 min. Belford Rd.* Note that a gate from the river path up to the gallery grounds is locked at 6pm during the summer & at dusk during the winter. See p 28, ⑤.

⑧ **The Gallery Cafe** at the National Gallery of Modern Art has a good deal of outdoor seating during the summer months, and serves a range of sandwiches and soup options. ☎ *0131/332-8600. $.*

⑨ **Dean Gallery.** On the grounds of this gallery, near Belford Road, is a sculpture by one of Scotland's most enduring modern/pop surrealist artists, Sir Eduardo Paolozzi (1924–2005). Beside it, over the yew hedge, is a fine (although private) garden full of fruit and vegetables. The gallery's neoclassical building dates back to 1831, and was once an orphanage. Today it holds a portion of the national collection of modern art. The clock face on the front exterior was originally part of the old Netherbow Port near the World's End Close in the city's Old Town. Around the side is historic Dean cemetery, which has some excellent examples of funerary monuments and sculpture. ⏲ *15 min.* See p 27, ③. ●

The spiraling Landform at the Scottish National Gallery of Art.

Dining in **Edinburgh**

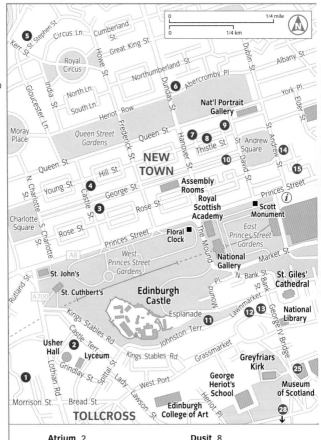

0   1/4 mile
0   1/4 km

Kerr St. · St. Stephen St. · Circus Ln. · Cumberland St. · Great King St. · Dublin St. · Albany St. · York Pl. · Elder St.

Royal Circus

India St. · Howe St. · Northumberland St.

Gloucester Ln. · North Ln. · South Ln. · Heriot Row · Abercromby Pl. · **6**

Moray Place

5

Nat'l Portrait Gallery

Queen Street Gardens · Queen St. · Hanover St. · **7** · **8** · Thistle St. · **9** · St. Andrew Square · **14**

NEW TOWN

Queen St. · Hill St. · George St. · **10** · David St. · **15**

N. Charlotte St. · Young St. · **4** · Castle St. · Rose St. · **3** · Frederick St. · Assembly Rooms · Royal Scottish Academy · Princes Street · **i**

Charlotte Square · S. Charlotte St. · Rose St. · Princes Street · Floral Clock · Scott Monument · East Princes Street Gardens · Market St.

West Princes Street Gardens · The Mound · National Gallery · N. Bank St. · Bank St. · St. Giles' Cathedral

St. John's · St. Cuthbert's · **Edinburgh Castle** · Lawnmarket · **12** · **13** · George IV Bridge · National Library

Rutland St. · Kings Stables Rd. · Esplanade · **11** · Johnston Terr.

Usher Hall · **2** · Lyceum · Castle Terr. · Kings Stables Rd. · Grassmarket · Greyfriars Kirk

1 · Lothian Rd. · Grindlay St. · Spittal St. · Lady Lawson St. · West Port · George Heriot's School · Heriot Pl. · **25** · Museum of Scotland

Morrison St. · Bread St. · **TOLLCROSS** · Edinburgh College of Art · **28**

Previous Page: Café Royal Oyster bar is justifiably renowned for its seafood offerings.

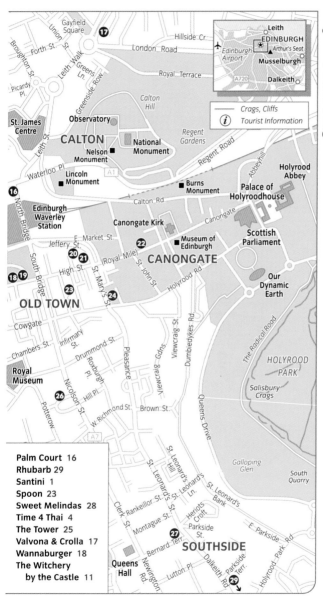

Palm Court 16
Rhubarb 29
Santini 1
Spoon 23
Sweet Melindas 28
Time 4 Thai 4
The Tower 25
Valvona & Crolla 17
Wannaburger 18
The Witchery
 by the Castle 11

Dining in **Leith**

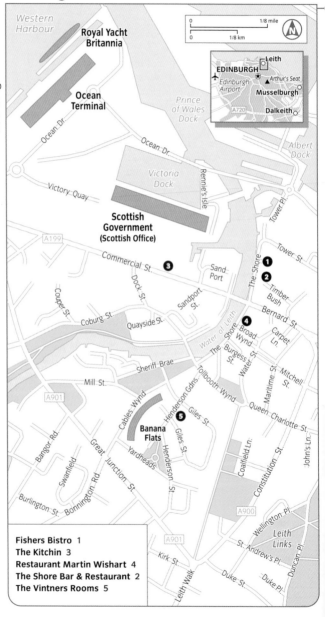

Fishers Bistro 1
The Kitchin 3
Restaurant Martin Wishart 4
The Shore Bar & Restaurant 2
The Vintners Rooms 5

Dining **Best Bets**

Best **Vegetarian**
★★ David Bann's Vegetarian Restaurant $ 56–58 St. Mary's St. (p 69)

Best **Hot Young Chef**
★★ The Kitchin $$$ 78 Commercial Quay (p 71)

Most **Romantic**
★ The Vintners Rooms $$$ The Vaults, 87 Giles St. (p 74)

Best **Burger**
★ Bell's Diner $ 17 St. Stephen St. (p 68)

Best **Outdoor Dining**
★ Oloroso $$–$$$ 33 Castle St. (p 72)

Best **Pre-Theatre Dining**
blue bar café $$ 10 Cambridge St. (p 68)

Best **Neighborhood Hangout**
★ Sweet Melindas $$ 11 Roseneath St. (p 73)

Best **Luxe Afternoon Tea**
Palm Court at the Balmoral Hotel $$ Princes St. (p 69)

Best for **Keeping Kids Happy**
★ Valvona and Crolla $ 19 Elm Row (p 74)

Best **Cheap Eats**
★ Kebab Mahal $ 7 Nicolson Sq. (p 71)

Best **French Brasserie**
★ Le Café St. Honoré $$ 34 NW Thistle St. Lane (p 71)

Best **Fresh Fish/Seafood**
★ Fishers Bistro $$ 1 The Shore (p 70)

Best **Views**
★★ Forth Floor $$–$$$ 30–34 St. Andrew Sq. (p 70)

Best **Cafe Diner**
★★ Spoon $ 15 Blackfriars St. (p 73)

Best **Spanish**
★ Barioja $ 19 Jeffrey St. (p 68)

Most **Atmospheric**
★ The Witchery by the Castle $$$ Castlehill (p 74)

Best **Extravagance**
★★★ Restaurant Martin Wishart $$$ 54 The Shore (p 72)

The 17th-century French dining room at the Vintners Rooms is a great setting for a romantic meal.

Edinburgh **Restaurants A to Z**

★★ **Atrium** WEST END
SCOTTISH/INTERNATIONAL Since
1993, this has been one of Edinburgh's most acclaimed and stylish
restaurants. Dishes use lots of local
and some organic ingredients, displaying flair but not excessive
amounts of fuss. *10 Cambridge St.
(adjacent to the Traverse Theatre).
☎ 0131/228-8882. www.atrium
restaurant.co.uk. Entrees £17–£22.
AE, MC, V. Lunch & dinner Mon–Fri,
dinner Sat. Bus: 1, 10, 15, or 24.
Map p 64.*

★ **Barioja** OLD TOWN *SPANISH*
Casual and staffed by natives of
Spanish-speaking nations, this tapas
bar is fun, friendly, and often lively.
Portions are reasonably substantial
for the price. *19 Jeffrey St. ☎ 0131/
557-3622. Entrees £4–£10. AE, MC, V.
Lunch & dinner Mon–Sat. Bus: 36.
Map p 64.*

★ **Bell's Diner** STOCKBRIDGE
AMERICAN If you're desperate for
a chargrilled patty of real ground
beef, seek out this wee diner. Open
for some 30-odd years, its burgers
are cooked to order with a variety of
toppings (from cheese to garlic butter). *17 St. Stephen St. ☎ 0131/225-
8116. Entrees £6.50–£9. Dinner daily,*

*Fresh lamb is just one of many locally
sourced options at the very stylish Atrium.*

*lunch Sat. Bus: 24, 29, or 42. Map
p 64.*

blue bar café WEST END *INTER-
NATIONAL/MODERN BRITISH* This
attractive bistro is the less expensive sibling of Atrium (see above),
with dishes that can serve as either
starters or a light main meal, as well
as a list of more substantial choices.
*10 Cambridge St. ☎ 0131/221-1222.
www.bluebarcafe.com. Entrees*

*Try the salmon Nicoise or one of the many light options on the menu at the blue bar
café.*

Tea for Two?

A traditional choice for the classically British experience of afternoon tea is **Clarinda's Tearoom,** 69 Canongate (☎ 0131/557-1888), where you'll find lace tablecloths, china, and Wedgwood plates on the walls—and light, affordable cakes and meals for under £10. If you want a formal venue with more substantial and filling choices (and a considerably higher price of £21), try the **Palm Court** at the Balmoral Hotel, Princes Street. Reservations are recommended for the Palm Court (☎ 0131/556-2414).

£10–£15. AE, MC, V. Lunch & dinner Mon–Sat. Bus: 1, 10, 15, or 24. Map p 64.

★ **Café Royal Oyster Bar** NEW TOWN *SEAFOOD/FISH* Many of this 140-year-old restaurant's splendid Victorian touches (think dark wood and stained glass) remain intact today. The main menu offers oysters, salmon, langoustines, and lobsters—as well as beef and rabbit. *17a W. Register St.* ☎ *0131/556-4124. Entrees £15–£20. AE, MC, V. Lunch & dinner daily. Bus: 8 or 29. Map p 64.*

Calistoga SOUTHSIDE *AMERICAN* Unique in Scotland, this casual and relaxed restaurant attempts to re-create California cuisine, focusing on Pacific Rim–inspired recipes. The wine list is devoted to vintages from the Golden State (plus two from Oregon). *93 St. Leonard St.* ☎ *0131/668-4207. www.calistoga.co.uk. Entrees £13–£15. AE, MC, V. Dinner daily, lunch Fri–Mon. Bus: 14, 30, or 33. Map p 64.*

★★ **David Bann's Vegetarian Restaurant** OLD TOWN *VEGETARIAN* Chef David Bann has been at the forefront of meat-free cooking in Edinburgh for more than a decade, and his vegetarian meals are tasty and healthy. The dining room is as stylish as the cooking. *56–58 St.*

Mary's St. ☎ *0131/556-5888. www.davidbann.com. Entrees £7.50–£10. AE, MC, V. Lunch & dinner daily. Bus: 36. Map p 64.*

Dome Grill Room and Bar NEW TOWN *INTERNATIONAL* Corinthian columns, intricate mosaic tile flooring, a marble-topped bar, potted palms, and towering flower arrangements—all housed under an elaborate domed ceiling. Many people come here for the decor and ambience, although the food is fine. *14 George St.* ☎ *0131/624-8624. www.thedomeedinburgh.com. Entrees £10–£22. AE, DC, MC, V. Lunch & dinner daily. Bus: 45. Map p 64.*

The splendid Victorian dining room at Café Royal Oyster Bar has been seating diners for more than century.

The food isn't bad, but most people come to the Dome Grill Room and Bar for the posh ambience. See p 69.

★ **Dusit** NEW TOWN *THAI* An unassuming restaurant with a reputation for serving some of the best Thai cuisine in the city. A number of dishes use Scottish produce, such as venison, and the seafood options are plentiful. *49a Thistle St.* ☎ *0131/220-6846. www.dusit.co.uk. Entrees £10–£16. AE, MC, V. Lunch & dinner daily. Bus: 24, 29, or 42. Map p 64.*

★ **Fishers Bistro** LEITH *FISH* A favorite for its seafood—and its views of the harbor at Leith. The chefs here offer such enticing dishes as fresh Loch Fyne oysters and breaded and crispy fish cakes. *1 The Shore.* ☎ *0131/554-5666. Entrees £12–£16. AE, MC, V. Lunch & dinner daily. Bus: 16, 22, 35, or 36. Map p 66.*

★★ **Forth Floor** NEW TOWN *SCOTTISH/MODERN BRITISH* This restaurant and brasserie at the top of the Harvey Nichols department store, with excellent city views (and of the Firth of Forth), dishes out excellent contemporary Scottish cooking. The brasserie menu, while less extensive, serves just as tasty

dishes that are cheaper than the restaurant's. *In Harvey Nichols, 30–34 St. Andrew Sq.* ☎ *0131/524-8350. www.harveynichols.com. Entrees £15–£25. AE, DC, MC, V. Lunch & dinner daily. Bus: 8, 10, 12, or 45. Map p 64.*

★ **The Grain Store** OLD TOWN *SCOTTISH/MODERN BRITISH* In its upstairs dining room, the Grain Store delivers ambitious, innovative cooking, including such dishes as a saddle of Scottish venison with a beetroot fondant, and a medley of sea bass and scallops. *30 Victoria St.* ☎ *0131/225-7635. www.grain store-restaurant.co.uk. Entrees £17–£25. AE, MC, V. Lunch & dinner daily. Bus: 2, 41, or 42. Map p 64.*

Haldanes Restaurant NEW TOWN *SCOTTISH* Dinners here are choreographed like meals in a private country house, with polite and deferential service. Excellent for a romantic meal. *13b Dundas St.* ☎ *0131/556-8407. www.haldanes restaurant.com. Entrees £16–£23. MC, V. Lunch & dinner Tues–Sat. Bus: 23 or 27. Map p 64.*

Henderson's Salad Table is a great spot for tasty and inexpensive vegetarian cuisine.

Sample imaginative cooking in a swanky setting at the rooftop Oloroso. See p 72.

kids Henderson's Salad Table
NEW TOWN *VEGETARIAN* This is Edinburgh's longtime stalwart of healthy, inexpensive, and totally vegetarian cuisine. Dinner features table service and an expanded menu. Wines include organic options. *94 Hanover St.* ☎ *0131/225-2131. www.hendersonsofedinburgh.co.uk. Entrees £6–£8. MC, V. Breakfast, lunch & dinner Mon–Sat. Bus: 13, 23, or 27. Map p 64.*

Howies OLD TOWN *SCOTTISH/ MODERN BRITISH* Of this local chain's four branches, the one near the Royal Mile is most convenient. The Howies motto is "fine food without the faff"—and it's sold at reasonable prices, too. *10–14 Victoria St.* ☎ *0131/225-1721. www.howies. uk.com. Set dinner £18. AE, MC, V. Lunch & dinner daily. Bus: 2, 41, or 42. Map p 64.*

★ Kebab Mahal SOUTHSIDE *INDIAN* Drawing a cross section of the city, this basic, inexpensive Indian restaurant—where you may have to share your table with others—is a local landmark. No alcohol is served (or allowed inside), but it is

open late. *7 Nicolson Sq.* ☎ *0131/ 667-5214. Entrees £4–£6. Lunch & dinner daily. No credit cards. Bus: 3, 5, 29, 31, or 35. Map p 64.*

★★ The Kitchin LEITH *MODERN SCOTTISH/FRENCH* After opening this contemporary restaurant in 2006, appropriately named chef/owner Tom Kitchin quickly garnered a Michelin star, among other awards. The 20-something chef's French-inspired recipes use top seasonal Scottish ingredients. *78 Commercial Quay.* ☎ *0131/555-1755. www.thekitchin.com. Entrees £22. MC, V. Lunch & dinner Tues–Sat. Bus: 16, 22, 35, or 36. Map p 66.*

★ La Garrigue OLD TOWN *FRENCH* Its chef and owner hails from southern France, and here he re-creates that region's fresh and rustic cooking. The feeling of the dining room is casual but still stylish. *31 Jeffrey St.* ☎ *0131/557-3032. www.lagarrigue.co.uk. Set lunch £13, dinner £20. AE, MC, V. Lunch & dinner Mon–Sat. Bus: 36. Map p 64.*

★ Le Café St. Honoré NEW TOWN *FRENCH* This Parisian-style brasserie is a rapid-paced place at

The prices are high, but the food is worth the splurge at Restaurant Martin Wishart. See p 72.

King o' the Puddin' Race

Haggis, the much-misunderstood traditional dish of Scotland, can be an acquired taste, but it's honestly tasty. **Macsween of Edinburgh** (www.macsween.co.uk) is a long-established family business specializing in what poet Robert Burns lionized as the "King o' the Puddin' Race." Their version includes lamb, beef, oatmeal, onions, and various seasonings and spices—all cooked together in a natural casing. You can buy it at many supermarkets and food stores in Edinburgh. They also make a popular vegetarian version.

lunchtime and more sedate at dinner, with cuisine that might include venison with juniper berries or pheasant in wine. *34 NW Thistle St. Lane.* ☎ *0131/226-2211. Entrees £16–£20. AE, MC, V. Lunch & dinner daily. Bus: 24, 29, or 42. Map p 64.*

★ **Number One** NEW TOWN *SCOTTISH/MODERN BRITISH* The premier restaurant in the city's premier central hotel has a well-earned Michelin star for its superior cuisine and service. A special treat that's worth the price. *In the Balmoral Hotel, 1 Princes St.* ☎ *0131/557-6727. www.thebalmoralhotel.com. Set dinner £60. AE, DC, MC, V. Dinner daily. Bus: 3, 8, 19, or 30. Map p 64.*

★ **Oloroso** NEW TOWN *SCOTTISH/INTERNATIONAL* At this rooftop restaurant, with an ample veranda and excellent panoramic views, the atmosphere is contemporary and swanky, and the cooking imaginative. The bar, which mixes some mean cocktails, is usually open until 1am. *33 Castle St.* ☎ *0131/226-7614. www.oloroso.co.uk. Entrees £15–£25. MC, V. Lunch & dinner daily. Bus: 24, 29, or 42. Map p 64.*

★★★ **Restaurant Martin Wishart** LEITH *MODERN FRENCH* One of Scotland's leading chefs, Wishart takes his accolades in stride and constantly strives to improve

the quality of this high-priced establishment, where the menu is seasonal and the wine list superb. If it's an option, try the John Dory with leeks, salsify, mussel, and almond gratin. *54 The Shore.* ☎ *0131/553-3557. www.martin-wishart.co.uk. Entrees £20–£25, set dinner £60. AE, MC, V. Lunch & dinner Tues–Sat. Bus: 22 or 36. Map p 66.*

Rhubarb SOUTHSIDE *SCOTTISH/MODERN BRITISH* Housed in 17th-century Prestonfield House, this posh, theatrical restaurant offers a sense of drama and flair. The menu is a bit fancy as well. *Priestfield Rd.*

For dramatic dining, both on and off your plate, Rhubarb is an excellent choice.

The setting might be simple at The Shore Bar & Restaurant, but the tasty seafood's always fresh.

☎ 0131/225-1333. www.preston field.com. Entrees £18–£25. AE, DC, MC, V. Lunch & dinner daily. Bus: 2, 14, or 30. Map p 64.

Santini WEST END *ITALIAN* This modern restaurant, set in a building adjacent to the Sheraton Grand Hotel, has some of the capital's classiest Italian cooking. *8 Conference St.* ☎ 0131/221-7788. Entrees £15–£22. AE, MC, V. Lunch & dinner Mon–Fri, dinner Sat. Bus: 1, 2, 10, 24, or 34. Map p 64.

★ **The Shore Bar & Restaurant** LEITH *FISH* Whether eating in the unassuming pub or the slightly more formal dining room, you'll appreciate the simplicity and ease of this operation, dedicated to fresh fish and seafood. *3/4 The Shore.* ☎ 0131/553-5080. Entrees £12–£18. AE, MC, V. Lunch & dinner daily. Bus: 16, 22, 35, or 36. Map p 66.

kids ★★ **Spoon** OLD TOWN *CAFE* This particular spoon is far from greasy. Instead, this contemporary cafe combines a relaxed ambience, first-rate espresso-based coffees, and the sure hand of a classically trained chef on sandwiches, soups, and cakes. *15 Blackfriars St.* ☎ 0131/556-6922. Entrees £4.50. MC, V. Lunch Mon–Sat. Bus: 35. Map p 64.

★ **Sweet Melindas** SOUTHSIDE *SCOTTISH/FISH* South of the Meadows, this is a neighborhood favorite but merits a visit from anyone admiring simple and amiable surroundings. The menu emphasizes fish, which the chefs purchase from the shop next door. *11 Roseneath St.* ☎ 0131/229-7953. Entrees £10–£15. AE, MC, V. Lunch & dinner Tues–Sat, dinner Mon. Bus: 24 or 41. Map p 64.

Time 4 Thai NEW TOWN *THAI* Come to this stylish, relatively new restaurant for well-made and attractively presented East Asian curries, and other Thai specialties. Everything is served with grace and courtesy. *45 N. Castle St.* ☎ 0131/225-8822. Entrees £8–£16. AE, MC, V. Lunch & dinner daily. Bus: 24, 29, or 42. Map p 64.

★ **The Tower** OLD TOWN *SCOTTISH/MODERN BRITISH* A window seat (request it when you make your reservation) at this restaurant, atop the Museum of Scotland, makes a meal here more special. Hearty portions of steak, roast venison, and excellent seafood are featured on the menu. *Chambers St.* ☎ 0131/225-3003. www.tower-restaurant.com. Entrees £14–£22. AE, DC, MC, V. Lunch & dinner daily. Bus: 2, 41, or 42. Map p 64.

To complement the excellent food at The Tower, request a window seat so you can also sample the fabulous views.

Family-Friendly Fare

If you're looking for a friendly lunch spot, children generally love the **Baked Potato Shop,** 56 Cockburn St. (☎ **0131/225-7572**), just off the High Street in Old Town. Kids can order fluffy baked potatoes with a choice of half a dozen hot fillings.

kids ★ **Valvona & Crolla,** 19 Elm Row (☎ **0131/556-6066**), is best known as one of the U.K.'s finest delis, but the cafe in the back handles children in a way that bambini-loving Italians do best.

★ **The Vintners Rooms** LEITH *FRENCH*   Housed in a 17th-century French wine store, this romantic restaurant's reputation has never been higher. The chef, born in France, uses Scottish produce in a host of confidently Gallic dishes. *In The Vaults, 87 Giles St.* ☎ *0131/554-6767. www.thevintnersrooms.com. Entrees £18–£23. AE, MC, V. Lunch & dinner Tues–Sat, lunch Sun. Bus: 22 or 36. Map p 66.*

kids **Wannaburger** OLD TOWN *AMERICAN*   A modern diner in the heart of Old Town serves what it says on the label: burgers. Made of 100% Scottish beef (and grilled medium rare instead of the city's usual well-done), they come with a variety of toppings, presented on hefty sesame seed buns. *217 High St.* ☎ *0131/225-8770. www.wannaburger.com. Entrees £5.50. MC, V. Lunch & dinner daily. Bus: 35. Map p 64.*

★ **The Witchery by the Castle** OLD TOWN *SCOTTISH/MODERN BRITISH*   In a historic building that's associated with nearby Medieval sites of execution (and a ghost or two), this restaurant near Edinburgh castle serves classy Scottish food in even classier surroundings. Great for special occasions. *Castlehill, Royal Mile.* ☎ *0131/225-5613. www.thewitchery.com. Entrees £18–£25. AE, DC, MC, V. Lunch & dinner daily. Bus: 28. Map p 64.* ●

Head to The Witchery By the Castle for well-constructed dishes served in classy surroundings.

Nightlife in Edinburgh

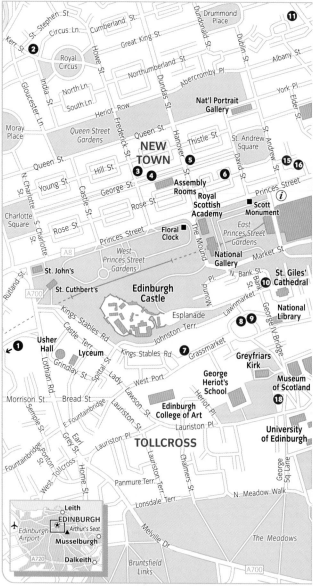

Previous Page: Most of Edinburgh's have a number of Scottish ales on tap, so be sure to sample the local brew.

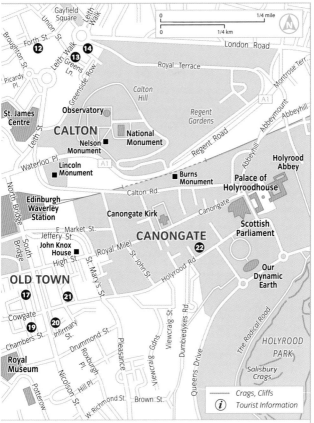

The Abbotsford 6
All Bar One 5
The Bailie Bar 2
The Beehive Inn 7
Black Bo's 21
Bongo Club 22
Bow Bar 8
C. C. Bloom's 13
Caberet Voltaire 17
Café Royal
    Circle Bar 15
Corn Exchange 1

Deacon Brodie's
    Tavern 10
Guildford Arms 16
The Jazz Bar 19
The Liquid Room 9
Opal Lounge 4
The Outhouse 12
Planet Out 14
Po Na Na 3
The Royal Oak 20
Sala 11
Sandy Bell's 18

Nightlife in Leith

The Pond Bar 2
The Shore 1

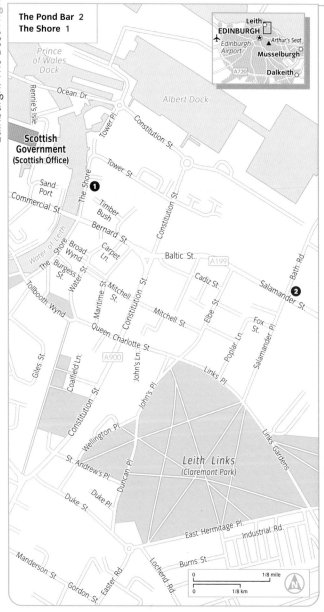

Nightlife Best Bets

Best for Real Ale
★ Bow Bar, *80 West Bow (p 80)*

Best Grassmarket Pub
The Beehive Inn, *18–20 Grassmarket (p 80)*

Best Victorian Bar
★★ Café Royal Circle Bar, *17 W. Register St. (p 80)*

Best Beer Garden
★ The Outhouse, *12a Broughton St. Lane (p 82)*

Best See and be Seen Bar
Opal Lounge, *51a George St. (p 82)*

Best for Bottle Lager
★★ The Pond Bar, *2–4 Bath Rd. (p 83)*

Best Old-Style Pub
★ Guildford Arms, *1–5 W. Register St. (p 81)*

Best Leith Pub
★★★ The Shore, *3–4 The Shore. (p 83)*

Best Scottish Folk Hangout
★ Sandy Bell's, *25 Forrest Rd. (p 84)*

Best Jazz Joint
★ The Jazz Bar, *1A Chambers St. (p 84)*

Best Rock Club
★ The Liquid Room, *9c Victoria St. (p 83)*

Best Gay Bar
Planet Out, *6 Baxters Place. (p 84)*

Best Dive Bar
★ Black Bo's, *57 Blackfriars St. (p 80)*

Best Neighborhood Hangout
★ The Bailie Bar, *2 St. Stephen St. (p 80)*

Best Rose Street Pub
★ The Abbotsford, *3 Rose St. (p 80)*

Best for Funky Dancing Cabaret
Cabaret Voltaire, *36–38 Blair St. (p 83)*

For live Scottish folk music, you won't do better than Sandy Bell's. See p 84.

Edinburgh Nightlife A to Z

If Bow Bar's cask-conditioned ales don't work for you, down a dram of one of its whiskies.

Bars & Pubs

★ **The Abbotsford** NEW TOWN Bartenders have been pouring pints here since around 1900, and the gaslight era is preserved thanks to dark paneling and an ornate plaster ceiling. The ales on tap change about once a week. *3 Rose St.* ☎ *0131/225-5276. Bus: 3, 28, or 45. Map p 76.*

All Bar One NEW TOWN All Bar One is a well-run U.K. chain with modern decor and an excellent selection of wines by the glass. Food—global tapas and impressive entrees—is available daily until 9 or 10pm. *29 George St.* ☎ *0131/226-9971. Bus: 24, 28, or 45. Map p 76.*

★ **The Bailie Bar** STOCKBRIDGE This traditional pub is in the heart of Stockbridge village and feels as if it could serve as the public meeting hall for the neighborhood, with plenty of banter between the regulars and the staff. *2 St. Stephen St.* ☎ *0131/225-4673. Bus: 24, 29, or 42. Map p 76.*

The Beehive Inn OLD TOWN The Grassmarket is chockablock with pubs. This one offers plenty of

space in three different rooms and, unlike so many others nearby, it doesn't try to flog any dubious historic connections. There's a beer garden in back and streetside seating in good weather. *18–20 Grassmarket.* ☎ *0131/225-7171. Bus: 2. Map p 76.*

★ **Black Bo's** OLD TOWN This bar is slightly unconventional and one of my personal faves. It is neither a traditional pub nor a particularly stylish place, but it does have an easy air of hipness. *57 Blackfriars St.* ☎ *0131/557-6136. Bus: 35. Map p 76.*

★ **Bow Bar** OLD TOWN It feels like a classic time-honored Edinburgh pub, but is actually just over a dozen years old. Still, it looks the part and features some eight cask-conditioned ales. *80 West Bow.* ☎ *0131/226-7667. Bus: 2 or 35. Map p 76.*

★★ **Café Royal Circle Bar** NEW TOWN Another personal favorite. The high Victorian design of Café Royal was nearly demolished in the

The wonderful Victorian character of Café Royal Circle Bar makes it an atmospheric place for a drink.

The exquisite decor of the Guildford Arms makes it a great stop on a pub crawl.

late 1960s, and thank goodness the wrecking ball wasn't used. Spacious booths and plenty of room around the bar combine to make this a comfortable place to drink. *17 W. Register St.* ☎ *0131/556-1884. Bus: 8 or 17. Map p 76.*

Deacon Brodie's Tavern OLD TOWN This Royal Mile pub is primarily populated by tourists and local lawyers. Its name, of course, perpetuates the memory of William Brodie (1741–88), good citizen by day and nasty robber by night (and the inspiration behind Dr. Jekyll and Mr. Hyde). *435 Lawnmarket.* ☎ *0131/ 225-6531. Bus: 35. Map p 76.*

★ **Guildford Arms** NEW TOWN Head through this pub's revolving doors, and you will find seven arched windows with etched

glass and exquisite cornices. It's reasonably large and bustling, with a good deal of character. *1–5 W. Register St.* ☎ *0131/556-4312. www. guildfordarms.com. Bus: 8 or 17. Map p 76.*

Deacon Brodie's Tavern is a tourist haven for the inspiration behind Dr. Jekyll and Mr. Hyde.

Late Night Noshing

Okay, you've been out to play and it's late but you're famished. If you're in the West End, Lothian Road is your best bet. Try **Lazio,** 95 Lothian Rd. (☎ **0131/229-7788**), for a bit of pizza or pasta. It's open until midnight during the week and until 2am on Friday and Saturday nights (that is, Sat and Sun mornings). For something a bit more modern and trendy, **Favorit,** Teviot Place. (☎ **0131/220-6880**), is an NYC-style diner open until 3am, with food served until 2am.

For a stylish place where you can drink and dance, try Opal Lounge.

Opal Lounge NEW TOWN   If you want to experience a so-called Scottish "style bar," then this is an excellent example of the genre. After opening in 2001, it became the haunt of Prince William, when the handsome heir to the British throne attended St. Andrew's University. The Opal draws a predominantly young, well-dressed, and affluent crowd. *51a George St.* ☎ *0131/226-2275.*

www.opallounge.co.uk. *Bus: 24, 29, or 42. Map p 76.*

★ **The Outhouse** NEW TOWN   Down a cobbled lane off Broughton Street, this contemporary bar, renovated in 2003, has a popular beer garden (equipped with outdoor heaters) out back. *12a Broughton St. Lane.* ☎ *0131/557-6688. Bus: 8 or 17. Map p 76.*

Whisky: The Water of Life

When you're in Scotland, you don't need to ask for a *Scotch* whisky. Everyone here just calls it whisky. Connoisseurs prefer varieties of single malt whisky rather than blended versions, such as Johnnie Walker. The taste of malt whisky depends largely on where it's distilled: Those from one of the Islands, such as Talisker on Skye or Ardbeg on Islay, are best known for their strong peaty and slightly briny flavors. Those from the Highlands, say the lovely Glenmorangie, can have less of the smoky, peaty element, tasting a bit sweeter. My all-time favorite would probably be Highland Park from the far reaches of Orkney: well-balanced and very drinkable. If you're ordering whisky, simply ask for a "wee dram" and the bartender may think you've been drinking in Scotland your whole life. But if you want to maintain the illusion, you must order it neat—that is, no ice or mixers. Only a few drops of tap water are allowed, to help lift the aromas and flavors.

★★ **The Pond Bar** LEITH As bohemian as Black Bo's (p 80), the decor of this bar is eclectic—it looks like it was furnished by the purchase of a lot in a blind auction. The highlights of the drinks selection are draft and bottled European lagers. *2–4 Bath Rd., at Salamander St.* ☎ *0131/467-3825. Bus: 12. Map p 78.*

★★★ **The Shore** LEITH Probably my overall favorite, this pub fits seamlessly into Leith's seaside port ambience, without the usual cork and netting decorations. On 3 nights of the week, you'll find live folk and jazz music. *3–4 The Shore.* ☎ *0131/553-5080. www.theshore.biz. Bus: 16 or 36. Map p 78.*

Dance Clubs

Bongo Club OLD TOWN Offering a varied program of music throughout the week—funk, dub, and experimental—this venue has more reasonably priced drinks than many. *Moray House, 37 Holyrood Rd.* ☎ *0131/558-7604. www.the bongoclub.co.uk. Up to £7 cover. Bus: 35. Map p 76.*

Cabaret Voltaire OLD TOWN This club's mix includes house, indie, and techno—plus live bands 10 times a month. *36–38 Blair St.* ☎ *0131/220-6176. www.thecabaret voltaire.com. Up to £12 cover. Bus: 35. Map p 76.*

The Liquid Room OLD TOWN This busy but smallish space is a dance club when not hosting rock groups. It's popular with guest DJs. *9c Victoria St. See p 84. Map p 76.*

Opal Lounge NEW TOWN Patronized by the well-dressed New Town set, this stylish bar doubles as a late-night club, with a small dance floor sandwiched between the main bar and a low-lit lounge. *51a George St. See p 82. Map p 76.*

Po Na Na This is the Edinburgh branch of a successful chain of clubs in Britain with a Moroccan casbah theme. The dance mix is hip-hop and funk, or disco and the sounds of the '80s. *43B Frederick St.* ☎ *0131/226-2224. www.ponana. co.uk. Up to £8 cover. Bus: 80. Map p 76.*

The Royal Oak is a bi-level pub where the selection of whiskies is vast, and live folk music plays into the wee hours of the night. See p 84.

Gay & Lesbian Edinburgh

The heart of the gay community is an area below Calton Hill, incorporating the top of Leith Walk around the Playhouse Theatre and nearby Broughton Street—though it is hardly a district such as Manhattan's Christopher Street or San Francisco's Castro. **C. C. Bloom's** (apparently named after Bette Midler's character in *Beaches*), 23–24 Greenside Place. (☎ **0131/556-9331;** bus: 7 or 22), is one of Edinburgh's long-running and enduringly popular gay nightspots. **Planet Out,** 6 Baxters Place. (☎ 0131/524-0061), draws a mixed crowd, attracting a slightly higher percentage of lesbians than most of its nearby competitors. **Sala,** 60 Broughton St. (☎ **0131/556-5758**), is the focus of gay cultural life on Broughton Street, and linked to the Lesbian, Gay, and Bisexual Centre, which is a useful resource for residents and visitors alike.

Folk Music

The Royal Oak SOUTHSIDE This two-level pub, often open until 2am, is the home of live Scottish folk music. On Sunday from 8:30pm, various guests play at the "Wee Folk Club." *1 Infirmary St.* ☎ *0131/557-2976. www.royal-oak-folk.com. £3 cover Sun. Bus: 3, 5, 8, or 29. Map p 76.*

★ **Sandy Bell's** OLD TOWN This small, corner pub near the Museum of Scotland is a landmark for Scottish and Gaelic culture, with live acts nearly every night and all day Saturday. Surprisingly, when it's

If you want to get up close to the performers, The Liquid Room is the best place to catch a rock band.

not hosting folk or traditional musicians, music rarely plays at all. *25 Forrest Rd.* ☎ *0131/225-2751. No cover. Bus: 2 or 42. Map p 76.*

Rock & Jazz

Corn Exchange SLATEFORD A bit of a haul from the city center, this medium- to small-size hall (3,000 capacity) books rock and pop performers from Radiohead to Justin Timberlake. *11 New Market Rd.* ☎ *0131/477-3500. www.ece.uk.com. Ticket prices vary. Bus: 4 or 28. Suburban train: Slateford. Map p 76.*

★ **The Jazz Bar** OLD TOWN This basement bar is owned by a practicing jazz drummer, who occasionally sits in with performers (a few of them internationally renowned). The only purpose-built space dedicated to jazz in the city. *1A Chambers St.* ☎ *0131/ 220-4298. www.thejazzbar.co.uk. Cover £3–£10. Bus: 3, 5, 8, or 29. Map p 76.*

★ **The Liquid Room** OLD TOWN With space for fewer than 1,000, this is Edinburgh's best venue for seeing the sweat off the brows of bands. *9c Victoria St.* ☎ *0131/225-2564. www.liquidroom.com. Ticket prices vary. Bus: 35. Map p 76.* ●

A&E in Edinburgh

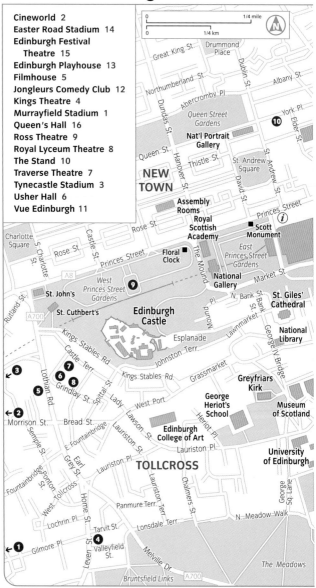

Cineworld 2
Easter Road Stadium 14
Edinburgh Festival
   Theatre 15
Edinburgh Playhouse 13
Filmhouse 5
Jongleurs Comedy Club 12
Kings Theatre 4
Murrayfield Stadium 1
Queen's Hall 16
Ross Theatre 9
Royal Lyceum Theatre 8
The Stand 10
Traverse Theatre 7
Tynecastle Stadium 3
Usher Hall 6
Vue Edinburgh 11

Previous Page: The 1,300-seat Kings Theatre hosts everything from ballet to opera to productions by the Scottish National Theatre.

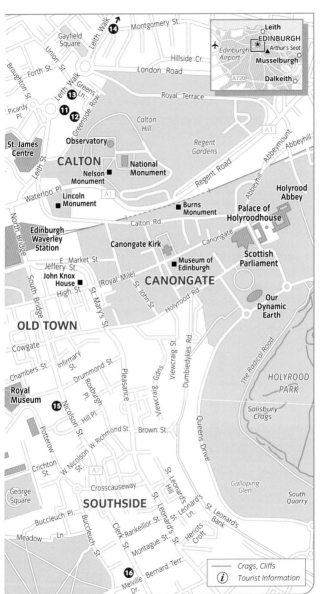

Arts & Entertainment **Best Bets**

Best **Comedy Club**
★★ The Stand, *5 York Place (p 89)*

Best **Art House Cinema**
★★ Filmhouse, *88 Lothian Rd. (p 89)*

Best **Multiplex**
Vue Edinburgh, *Greenside Place. (p 89)*

Best **Concert Hall**
★★ Usher Hall, *71 Lothian Rd. (p 90)*

Best for **Contemporary Drama**
★★ Traverse Theatre, *10 Cambridge St. (p 91)*

Best for **Shakespeare Productions**
★ Royal Lyceum Theatre, *Grindlay St. (p 91)*

Best for **Family Entertainment**
Edinburgh Playhouse, *18–22 Greenside Place (p 91)*

Best for **Ballet**
Edinburgh Festival Theatre, *13–29 Nicolson St. (p 89)*

Best **Victorian Theater**
Kings Theatre, *2 Leven St. (p 91)*

Best **Outdoors Performance Space**
Ross Theatre, *W. Princes Street Gardens. (p 90)*

Best **Annual Festival**
Edinburgh Festival Fringe *(p 91)*

Best **Fireworks Display**
Edinburgh Hogmanay, *Edinburgh Castle (p 90)*

Best **Precision Marching**
Military Tattoo, *Edinburgh Castle (p 92)*

Best **Sports Spectacle**
Six Nations Rugby, *Murrayfield Stadium (p 92)*

Best **Place to Hear Authors**
Edinburgh International Book Festival, *Charlotte Sq. (p 91)*

Best **Small Concert Hall**
Queen's Hall, *Clerk St. (p 90)*

Best **Street Party**
Edinburgh's Hogmanay, *Princes St. (p 90)*

Built specifically as a comedy club, The Stand is the best place for comedy in the city. See p 89.

Arts & Entertainment **A to Z**

Ballet & Opera
Edinburgh Festival Theatre
SOUTHSIDE   This 1,915-seat venue, once known as the Art Deco–style Empire Theatre, dates back to the 1920s, though a theater has stood on this site since 1830. It reopened after major renovations for the 1994 Edinburgh Festival (hence its name). It hosts the national opera and ballet, as well as touring companies and orchestras. *13–29 Nicolson St.* ☎ *0131/529-6000. www.eft.co.uk. Tickets £6–£45. Bus: 5, 7, 8, or 29. Map p 86.*

Cinema
Cineworld WEST END   A branch of a chain of multiplex cinemas across the U.K. It combines big releases and Hollywood blockbusters with art house and some foreign films, as well. *130 Dundee St.* ☎ *0871/200-2000. www.cineworld.co.uk. Tickets £6. Bus: 34 or 38. Map p 86.*

★★ **Filmhouse** WEST END   A must stop for any visiting film buffs, this is Edinburgh's most important movie house. The film genres shown on its three screens include foreign and art house, classic and experimental, and documentaries and shorts. The Filmhouse also hosts discussions and lectures with directors. *88 Lothian Rd.* ☎ *0131/228-2688. www.filmhouse cinema.com. Tickets £1.50–£6. Bus: 10, 22, or 30. Map p 86.*

Vue Edinburgh NEW TOWN   This big glass-fronted multiplex below Calton Hill is the most recent addition to the Edinburgh movie scene. It offers first-run, big commercial releases. *Greenside Place (at top of Leith Walk).* ☎ *0871/224-0240. www.myvue.com. Tickets £6. Bus: 7 or 22. Map p 86.*

Edinburgh likes its comedy clubs and Jongleurs Comedy Club hosts both local and international talent.

Comedy
Jongleurs Comedy Club NEW TOWN   A corporate-owned entity based in England, with more than a dozen venues across the U.K., Jongleurs has a cadre of house funny men (and women), and also presents touring comedians from overseas. *Omni Centre, Greenside Place (top of Leith Walk).* ☎ *0870/787-0707. www.jongleurs.com. Tickets £5–£20. Bus: 7 or 22. Map p 86.*

★★ **The Stand** NEW TOWN   Pardon the pun, but stand-up comedy is taken seriously in the Scottish capital. Just down the hill from St. Andrew Square, this is the premier, purpose-built local venue for comedians. Big acts are reserved for weekends, while local talent takes the stage during the week. *5 York Place (near Queen St.).* ☎ *0131/558-7272. www.thestand.co.uk. Tickets £1.50–£10. Bus: 8 or 17. Map p 86.*

Happy Hogmanay!

What's that you say? Hogmanay is what the Scots call New Year's Eve. Traditionally and culturally it is actually bigger than Christmas (though the commercialization of the latter is slowly altering the equation). Edinburgh hosts one of the biggest December 31 parties on the planet, and the celebrations usually begin a few days in advance with street parties and big bonfires. When the clock strikes midnight, and the new year begins, however, people really let their hair down, while rock bands play in Princes Street Gardens and fireworks fill the skies, launched from most of the city's hills. Quite a sight. For information, visit **www. edinburghshogmanay.com**.

For the best Hogmanay fireworks, head to Princes Street Gardens, just below Edinburgh Castle.

Concert Halls

Queen's Hall SOUTHSIDE   About a mile south of Old Town, the Queen's Hall began life as the Hope Park Chapel, but was altered in the 1970s (coinciding with Queen Elizabeth's silver jubilee) to accommodate

Just under a century old, Usher Hall is Edinburgh's top concert hall.

concerts. It's primarily a venue for classical works. *Clerk St. (at Hope Park Terrace).* ☎ *0131/668-2019. www.thequeenshall.net. Ticket prices vary. Bus: 5, 7, 8, or 29. Map p 86.*

Ross Theatre NEW TOWN   The bandstand at this open-air theater on the western end of Princes Street Gardens, in the shadow of Edinburgh Castle, is open during the summer for outdoor concerts. *W. Princes Street Gardens.* ☎ *0131/220-4351. Ticket prices vary. Bus: 3, 4, or 25. Map p 86.*

★★ **Usher Hall** WEST END   This Beaux Arts building opened in 1914 and is Edinburgh's equivalent to New York's Carnegie Hall. During the annual Edinburgh Festival, the 2,900-seat auditorium hosts orchestras such as the London Philharmonic. But it's not only for classical music—top touring jazz, world music, and pop acts play here, too. *71 Lothian Rd. (at Cambridge St.).* ☎ *0131/228-1155. www.usherhall.co.uk. Ticket prices vary. Bus: 1, 10, 15, or 34. Map p 86.*

Drama

Edinburgh Playhouse NEW TOWN   Arguably the largest theater in Great Britain (with more than 3,000 seats), this is Edinburgh's best-known venue for popular plays and touring blockbuster/Broadway-style musicals, such as *Miss Saigon*. The Playhouse also hosts other mainstream acts, such as *Lord of the Dance*. *18–22 Greenside Place (top of Leith Walk).* ☎ *0131/524-3333. www.edinburgh-playhouse.co.uk. Tickets £6–£40. Bus: 5 or 22. Map p 86.*

Kings Theatre TOLLCROSS   This late Victorian venue with a domed ceiling and red-stone frontage turned 100 years old in 2006. The 1,300-seat venue offers a wide repertoire, including productions of the Scottish National Theatre, plus classical entertainment, ballet, and opera. *2 Leven St.* ☎ *0131/ 529-6000. www.eft.co.uk. Tickets £6–£30. Bus: 11, 15, or 17. Map p 86.*

★ **Royal Lyceum Theatre** WEST END   The Lyceum, built in 1883, has a most enviable reputation thanks to presentations that range from the most famous works of Shakespeare to hot new Scottish playwrights. It is home to the leading theatrical production company in the city, often hiring the best Scottish actors. *Grindlay St. (off Lothian Rd.).* ☎ *0131/248-4848 box office; 0131/238-4800 general inquiries. www.lyceum.org. Tickets £8–£30. Bus: 1, 10, 15, or 34. Map p 86.*

★★ **Traverse Theatre** WEST END   This local legend began in the 1960s as an experimental theater company that doubled as bohemian social club; it still produces contemporary drama at its height. The theater's bar is where you'll find the hippest

The World Comes to Edinburgh

The **Edinburgh Festival** (which is actually a few festivals running at once), held in August, is the cultural highlight of the year. Since 1947, the ★ **International Festival** has attracted internationally accomplished performers in classical music, opera, ballet, and drama. But the ★★★ **Fringe** has overtaken it in scope and popularity with its international and first-rate comic acts, plus contemporary drama and performance art. As if all that weren't enough, Edinburgh also hosts an international ★★ **Book Festival, Jazz Festival, and Television Festival.** The town is overrun during this time of year, so if you plan to arrive in August, reserve your hotel well in advance.

The International Festival box office is at The Hub, Castle Hill (☎ 0131/473-2000; www.eif.co. uk). The Fringe is based at 180 High St. (☎ 0131/226-0000; www. edfringe.com). Information on all the festivals is available at **www. edinburghfestivals.co.uk**. Ticket prices vary.

Top-notch theatrical performances are staged all over the city during the Edinburgh Festival.

dramatists and actors in the city. *10 Cambridge St. (off Lothian Rd.). ☎ 0131/228-1404. www.traverse. co.uk. Tickets £5–£16. Bus: 1, 10, 15, or 34. Map p 86.*

A Special Event

Military Tattoo   Occurring at the same time as the Edinburgh Festival (see above), this is one of the city's more popular traditional spectacles. It features precision marching of not only Scottish regiments, but also soldiers and performers (including bands, drill teams, and gymnasts) from dozens of countries on the floodlighted esplanade of Edinburgh Castle. *Tattoo Office, 32 Market St. ☎ 0131/225-1188. www.edinburgh-tattoo.co.uk. Tickets £12–£40.*

Precision marching and piping are a hallmark of the city's world-renowned Military Tattoo.

Spectator Sports

Easter Road Stadium   This 17,500-seat stadium, opened in 1893, is where the Hibernian Football Club (or simply Hibs, for short), one of Edinburgh's two soccer teams, plays. The club dates back to 1875, having first been organized by Irish immigrants (Hibernia's the Latin name for Ireland), and today is a feisty underdog in League matches. *Easter Road, toward Leith. ☎ 0131/661-2159. www.hibs.co.uk. Tickets £10–£50. Bus: 1 or 35. Map p 86.*

Murrayfield Stadium   Opened in 1925, this is the country's national home for rugby and the largest stadium in Scotland, seating almost 68,000. The sport, which has an especially passionate following in Edinburgh, is usually played from autumn to spring, usually on Saturdays. Some of the most celebrated matches are those among teams in the annual Six Nations competition comprising Scotland, Wales, England, Ireland, Italy, and France. *About 3km (1¾ miles) west of Edinburgh's city center (within walking distance from Haymarket station). ☎ 0131/346-5000. www.scottishrugby.org. Tickets £25–£45. Bus: 12, 26, or 31. Map p 86.*

Tynecastle Stadium   Near Haymarket railway station, this large facility (first opened in 1886) is where Edinburgh's other soccer team, the evocatively named Heart of Midlothian Football Club, plays. If that seems like a mouthful, just call them Hearts. Like Hibs, they haven't been a major force in Scottish sport for some time, but they do play entertaining football. *Gorgie Rd. ☎ 0131/200-7201. www.heartsfc.co.uk. Tickets £10–£50. Bus: 1, 2, 3, 21, 25, or 33. Map p 86.* ●

Edinburgh Hotels

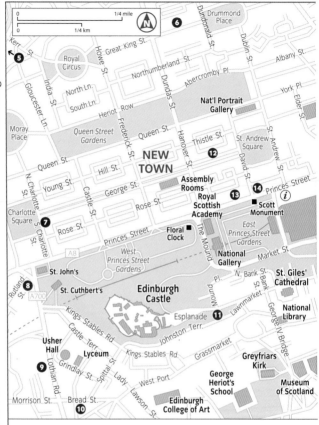

0   1/4 mile
0   1/4 km

Drummond Place
Dundonald St.
Dublin St.
Albany St.
York Pl.
Elder St.
St. Andrew Square
David St.
Princes Street
Scott Monument
East Princes Street Gardens
Market St.
National Gallery
St. Giles' Cathedral
National Library
George IV Bridge
Lawnmarket
N. Bank St.
S. Bank St.
The Mound
Floral Clock
Royal Scottish Academy
Assembly Rooms
Nat'l Portrait Gallery
Thistle St.
Hanover St.
Frederick St.
Queen St.
Hill St.
George St.
Rose St.
Princes Street
West Princes Street Gardens
A8
Castle St.
Young St.
N. Charlotte St.
S. Charlotte St.
Charlotte Square
Rose St.
St. John's
St. Cuthbert's
Rutland St.
A700
Kings Stables Rd.
Castle Terr.
Usher Hall
Lyceum
Grindlay St.
Spittal St.
Lothian Rd.
Morrison St.
Bread St.
Lady Lawson St.
West Port
Kings Stables Rd.
Johnston Terr.
Esplanade
Edinburgh Castle
Grassmarket
George Heriot's School
Greyfriars Kirk
Museum of Scotland
Edinburgh College of Art
Kerr St.
Gloucester Ln.
India St.
Royal Circus
Howe St.
Great King St.
North Ln.
South Ln.
Heriot Row
Moray Place
Queen Street Gardens
Queen St.
Northumberland St.
Dundas St.
Abercromby Pl.
Great King St.
NEW TOWN

6 5 12 13 14 7 8 9 10 11

Balmoral Hotel 16
The Bank Hotel 19
The Bonham 3
Caledonian Hilton 8
The Carlton Hotel 18
Channings 4
The Chester Residence 1
The Edinburgh
 Residence 2
The George Hotel 12
The Glasshouse 15
Holyrood Hotel 21

The Howard 6
Macdonald
 Roxburghe Hotel 7
Old Waverley Hotel 14
Point Hotel 10
Radisson SAS Hotel 20
Ramada Mount Royal 13
The Scotsman 17
Seven Danube Street 5
Sheraton Grand Hotel 9
The Witchery
 by the Castle 11

Previous Page: The Georgian charm and elegance of the Howard makes it one of the best hotels in the city.

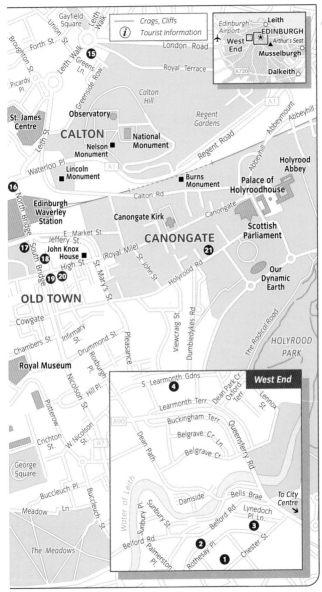

Crags, Cliffs
ⓘ Tourist Information

Edinburgh Airport
West End
Leith
EDINBURGH
★ Arthur's Seat
Musselburgh
Dalkeith
A720

London Road
Royal Terrace

Gayfield Square
Leith Walk
Union St.
Forth St.
Broughton St.
Leith Walk
Greenside Row
Greens Ln.
⑮
Picardy Pl.
Broughton St.

Calton Hill

St. James Centre

Observatory
CALTON
Nelson Monument
National Monument
Regent Gardens
A1
Abbeymount
Abbeyhill
Abbeyhill

Leith St.
Lincoln Monument
A1
Regent Road
Abbeyhill

Waterloo Pl.
Burns Monument
Palace of Holyroodhouse
Holyrood Abbey

⑯
North Bridge
Edinburgh Waverley Station
Calton Rd.
Canongate
Scottish Parliament

E. Market St.
Canongate Kirk
Jeffery St.
⑰
South Bridge
John Knox House
(Royal Mile)
St. John St.
High St.
CANONGATE
㉑
Canongate
⑱
St. Mary's St.
Holyrood Rd.
Our Dynamic Earth
⑲ ⑳

OLD TOWN
Cowgate
Infirmary St.
Viewcraig St.
Dumbiedykes Rd.
The Radical Road

Chambers St.
Drummond St.
Roxburgh Pl.
Pleasance
HOLYROOD PARK

Royal Museum
Hill Pl.
Nicolson St.
Potterow
Crichton St.
W. Nicolson St.
A7
West End
S. Learmonth Gdns.
❹
Dean Park Cr.
Oxford Terr.
Lennox St.

George Square
Buccleuch Pl.
Buccleuch St.
Learmonth Terr.
Buckingham Terr.
A90
Belgrave Cr. Ln.
Queensferry Rd.

Meadow Ln.
Dean Path
Belgrave Cr.

The Meadows
Water of Leith
Damside
Bells Brae
To City Centre →

Belford Rd.
Sunbury Pl.
Sunbury St.
❷
Belford Rd.
Lynedoch Pl. Ln.
❸
Belford Rd.
Palmerston Pl.
Rothesay Pl.
❶
Chester St.

Southside Hotels

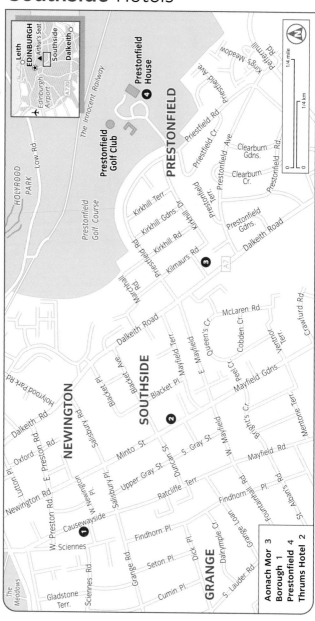

Aonach Mor 3
Borough 1
Prestonfield 4
Thrums Hotel 2

Leith Hotels

A-Haven Townhouse 2
Ardmor House 4
Malmaison 1
Pilrig House Apartment 3

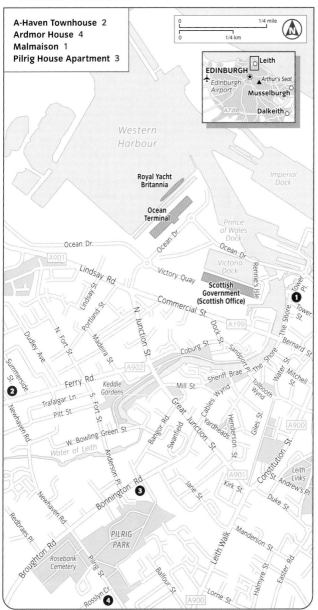

Hotel **Best Bets**

Best **Boutique Hotel**
★★ The Bonham $$$$ 35
Drumsheugh Gardens (p 100)

Best **Traditional Hotel**
★ Caledonian Hilton $$$$ Princes
St. (p 100)

Best **Hotel Restaurant**
★★ Balmoral Hotel $$$$ 1 Princes
St. (p 99)

Best **Hotel to see Celebrities**
★★★ The Witchery by the Castle
$$$$$ Castlehill (p 104)

Best **Hotel Health Spa**
★★ Sheraton Grand Hotel $$$
1 Festival Sq. (p 103)

Best **Old Town Hotel**
★ The Scotsman $$$$ 20 N. Bridge.
(p 103)

Best **New Town Hotel**
★★ The Howard $$$$ 34 Great
King St. (p 101)

Best **West End Hotel**
★ The Edinburgh Residence
$$$–$$$$ 7 Rothesay Terrace (p 100)

Best Hotel **in Leith**
★★ Malmaison $$ 1 Tower Place
(p 102)

Best **View of the Castle**
Point Hotel $$$ 34 Bread St. (p 102)

Best **B&B**
★★ Ardmor House $ 74 Pilrig St.
(p 99)

Best **Family Hotel**
A-Haven Townhouse $ 180 Ferry Rd.
(p 99)

Best **Serviced Apartments**
★ The Chester Residence $$$
9 Chester St. (p 100)

Best **for Self-Catering**
★ Pilrig House Apartment $$
Bonnington Rd. (p 102)

Best **Guest House**
Aonach Mor $–$$ 14 Kilmaurs
Terrace (p 99)

Best **Hotel in a Quiet
Neighborhood**
★★ Channings $$$$ 12–16 S.
Learmonth Gardens (p 100)

Best **Country House Hotel**
★★ Prestonfield $$$$ Priestfield Rd.
(p 102)

A petite room at The Bonham, the best boutique hotel in Edinburgh.

Edinburgh **Hotels A to Z**

The sumptuously furnished rooms at the Balmoral Hotel are among the grandest in the city.

kids A-Haven Townhouse LEITH
The A-Haven is a semidetached gray-stone Victorian with traditionally furnished rooms, some of which are large enough to accommodate families. There's a park nearby. *180 Ferry Rd.* ☎ *0131/554-6559. www. a-haven.co.uk. 14 units. Doubles £60–£110. AE, MC, V. Bus: 14. Map p 97.*

Aonach Mor SOUTHSIDE   This well-priced and family-run guesthouse is located in a proud row of three-story Victorian terraced houses, away from the bustle of the city center. Some rooms have views of Arthur's Seat. *14 Kilmaurs Terrace (at Dalkeith Rd.).* ☎ *0131/667-8694. www.aonachmor.com. 7 units. Doubles £60–£140. MC, V. Bus: 3, 8, or 29. Map p 96.*

★★ **Ardmor House** LEITH   This gay-owned, straight-friendly boutique B&B offers modern renovations and plush furnishings amid bay

windows and period settees. The owners also have two highly rated self-catering apartments in New Town. *74 Pilrig St. (near Leith Walk).* ☎ *0131/554-4944. www.ardmor house.com. 5 units. Doubles £65–£110. MC, V. Bus: 11. Map p 97.*

★★ **Balmoral Hotel** NEW TOWN
Opened in 1902, this is one of the grandest hotels in Britain. Kilted doormen supply the Scottish atmosphere; rooms are sumptuously furnished. *1 Princes St.* ☎ *800/223-6800 in the U.S. or 0131/556-2414. www.thebalmoralhotel.com. 188 units. Doubles £225–£290. AE, DC, MC, V. Bus: 3, 8, 22, 25, or 30. Map p 94.*

The Bank Hotel OLD TOWN
This hotel—housed in a building that was once a branch of the Bank of Scotland—offers better value than many of its local competitors. The guest rooms are dedicated to the works of famous Scots, including

For good value and well-decorated guest rooms dedicated to famous Scots, check into The Bank Hotel.

Robert Burns and Alexander Graham Bell. *1 S. Bridge St.* ☎ *0131/622-6800. www.festival-inns.co.uk. 9 units. Doubles £110. AE, MC, V. Bus: 35. Map p 94.*

★★ **The Bonham** WEST END One of Edinburgh's most stylish hotels, the Bonham's individually decorated rooms have plush upholsteries, state-of-the-art bathrooms with expensive toiletries, and high ceilings. *35 Drumsheugh Gardens.* ☎ *0131/226-6050. www.thebonham. com. 48 units. Doubles £195–£240. AE, DC, MC, V. Bus: 19 or 37. Map p 94.*

Borough SOUTHSIDE While admittedly on the small side, the rooms at this boutique hotel are individually designed and have high ceilings, casement windows, and stylish looks. The bar on the ground floor is equally fashionable. *72 Causewayside.* ☎ *0131/668-2255. www.boroughhotel.com. 12 units. Doubles £80–£125. MC, V. Bus: 3, 5, 7, or 31. Map p 96.*

★ **Caledonian Hilton** WEST END This city landmark has commanding views of Edinburgh Castle. An elegant Edwardian atmosphere pervades its public areas and the first-class guest rooms are spacious (except on the fifth floor), but the hotel does lag behind its competitors in its recreational offerings. *Princes St. (at Lothian Rd.).* ☎ *0131/222-8888. www.caledonian.hilton.com. 251 units. Doubles £180–£380. AE, DC, MC, V. Bus: 12, 25, or 33. Map p 94.*

kids **The Carlton Hotel** OLD TOWN This baronial pile (a former department store) received a substantial upgrade, enlarging some units to create private bathrooms with a tub and shower. Furnishings are tasteful with a subdued modern simplicity. Light sleepers should request rooms at the rear. *19 N. Bridge.* ☎ *0131/472-3000. www. paramount-hotels.co.uk. 189 units. Doubles £180–£250. AE, DC, MC, V. Parking £6. Bus: 3, 8, 14, or 29. Map p 94.*

★★ **Channings** NEW TOWN Five Edwardian terrace houses in a tranquil residential area combine to create a hotel with the atmosphere of a Scottish country house. Guest rooms are modern; for the best views, ask for one in the front of the hotel. *12–16 S. Learmonth Gardens (near Queensferry Rd.).* ☎ *0131/623-9302. www.channings.co.uk. 46 units. Doubles £120–£185. AE, DC, MC, V. Bus: 37. Map p 94.*

★ **The Chester Residence** WEST END You can cook in these "serviced apartments," but someone else cleans up. These luxury apartments vary in size, but all (except the "Patio" apartment) come with a full kitchen; the "Garden" flat has its own private outdoor retreat. *9 Chester St.* ☎ *0131/226-2075. www.chester-residence.com. 5 units. £140–£230. MC, V. Bus: 12 or 31. Map p 94.*

★ **The Edinburgh Residence** WEST END Grand historic staircases and classic wood paneling in the public areas are complemented by completely up-to-date conveniences in the spacious rooms at this top-end hotel. *7 Rothesay Terrace.* ☎ *0131/226-3380. www.theedinburgh residence.com. 29 units. Doubles £150–£265. AE, MC, V. Bus: 13. Map p 94.*

The George Hotel NEW TOWN The buildings that house this elegant inn in the heart of the city were first erected in the 1780s, but a £12-million renovation has updated everything in order to provide modern comfort. *19–21 George St.* ☎ *0131/225-1251. 195 units. Doubles £100–£300. AE, DC, MC, V. Bus: 24, 28, or 45. Map p 94.*

★ **The Glasshouse** NEW TOWN Among the top boutique hotels of Edinburgh, The Glasshouse combines old and new, with an impressive stone church facade harmonizing with a modern glass structure. Many of the sleek, modern bedrooms offer great views of the city. *2 Greenside Place (Leith Walk).* ☎ *0131/525-8200. www.theetoncollection.com/hotels/glasshouse. 65 units. Doubles £175–£195. Bus: 5, 14, or 22. Map p 94.*

★ **Holyrood Hotel** OLD TOWN This impressive and stylish hotel is close to new Scottish Parliament, only minutes from the heart of Old Town. Bedrooms are luxurious, with

A suite bathroom at Channings hotel.

deluxe furnishings and elegant toiletries; the Club Floor is one of the best high-end retreats in town. *81 Holyrood Rd.* ☎ *0870/194-2106. www.macdonaldhotels.co.uk. 156 units. Doubles £150–£250. AE, DC, MC, V. Bus: 35. Map p 94.*

★★ **The Howard** NEW TOWN Made up of a set of Georgian houses—with a definite aura of privacy—this has been dubbed one of the most discrete five-star hotels in the city. The guest rooms are individually and rather elegantly decorated, and have some of the best bathrooms in town. *34 Great King*

If you're seeking unpretentious but hip digs in Leith, Malmaison is an excellent choice. See p 102.

St. ☎ 0131/557-3500. www.the howard.com. 18 units. Doubles £180–£275. AE, DC, MC, V. Bus: 23 or 27. Map p 94.

★ **Macdonald Roxburghe Hotel** NEW TOWN Its classy atmosphere starts in the elegant lobby, which has an ornate ceiling and antique furnishings. The largest rooms—in the hotel's original wing—have imposing fireplaces, but rooms in the newer wing have more modern plumbing. *38 Charlotte St. (at George St.). ☎ 0870/194-2108 or from U.S. 888/892-0038. www.macdonaldhotels. co.uk/roxburghe. 197 units. Doubles £140–£180. AE, DC, MC, V. Bus: 13, 19, or 41. Map p 94.*

★★ **Malmaison** LEITH A hip, unpretentious boutique hotel with a minimalist decor. Set in the old harbor district—in the 19th century it served as a seamen's dorm—Malmaison is a quick walk from the Water of Leith. Rooms are average in size but individually designed and well equipped. *1 Tower Place. ☎ 0131/468-5000. www.malmaison. com. 100 units. Doubles £135–£195. AE, DC, MC, V. Bus: 16, 35. Map p 97.*

Old Waverley Hotel NEW TOWN It opened in 1848 as a temperance hotel (not an issue today) and still has a very central location, opposite the Scott Monument. The guest rooms are comfortable; corner rooms are the most desirable. *43 Princes St. ☎ 0131/556-4648. www. oldwaverley.co.uk. 66 units. Doubles £130–£170. AE, DC, MC, V. Bus: 4, 12, 31, or 44. Map p 94.*

★ **Pilrig House Apartment** LEITH It was built in 1718, and in the 1800s, Robert Louis Stevenson played in this house's yard gardens as a child. Today, the self-contained two-bedroom apartment will suit those who want a bit of independence. *Pilrig House Close, Bonnington Rd. ☎ 0131/554-4794. www.pilrighouse apartment.co.uk. £80–£140. MC, V. Bus: 36. Map p 97.*

Point Hotel WEST END Standard rooms here may feel a bit small, but the premium units are spacious and several have views of the castle (those in the rear don't). If your taste in decor is more stainless steel and brushed chrome than Scottish tartan and antiques, this is the place to stay. *34 Bread St. ☎ 0131/221-5555. www.point-hotel.co.uk. 140 units. Doubles £125–£160. AE, DC, MC, V. Bus: 2 or 28. Map p 94.*

★★ **Prestonfield** SOUTHSIDE Boasting Jacobean splendor amid 5.3 hectares (13 acres) of gardens, pastures, and woodlands, this

The Terrace Suite bathroom at the Howard.

The guest rooms at Prestonfield may exude old-style character, but they have all the modern conveniences.

17th-century hotel has hosted luminaries ranging from Benjamin Franklin to Sean Connery. The guest rooms hide all their modern conveniences behind velvet-lined walls: Bose sound systems, DVD players, and plasma flatscreen TVs. *Priestfield Rd.* ☎ *0131/225–7800. www.prestonfield.com. 28 units. Doubles £195–£225. AE, MC, V. Free parking. Bus: 2, 14, or 30. Map p 96.*

★ Radisson SAS Hotel OLD

TOWN   The preferred major hotel in central Old Town, this thoroughly modern facility (don't let the baronial exterior fool you) is also one of the best equipped, with a leisure club and an indoor pool. Most bedrooms are spacious and well decorated. *80 High St.* ☎ *0131/473-6590. www.radisson.com. 238 units. Doubles £110–£230. AE, DC, MC, V. Bus: 35. Map p 94.*

Ramada Mount Royal NEW

TOWN   There aren't necessarily a lot of frills at the Ramada, but the comfort is genuine in its streamlined guest rooms. Just be aware that this hotel is a favorite of tour groups. *53 Princes St.* ☎ *0131/225-7161.*

www.ramadajarvis.co.uk. 158 units. Doubles £125–£180. AE, DC, MC, V. Bus: 4, 12, 31, or 44. Map p 94.

★ The Scotsman OLD TOWN

One of the brightest and most stylish hotels in Edinburgh. Traditional decor and cutting-edge design are harmoniously wed in the 1904 baronial building (which was once home to the newspaper that lent the hotel its name), a city landmark since it was first constructed. *20 N. Bridge.* ☎ *0131/556-5565. www.scotsmanhotels.com. 68 units. Doubles £200–£350. AE, DC, MC, V. Bus: 3, 8, 14, or 29. Map p 94.*

★ Seven Danube Street STOCK-

BRIDGE   This small three-unit B&B (one double, one twin, and one single) offers spacious rooms and lavish breakfasts that might include venison sausages, omelets made from free-range eggs, homemade scones, and jams and marmalades. *7 Danube St.* ☎ *0131/332-2755. www.sevendanubestreet.com. 3 units. Double £130. Bus: 24, 29, or 42. Map p 94.*

★★ Sheraton Grand Hotel WEST

END   Elegant, with soaring public rooms and rich carpeting, the Sheraton boasts an enviable location in the

The rooms at The Scotsman are a great combination of traditionalism and cutting edge design.

If your tastes trend to the theatrical, the rooms at The Witchery by the Castle will more than satisfy.

proverbial shadow of Edinburgh Castle. The spacious guest rooms are well equipped and the hotel also has the best spa and leisure facilities (including a rooftop indoor/outdoor pool) in the city. *1 Festival Sq. (at*

Lothian Rd.). ☎ *800/325-3535 in the U.S. & Canada, or 0131/229-9131. www.sheraton.com. 260 units. Doubles £150–£360. AE, DC, MC, V. Bus: 10, 22, or 30. Map p 94.*

kids Thrums Hotel SOUTHSIDE Located in the Newington district, Thrums has high-ceilinged guest rooms with some antique furnishings. Some units are set aside as family rooms (kids get a warm welcome), while the garden offers an outdoor play area. *14–15 Minto St.* ☎ *0131/ 667-5545. www.thrumshotel.com. 15 units. Doubles £55–£110. MC, V. Bus: 3, 8, or 29. Map p 96.*

★★★ **The Witchery by the Castle** OLD TOWN   Part of the famous restaurant (p 74), the overnight accommodations in the Witchery include romantic, sumptuous, and theatrically decorated suites with Gothic antiques and elaborate tapestries. The much-lauded property has played host to a long list of celebrity guests. *Castlehill.* ☎ *0131/225-5613. www.thewitchery. com. 7 units. Suites £295. AE, DC, MC, V. Bus: 28. Map p 94.* ●

"Inns" & Outs of Overnight Stays

A good source of information on different types of accommodations in Scotland is the tourist board's official website, **www.visit scotland.com**. The site lists a range of lodging options, from hotels and guesthouses to self-catering condos. Plus, it will take reservations, too.

Most of the time breakfast (and a big one at that) is included in the price of your hotel room. On the other hand, bellhops (porters) are less common, except in high-end hotels, such as Edinburgh's Balmoral. Smaller city hotels also sometimes lock their front doors at night, so you may have to ring to be let in after hours. This can also pose a problem the following morning, so be sure you understand issues of access. I recently heard about some visitors to Edinburgh missing a tour of the town because their personal guide couldn't get through the front door in the morning.

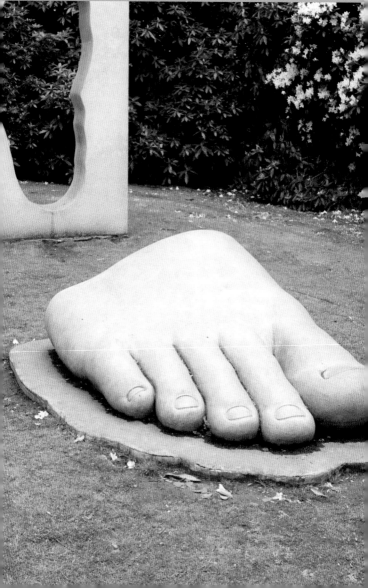

The Best in One Day

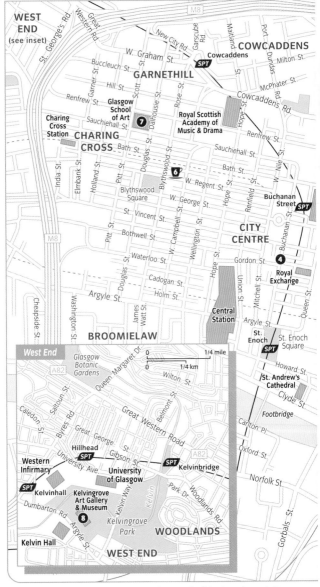

WEST END
(see inset)

COWCADDENS

Cowcaddens
SPT

GARNETHILL

Glasgow
School
of Art ⑦

Royal Scottish
Academy of
Music & Drama

Charing
Cross
Station

CHARING
CROSS

Blythswood
Square

⑥

Buchanan
Street
SPT

CITY
CENTRE

④
Royal
Exchange

BROOMIELAW

Central
Station

St.
Enoch
SPT

St. Enoch
Square

St. Andrew's
Cathedral

Footbridge

West End

Glasgow
Botanic
Gardens

0   1/4 mile
0   1/4 km

Great Western Road

Hillhead
SPT

Western
Infirmary

University
of Glasgow

SPT Kelvinbridge

Kelvinhall
SPT

Kelvingrove
Art Gallery
& Museum
⑧

Kelvingrove
Park

WOODLANDS

Kelvin Hall

WEST END

Previous Page: A modern art sculpture on the grounds of the House for an Art Lover.

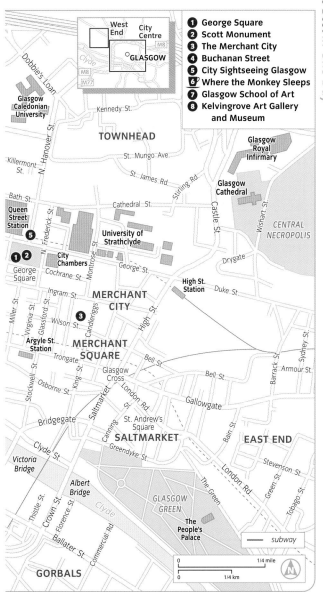

1 George Square
2 Scott Monument
3 The Merchant City
4 Buchanan Street
5 City Sightseeing Glasgow
6 Where the Monkey Sleeps
7 Glasgow School of Art
8 Kelvingrove Art Gallery
   and Museum

West End
City Centre
GLASGOW
M8
M77

Dobbie's Loan

Glasgow
Caledonian
University

Kennedy St.

TOWNHEAD

St. Mungo Ave.

Killermont St.

N. Hanover St.

St. James Rd.

Stirling Rd.

Bath St.

Frederick St.

Cathedral St.

Queen
Street
Station

5

University of
Strathclyde

Glasgow
Royal
Infirmary

Glasgow
Cathedral

Castle St.

Wishart St.

CENTRAL
NECROPOLIS

1 2

George
Square

City
Chambers

Cochrane St.

Montrose St.

George St.

Drygate

High St.
Station

Duke St.

Miller St.

Virginia St.

Glassford St.

Ingram St.

MERCHANT
CITY

High St.

Wilson St.

3

Candleriggs

Argyle St.
Station

Trongate

MERCHANT
SQUARE

Bell St.

Bell St.

Barrack St.

Armour St.

Sydney St.

Stockwell St.

Osborne St.

King St.

Glasgow
Cross

London Rd.

Gallowgate

EAST END

Bridgegate

Saltmarket

Canning St.

St. Andrew's
Square

SALTMARKET

Greendyke St.

London Rd.

Bain St.

Green St.

Stevenson St.

Tobago St.

Clyde St.

Victoria
Bridge

Thistle St.

Crown St.

Albert
Bridge

Florence St.

Clyde

GLASGOW
GREEN

The Green

Ballater St.

Commercial Rd.

The
People's
Palace

subway

GORBALS

0   1/4 mile
0   1/4 km

N

Scotland's largest city offers a very different feel than Edinburgh, but Glasgow's (pronounced *glaaz-go* by natives) reputation as a tourist destination is growing. Seeing all of this vibrant city in a single day is impossible, but you can take in the major highlights. Begin with the Victorian splendor of the city center, and finish your full schedule with a foray into the salubrious West End. START: **Buchanan St. underground station.**

❶ George Square. This is the city's central plaza (originally laid out in 1782, but significantly altered since then), named for King George III. A popular meeting place that's also seen several political demonstrations, it's home to a number of 19th-century statues commemorating famous Scots and Brits, as well as the opulent City Chambers (opened in 1888 and a great example of Victorian architecture), and the city's main tourist office. ⏱ *30 min. Open 24 hours.*

❷ Scott Monument. The most imposing of the statues in George Square, this 25m (82-ft.) Doric column (topped by the likeness of Sir Walter Scott) was the first monument built in honor of the author, about 5 years after his death in 1832. ⏱ *5 min. In George Sq. Open 24 hours.*

❸ ★ The Merchant City. This is urban Glasgow's equivalent of London's SoHo, with converted warehouses set amid trendy bars and restaurants. Begun as a New Town development in the 1700s, this district also abuts the historic core of Glasgow along the High Street—though all remnants of the city's Medieval past were long ago demolished. ⏱ *1 hr. Open 24 hours.*

❹ ★ Buchanan Street. This pedestrian-only boulevard often teems with people, and stretches from the River Clyde, up a gentle slope, to the Glasgow Royal Concert Hall. If you're a fan of retail therapy, your Glasgow shopping trip should probably begin—and possibly end—here. Otherwise, stroll it to see Glaswegians buzz about their

George Square is Glasgow's central plaza and a popular meeting place.

The impressive library of the Mackintosh-designed Glasgow School of Art.

business. ⏱ *30 min.–2 hr. Open 24 hours. Underground: Buchanan St.*

❺ ★★ City Sightseeing Glasgow. Tours on these brightly colored, open-topped buses hit many of the city's highlights and offer a good orientation. Though some visitors find the live tour guides difficult to follow (due to the Glaswegian accents), their patter is usually as humorous and as entertaining as it is informative. It beats the taped version by miles, so listen carefully. You can hop on and off at some 20-odd stops. ⏱ *1½ hr. George Sq.* ☎ *0141/204-0444. www.scotguide. com. Tickets £9. Daily Apr–Oct every 20 min. 9:30am–5pm; Nov–Mar every 30 min. 9:30am–4:30pm. Underground: Buchanan St.*

Owned and operated by artistic types (including two graduates from the nearby Art School), **❻ ★ Where the Monkey Sleeps,** a singular cafe-cum-gallery, is one of the best daytime stops for cappuccinos, soups, and sandwiches. *182 W. Regent St.* ☎ *0141/226-3406. www.wtms.co.uk. $.*

❼ ★★★ Glasgow School of Art. This magnificent building on Garnethill is the highlight of the Charles Rennie Mackintosh architecture trail that legions of tourists follow through the city. What's more amazing is that Mackintosh (1868–1928) wasn't even 30 when he designed the place. It remains a working—and much respected—school of art and design. I like the shop for gifts. ⏱ *1½ hr. See p 120,* ❷.

❽ ★★ 🄺🄸🄳🅂 Kelvingrove Art Gallery and Museum. The Spanish Baroque–style Kelvingrove (built in 1901 of red sandstone) is the stirring soul of the city's art collection, one of the best amassed by a municipality in Europe. It is the most visited gallery and museum in the U.K. outside of London. The art (ranging from French Impressionists to Spanish surrealists to Scottish modern) is pretty great, but there is more than that to see, with exhibits on Scottish and Glasgow history, armory and war, and on natural history, too. There's also some humor: Watch out for the furry haggis animal. ⏱ *2½ hr. Argyle St.* ☎ *0141/ 276-9599. www.glasgowmuseums. com. Free admission, except for some temporary exhibits. Mon– Thurs, Sat 10am–5pm; Fri, Sun 11am– 5pm. Underground: Kelvinhall. Bus: 9, 16, 42, or 62.*

The Kelvingrove Art Gallery and Museum is home to one of the best municipal art collections in Europe.

The Best in Two Days

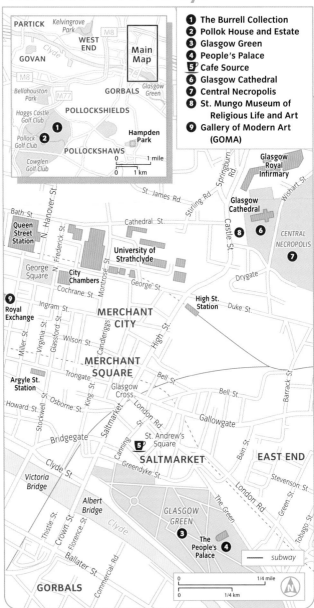

1. The Burrell Collection
2. Pollok House and Estate
3. Glasgow Green
4. People's Palace
5. Cafe Source
6. Glasgow Cathedral
7. Central Necropolis
8. St. Mungo Museum of Religious Life and Art
9. Gallery of Modern Art (GOMA)

The River Clyde runs through Glasgow, dividing the city into two sections. You spent your first day on the north side, but should start your second across the river, at the vaunted Burrell Collection (which hard-core art fans might try to see at the expense of other attractions on Day 1). After you're done sampling the world-class art, return to the north banks of the Clyde for a sampling of the city's hot spots for history and culture. START: **Take suburban train to Pollokshaws West or bus 45, 47, or 57.**

① ★★ The Burrell Collection.

This custom-built museum houses close to 9,000 treasures left to Glasgow by wealthy industrialist Sir William Burrell in 1958 (though the building itself didn't open until 1983). His tastes were eclectic: Chinese ceramics, French paintings from the 1800s, stained-glass church windows, medieval stone doorways, and tapestries. One major highlight is an original casting of Rodin's *The Thinker*. ⏱ *2 hr. Pollok Country Park, 2060 Pollokshaws Rd.* ☎ *0141/287-2550. www.glasgowmuseums.com. Free admission. Mon–Thurs, Sat 10am–5pm; Fri, Sun 11am–5pm.*

A ceramic Chinese statue from The Burrell Collection.

② Pollok House and Estate.

I suggest a quick stop here because it's so close to the Burrell (a 5- to 10-min. walk). This handsome 18th-century mansion, on an estate held by the Maxwell family for over 6 centuries, is accurately called a snapshot of historic county life on what once were the fringes of the city. It's also home to a first-rate collection of Spanish art, including works by Goya and El Greco. ⏱ *45 min. Pollok Country Park.* ☎ *0141/616-6410. www.glasgowmuseums.com. Free admission. Daily 10am–5pm, except Christmas & New Year's. Suburban Train: Pollokshaws West. Bus: 45, 47, or 57.*

③ ★ kids Glasgow Green.

This is the city's oldest park, dating in part to late medieval times (roughly the 15th c.). Its landmarks include the People's Palace and Winter Garden (see ④); and the 44m (143-ft.) Nelson's Monument, which was erected in 1806 in honor of Admiral Horatio Nelson—30 years before the more famous Nelson's Column in London was built. At the park's eastern end, the influence of the Doges' Palace in Venice can be seen in the colorful facade of the old Templeton Carpet Factory (1889). ⏱ *1 hr. Greendyke St. (east of Saltmarket).* ☎ *0141/287-5098. www.glasgow.gov.uk. Free admission. Open daily dawn–dusk. Underground: St. Enoch. Bus: 16, 18, 40, 61, 62, or 64.*

The music room at Pollok House and Estate.

The glass-enclosed Winter Garden at the People's Palace is a quiet retreat in busy Glasgow.

④ kids People's Palace. This museum, first opened in 1898, showcases Glasgow's social history, with displays on how "ordinary people" lived in the city, especially since the industrial age. In front of the museum is the heavily sculpted Doulton Fountain, the largest terra-cotta fountain in the world. In the rear, the cafe inside the spacious, glass-enclosed Winter Gardens is a good retreat from the city hubbub.

Glasgow Cathedral is the only intact medieval cathedral that remains in mainland Scotland.

🕐 1½ hr. Glasgow Green. ☎ 0141/554-0223. www.glasgowmuseums.com. Free admission. Mon–Sat 10am–5pm; Fri, Sun 11am–5pm. Bus: 16, 18, 43, 64, or 263.

Kill two proverbial birds with a single stop at **⑤ Cafe Source,** as the basement cafe is below the architecturally outstanding St. Andrew's in the Square church, now a performance space. The food emphasizes traditional Scottish ingredients, cooked in a modern fashion. 1 St. Andrew's Sq. ☎ 0141/548-6020. $. Bus: 16, 18, 64, or 263.

⑥ ★★ Glasgow Cathedral. Mainland Scotland's only complete medieval cathedral (it dates to the 13th c.), this is the country's most important ecclesiastical building of that era. Unlike others, this former Roman Catholic cathedral survived the Reformation practically intact. The lower church has a vaulted Gothic-style crypt that's among the finest in Europe and houses the tomb of St. Mungo (d. 614), patron saint of the city. 🕐 1½ hr. Castle St. (at High St.). ☎ 0141/552-6891. www.historic-scotland.gov.uk. Free admission. Apr–Sept Mon–Sat 9:30am–6pm, Sun 1–5pm; Oct–Mar

Mon–Sat 9:30am–4pm, Sun 1–4pm. Sun morning service. Suburban train: High St. Bus: 11, 36, 37, 38, 42, or 89.

❼ ★ Central Necropolis.

Built on a proud hill above Glasgow Cathedral and patterned on Paris's Père Lachaise, this graveyard was opened in the 1830s. You won't be able to miss the 62m (203-ft.) monument to John Knox at the top of the hill; it was erected in 1825. The cemetery's numerous Victorian-style monuments are excellent—as are the views of Glasgow. *🕐 1 hr. Adjacent to Glasgow Cathedral. Free admission. Daily dawn–dusk. Suburban train: High St. Bus: 11, 36, 37, 38, 42, or 89.*

❽ St. Mungo Museum of Religious Life and Art.

Opened in 1993, this eclectic museum of spirituality (treating all religions equally) is located next to Glasgow Cathedral on the site where the Bishop's Castle—the mansion in which the Catholic

An exterior plaque at the eclectic St. Mungo Museum of Religious Life and Art.

archbishops of Glasgow once resided—stood until the 17th century. *🕐 45 min. 2 Castle St. ☎ 0141/553-2557. Free admission. Mon–Thurs, Sat 10am–5pm; Fri, Sun 11am–5pm. Suburban train: High St. Bus: 11, 36, 38, 42, or 89.*

❾ Gallery of Modern Art (GOMA).

GOMA is housed in a neoclassical building that once served as the Royal Exchange, but was originally built as a mansion for an 18th-century tobacco magnate. Opened in 1996, the gallery focuses on artwork from 1950 onward. The permanent collection has works by Stanley Spencer and John Bellany, as well as art from the 1980s "new Glasgow boys." *🕐 1 hr. Royal Exchange Sq., Queen St. ☎ 0141/229-1996. www.glasgowmuseums.com. Free admission. Mon–Wed, Sat 10am–5pm; Thurs 10am–8pm; Fri, Sun 11am–5pm. Underground: Buchanan St.*

Glasgow's Gallery of Modern Art is home to a collection that focuses on art from the mid-20th-century onward.

The Best in Three Days

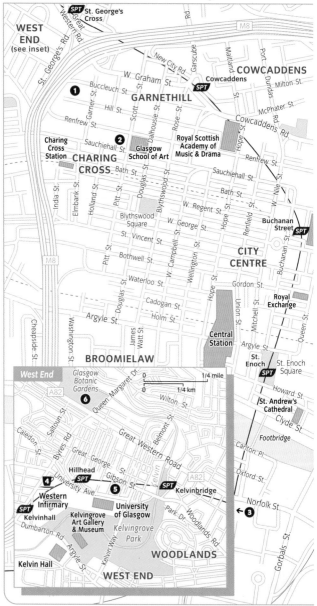

WEST END (see inset)

COWCADDENS

M8

St. George's Cross

Western Rd.

New City Rd.

W. Graham St.

Cowcaddens

Garscube

Maitland

Port Dundas St.

Milton St.

Buccleuch St.

Garnet St.

Hill St.

Scott St.

Dalhousie St.

Rose St.

McPhater St.

GARNETHILL

Cowcaddens Rd.

Renfrew St.

Sauchiehall St.

Charing Cross Station

CHARING CROSS

Glasgow School of Art

Royal Scottish Academy of Music & Drama

Hope St.

Renfrew St.

Sauchiehall St.

Bath St.

India St.

Elmbank St.

Holland St.

Pitt St.

Douglas St.

Blythswood St.

W. Regent St.

Hope St.

Renfield St.

W. Nile St.

Bath St.

Buchanan Street

Blythswood Square

St. Vincent St.

W. George St.

Pitt St.

Bothwell St.

St. Campbell St.

Wellington St.

CITY CENTRE

Buchanan St.

Waterloo St.

Gordon St.

Douglas St.

Cadogan St.

Hope St.

Union St.

Mitchell St.

Queen St.

Royal Exchange

Argyle St.

Holm St.

James Watt St.

Central Station

Argyle St.

BROOMIELAW

St. Enoch

St. Enoch Square

Cheapside St.

Washington St.

M8

West End

Glasgow Botanic Gardens

Queen Margaret Dr.

Wilton St.

0 ___ 1/4 mile
0 ___ 1/4 km

Howard St.

St. Andrew's Cathedral

Clyde St.

A82

Caledon St.

Saltoun St.

Byres Rd.

Great George St.

Belmont St.

Great Western Road

Kelvin St.

Footbridge

Carlton Pl.

Oxford St.

Hillhead

University Ave.

Gibson St.

A82

Kelvinbridge

Norfolk St.

Western Infirmary

Kelvinhall

Dumbarton Rd.

Kelvingrove Art Gallery & Museum

University of Glasgow

Kelvingrove Park

Park Dr.

Woodlands Rd.

Gorbals St.

WOODLANDS

Kelvin Hall

Kelvin Way

Argyle St.

WEST END

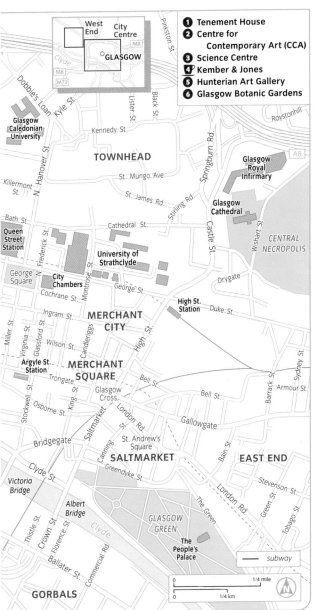

1 Tenement House
2 Centre for Contemporary Art (CCA)
3 Science Centre
4 Kember & Jones
5 Hunterian Art Gallery
6 Glasgow Botanic Gardens

The history of Glasgow is a bit checkered, from a tourist point of view. In the early 18th century, visitors such as the traveler/writer Daniel Dafoe described it as one of the most charming cities in Great Britain. By the end of the 19th century, it was the fourth-largest city in Europe: a sooty, smoke-ridden industrial powerhouse rather than a place of beauty. Today, the grime has been removed and heavy manufacturing has moved on, leaving a modern metropolis for visitors to enjoy. START: **Garnethill; take underground to Cowcaddens or bus 11, 20, or 66.**

Tenement House shows what Glaswegian home life was like in the early 20th century.

❶ ★ Tenement House. Tenements (or apartment buildings) are what many Glaswegians lived in from the middle of the 19th century onward. This "museum" is a typical tenement flat, preserved with all the old fixtures and fittings: coal fires, box bed in the kitchen, and gas lamps. Its former resident, Miss Agnes Toward, rarely threw anything out from 1911 to 1965, so there are displays of all sorts of historic memorabilia. ⏲ *1 hr. 145 Buccleuch St.* ☎ *0141/333-0183. www.nts.org.uk. Admission £5 adults, £4 kids, £14 family. Mar 1–Oct 31 daily 1–5pm. Closed Nov–Feb. Underground: Cowcaddens. Bus: 11, 20, 66, 118, or 159.*

❷ Centre for Contemporary Art (CCA). A leading proponent of conceptual art in Glasgow, the CCA was established in 1992 and is home to a diverse (and often-changing) lineup of experimental art and films. The center's modern interiors are contained in a building designed by Alexander "Greek" Thomson in the mid-1800s. Its central, atrium-like space has an excellent cafe. ⏲ *1 hr. 350 Sauchiehall St.* ☎ *0141/352-4900. www.cca-glasgow.com. Free admission. Tues–Fri 11am–6pm; Sat 10am–6pm. Underground: Cowcaddens. Bus: 16, 18, 44, or 57.*

❸ 𝐤𝐢𝐝𝐬 Science Centre. The futuristic-looking edifice of the center's main building is a focal point of Glasgow's drive to redevelop the rundown former dock lands. The

One of many entertaining hands-on exhibits at the Science Centre.

The Hunterian Art Gallery is the oldest public museum in Scotland.

main themes inside this "Science Mall" are 21st-century challenges and Glasgow's contribution to science and technology in the past, present, and future. Many exhibits are of the hands-on variety; kids can even star in their own digital video. The center also has a planetarium, Scotland's only IMAX theater, and an observation tower that's sadly rarely open due to problems with its construction. ⏱ *2 hr. 50 Pacific Quay.* ☎ *0141/420-5010. www.glasgowsciencecentre.org. Admission £7.95 adults, £5.95 kids, £2 car parking. Daily 10am–6pm (Nov to mid-Mar Mon–Sat 10am–5pm). Underground: Cessnock. Suburban train: Exhibition Centre & walk across the footbridge over the Clyde. Bus: 89 or 90.*

Part deli and part cafe, **4 Kember & Jones** is set in the heart of the West End's main street and is a fine stop for freshly made sandwiches, soups, salads, and cakes. *134 Byres Rd.* ☎ *0141/337-3851. www.kemberandjones.co.uk. $.*

5 ★ Hunterian Art Gallery.

A part of the University of Glasgow's Hunterian Museum, the oldest public museum in Scotland (opened in 1803). The gallery inherited the artistic estate of Scottish-American James

McNeill Whistler (1834–1903) and many of his paintings hang here. You'll also find a selection of Scottish Colourists, as well as a collection of 17th- and 18th-century European masters (from Rembrandt to Rubens). One wing of the building has a re-creation of Charles Rennie Mackintosh's Glasgow home (p 123, 9). ⏱ *1½ hr. University of Glasgow, 22 Hillhead St.* ☎ *0141/330-5431. www.hunterian.gla.ac.uk. Free admission (gallery), £3 (Mackintosh House). Mon–Sat 9:30am–5pm. Underground: Hillhead. Bus: 44.*

6 ★ Glasgow Botanic Gardens.

Not as extensive or exemplary as the Royal Botanic Gardens in Edinburgh, these gardens and glasshouses—opened in 1811 and spread over some 11 hectares (27 acres)—are nevertheless inviting. Especially noteworthy is the Kibble Palace, a restored Victorian cast-iron glasshouse that's home to an extensive collection of tropical plants, including some Australian tree ferns that are more than 120 years old. ⏱ *1 hr. 730 Great Western Rd. (at Queen Margaret Dr.).* ☎ *0141/334-2422. www.glasgow.gov.uk. Free admission. Daily 7am–dusk (glasshouses 10am–4pm). Underground: Hillhead.*

The Kibble Palace at the Glasgow Botanic Gardens.

Glasgow's Best Architecture

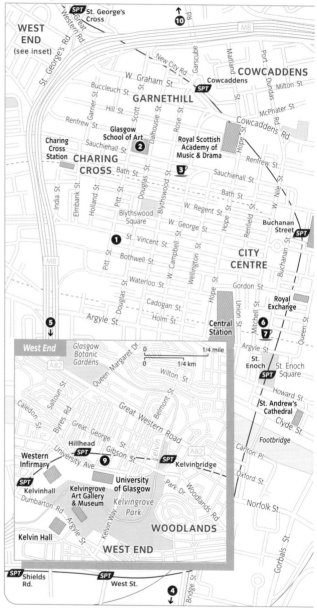

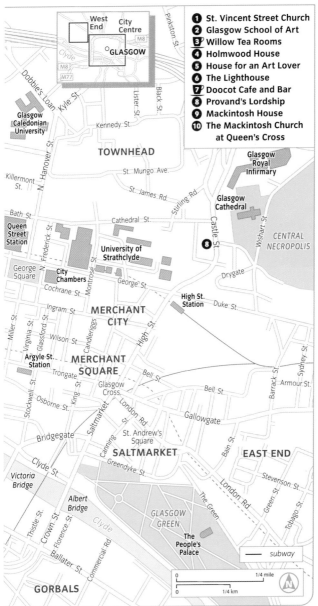

1. St. Vincent Street Church
2. Glasgow School of Art
3. Willow Tea Rooms
4. Holmwood House
5. House for an Art Lover
6. The Lighthouse
7. Doocot Cafe and Bar
8. Provand's Lordship
9. Mackintosh House
10. The Mackintosh Church at Queen's Cross

Amazingly, after Glasgow survived the Nazis' World War II bombing raids mostly intact, some city planners nearly decided to knock down all its surviving Victorian buildings for the sake of new development. Too much has been demolished, but the city remains a paragon of 19th-century architecture. This tour will give you the highlights, but just a stroll around the city center is an eye-opener.

START: **Take Bus 62 to St. Vincent Street Church at 265 St. Vincent St.**

St. Vincent Street Church is noteworthy for its Greek-influenced exterior, designed by Alexander Thomson.

❶ ★ St. Vincent Street Church. This should be a three-star, must-see attraction, but the congregation that worships here limits public access. Nevertheless, the church remains the most visible landmark attributed to one of the city's two greatest architects, Alexander "Greek" Thomson (1817–75). Two classic Greek porticos enclose a clock tower decorated in curiously sympathetic Egyptian, Assyrian, and even Indian-looking motifs and designs. ⏱ *15 min. (unless attending services). 265 St. Vincent St. Free admission. Sunday services at 11am, 6:30pm. www.greekthomson church.com. Bus: 62.*

❷ ★★★ Glasgow School of Art. This building, a blend of the Arts and Craft and Art Nouveau movements completed in 1909, is arguably Charles Rennie Mackintosh's finest masterpiece. Take the tour to see the finer details, such as the sun porch looking back over the city and what I think is the most impressive small library ever devised (plus some original watercolor paintings by the great architect). ⏱ *1½ hr. 167 Renfrew St.*

The gift shop at the Glasgow School of Art is a great place to pick up a memorable souvenir.

The Lighthouse is the home of Scotland's Centre for Architecture and Design.

☎ 0141/353-4526. www.gsa.ac.uk. Tours £6.50. Daily Apr–Sept every half-hour 10:30–11:30am, 1:30– 2:30pm; Mon–Sat Oct–Mar 11am, 2:30pm. Underground: Cowcaddens.

Where else to get a cuppa but the **3⃣ Willow Tea Rooms?** Designed by Mackintosh for the infamous Kate Cranston—a temperance advocate and Mackintosh patron—in 1904, some of the establishment's original features remain in the Room de Luxe and the exterior's fully intact. *217 Sauchiehall St.* ☎ *0141/332-0521. www.willowtearooms.co.uk.* $.

4⃣ ★★ Holmwood House. This villa, designed by Thomson and built in 1858, is probably the best example of his innovative style in Victorian homes. Magnificently original, its restoration (which is ongoing) has revealed that Thomson concerned himself with every detail, down to the wallpaper. Most impressive is the overall exterior design, as are the interior parlor and the cornices in the dining room. 🕑 *1½ hr. 61–63 Netherlee Rd., Cathcart, about 6km (4 miles) south of the city center.* ☎ *0141/637-2129. www.nts.org.uk. Admission £5 adults, £4 kids, £14 family. Apr–Oct Thurs–Mon noon–5pm. Suburban train: Cathcart. Bus: 44 or 66.*

Ahead of His Time: Charles Rennie Mackintosh

Although legendary today, his works recognized as the city's great architectural and design treasures, Charles Rennie Mackintosh (1868–1928) was largely forgotten in Scotland at the end of his life. Forms of nature, especially plants, inspired his elegant motifs, which were far from the fashion of the day. Forty kilometers (25 miles) west of Glasgow, in Helensburgh, is perhaps his greatest singular achievement: Hill House was designed for publisher Walter Blackie in 1902 (see p 174, 🔞). For more information on all the buildings you can visit, visit the website of the Charles Rennie Macintosh Society at **www. crmsociety.com**, or call ☎ **0141/946-6600**.

Holmwood House is the best example of Alexander Thomson's innovative Victorian style. See p 121.

❺ House for an Art Lover.

Although Mackintosh devotees flock here, I am not a big fan of this building, built in the mid-1990s. It was constructed using only drawings that Charles Rennie Mackintosh did for a 1901 architecture competition: a modern architect's interpretation of what Mackintosh had in mind. ⏱ *1 hr. Bellahouston Park, 10 Dumbreck Rd.* ☎ *0141/353-4770. www. houseforanartlover.co.uk. Admission £3.50 adults, £2.50 kids. Apr–Sept Mon–Wed 10am–4pm, Thurs–Sat 10am–1pm; Oct–Mar Sat–Sun 10am–1pm (weekday times by arrangement). Underground: Ibrox. Bus: 3, 9, 54, or 55.*

❻ ★ The Lighthouse.

Scotland's Centre for Architecture and Design is housed in Mackintosh's first public commission (in 1895), a former home of the *Glasgow Herald* newspaper. The Mackintosh Interpretation Centre on the 3rd level is the only permanent exhibit, providing an overview of his art, design, and architecture. A viewing platform on the roof offers a unique panorama of the city. ⏱ *1½ hr. 11 Mitchell Lane.* ☎ *0141/221-6362. www.the lighthouse.co.uk. Admission £3 adults, £1 kids, £7.50 family. Mon, Wed–Sat 10:30am–5pm; Tues 11am–5pm; Sun noon–5pm. Underground: St. Enoch.*

On the sixth level of the Lighthouse, ❼ **Doocot Cafe and Bar,** a modern diner, offers a good retreat and simple but effective dishes. *11 Mitchell Lane.* ☎ *0141/221-1821. $. Underground: St. Enoch.*

❽ Provand's Lordship.

Glasgow's oldest surviving house, built in the 1470s, is the only survivor from what would have been clusters of medieval homes near Glasgow Cathedral. Thanks to the 17th-century furniture (from the original collection of Sir William Burrell), you get a feel for what the interiors once were like. But the tiny doors (don't bump your head) are the best evidence of this building's true age.

Provand's Lordship, built in the 15th century, is Glasgow's oldest house.

Unappreciated Genius: Alexander "Greek" Thomson

Perhaps even more important than Mackintosh, Alexander "Greek" Thomson (1817–75) also brought an unrivaled vision to Glasgow. While the influence of classical Greece was nothing new to Victorian architects, Thomson honed it to essentials, and then mixed in Egyptian, Assyrian, and other Eastern-influenced motifs. Like Mackintosh, he increasingly found himself out of step with (and well ahead of) others. While a number of his structures have been tragically lost to the wrecker's ball, some key works remain: Terraced houses such as Moray Place (where he lived) or Eton Terrace (p 126, ❾); churches, such as the embarrassingly derelict Caledonian Road Church; and commercial structures such as the Egyptian Halls near Central Station. Just as a Mackintosh heritage trail has been created, Thomson deserves no less.

🕐 1 hr. 3 Castle St. ☎ 0141/552-8819. www.glasgowmuseums.com. Free Admission. Mon–Thurs, Sat 10am–5pm; Fri, Sun 11am–5pm. Suburban train: High St. Bus: 11, 36, 37, 38, 42, or 89.

❾ ★★ **Mackintosh House.** Part of the Hunterian Art Gallery, this is a literal re-creation of Mackintosh's Glasgow home from 1906 to 1914. It covers three levels, decorated in the original style of the famed architect and his artist wife Margaret Macdonald. All salvageable fittings and fixtures were recovered from the original home before it was demolished in the mid-1960s. It was startling then and little less so today. *For details see p 117, ❺.*

❿ ★ **The Mackintosh Church at Queen's Cross.** This restored attraction entails a bit of a trek, but in addition to showing off the architect's penchant for simple beauty and his timeless vision (the stained-glass windows are characteristic of his design aesthetic), it is the official Mackintosh Society's HQ, with a good resource center and shop. The church, completed in 1899, is the only one ever designed by Mackintosh that was actually built. 🕐 1 hr. 870 Garscube Rd. ☎ 0141/946-6600. www.crmsociety.com. Admission £2 adults, kids free. Mon–Fri 10am–4:30pm; Sun (Mar–Oct) 2–4:30pm. Bus: 40 or 61.

A bedroom at Mackintosh House, a recreation of the home of famed architect Charles Rennie Mackintosh.

A West End Hike

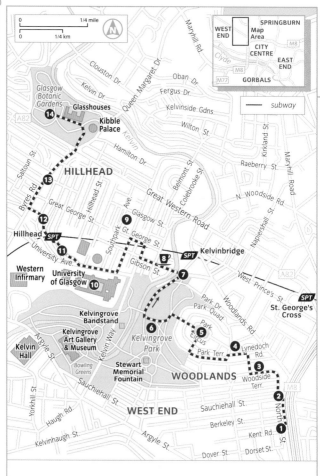

1. Mitchell Library
2. Cameron Fountain
3. Woodside Terrace
4. Trinity College and Park Church Tower
5. Park Circus
6. Kelvingrove Park
7. Gibson Street
8. Offshore
9. Eton Terrace
10. University of Glasgow
11. University Gardens
12. Ashton Lane
13. Byres Road
14. Botanic Gardens

This walk will give you a sense of Glasgow's leafy and trendy West End, while seeing some of its landmarks, too. The West End's urban development began in the 19th century, as Glasgow, a booming center for manufacturing, needed more space to house its ever-growing population; it soon became the Second City of the British Empire—in both number of residents and industrial might.
START: **Take train to Charing Cross, Underground to St. George's Cross, or bus 16, 44A, or 59.**

1 Mitchell Library. The largest public reference library (over 1.2 million volumes) in Europe opened in 1877 thanks to a bequest from Stephen Mitchell, a tobacco magnate who is commemorated with a bust in the library's entrance hall. A major highlight of the library's holdings is the world's largest collection of Robert Burns materials. The current building dates to 1911 and its most striking feature is its immense copper dome, upon which stands a statue of Minerva, the Roman goddess of wisdom. ⏱ *5–30 min., depending on whether you go inside. North St., at Kent Rd.* ☎ *0141/287-2999. www.mitchelllibrary.org. Free admission. Mon–Thurs 9am–8pm; Fri–Sat 9am–5pm.*

2 Cameron Fountain. This red stone fountain, completed in 1896 (though its clock was replaced in

The Cameron Fountain leans to the east because of issues with its foundation.

1908), leans considerably eastward, possibly because of the foundation works on the nearby freeway. It's dedicated to Sir Charles Cameron (1841–1925), a noted Glaswegian politician and newspaper editor. ⏱ *5 min. Sauchiehall St., at Woodside Terrace.*

3 ★ Woodside Terrace. This late Georgian row of homes (designed by George Smith in the 1830s) began an exemplary New Town development. But credit for the overall elegance and charm goes to Charles Wilson, who continued the neighborhood design into the middle of the 19th century. ⏱ *10 min. From Sauchiehall St. to Lynedoch Terrace.*

The Georgian row house that make up Woodside Terrace.

The immense towers of the former Trinity College are visible from many locations in Glasgow.

❹ ★ Trinity College and Park Church Tower. The former Trinity College (now Trinity House) is a landmark whose three towers are visible from many approaches to the city. Designed by Charles Wilson in 1856, most of the original interiors were lost when it was converted into condos in the 1980s. Across the broad triangular intersection is the cream-colored Park Church Tower. Part of J. T. Rochead's 1856 design, it is the other feature of the neighborhood recognizable from some distance. The church that went with the tower was razed in the 1960s. ⏱ *15 min. Lynedoch St., running to Woodlands Terrace.*

❺ ★★ Park Circus. This oval of handsome and uniform three-story buildings around a small central garden is the heart of Wilson's plans, designed in 1855. No. 22, known today as the Marriage Suites because civil wedding services are conducted here, offers the most remarkable interiors, with Corinthian columns and an Art Nouveau billiard room. You might poke your head in the front door, although the security guards are not the most friendly. At the western end of Park Circus is Park Gate, offering good views and an entrance to Kelvingrove Park. ⏱ *20 min. Runs to Park Gate.*

❻ ★★ Kelvingrove Park. This hilly park on the banks of the River Kelvin was commissioned to Sir Joseph Paxton in 1854, although construction apparently began a year before he produced his plans. Down the hill to your left, the Gothic Stewart Memorial Fountain (honoring Robert Stewart, the Lord Provost who helped supply the city with drinking water) includes signs of the Zodiac and scenes that depict the source of the city's main supply of water, Loch Katrine. ⏱ *30 min. Free admission. Daily dawn–dusk.*

❼ Gibson Street. One of the calmer commercial streets in the West End, with a good selection of cafe/bars and restaurants. You're now inside the Hillhead district, which includes the main campus of the University of Glasgow on Gilmorehill, and the Western Infirmary. ⏱ *10 min. From Eldon St. to Oakfield Ave.*

❽ Offshore is a cafe with numerous sofas that often exhibits art. It's a casual spot for a cup of strong cappuccino, an herbal tea, or a light meal. *3–5 Gibson St. No phone. $.*

❾ ★ Eton Terrace. The unmistakable hand of architect Alexander Thomson is apparent on this impressive (if rather poorly kept) row of eight connected houses, completed in 1864. Note the two temple-like facades serving as bookends; their double porches are fashioned after the Choragic Monument of Thrasyllus in Athens. For all his admiration of Eastern design, Thomson never traveled outside the U.K. ⏱ *15 min. Oakfield Ave., off Great George St.*

⑩ ★★ University of Glasgow.
Founded in 1451 (fourth-oldest in the U.K.), the university moved to its current location in the 1860s. English architect Sir George Gilbert Scott (1811–78), who designed London's Albert Memorial, did the campus's Gothic Revival main building, punctuated by a 30m (98-ft.) tower—a virtual beacon on the horizon of the West End. Between the two central quadrangles are cloistered vaults, evoking a sense of meditation and reflection. ⏱ *20 min. University Ave. www.gla.ac.uk.*

⑪ University Gardens. This fine street of houses was designed primarily by Scottish architect J. J. Burnet (1857–1938) in the 1880s. Stop particularly to admire No. 12, done by J. Gaff Gillespie in 1900-classic "Glasgow Style," with Mackintosh and Art Nouveau influences. ⏱ *20 min.*

⑫ ★ Ashton Lane. This cobbled mews is the heart of West End's nightlife, although it bustles right through the day, too. Its host of bars, cafes, and restaurants

You can spot Glasgow University Tower rising high above beautiful Kelvingrove Park.

includes the venerable Ubiquitous Chip (see p 133), which is housed in a building that once functioned as the stables for an undertaker. ⏱ *5 min.*

⑬ ★ Byres Road. The proverbial Main Street of the West End, with more bars, cafes, restaurants, and shops to enjoy. If you look up as you approach Downside Road and Byres, note the Victoria Cross sign; it's a remnant of a time when an attempt—derailed by locals—was made to change the name of the street to Victoria Road. ⏱ *15 min. From University Ave. to Great Western Rd. www.byres-road.co.uk.*

⑭ ★ Botanic Gardens. On dour days, Kibble Palace—a domed, cast-iron-and-glass greenhouse with exotic plants—is a welcome escape. Greenhouses at the gardens contain orchid and cactus collections, while the outdoor plantings include a working vegetable plot, a rose garden, and a 200-year-old weeping ash. ⏱ *1 hr. 730 Great Western Rd. (at Queen Margaret Dr.). See p 117, ⑥.*

Grand Bute Hall is used for graduation ceremonies at the University of Glasgow.

Dining in Glasgow

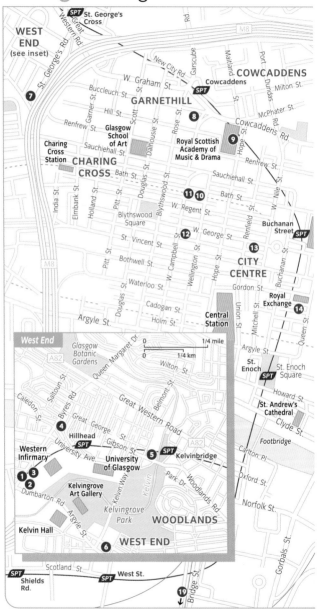

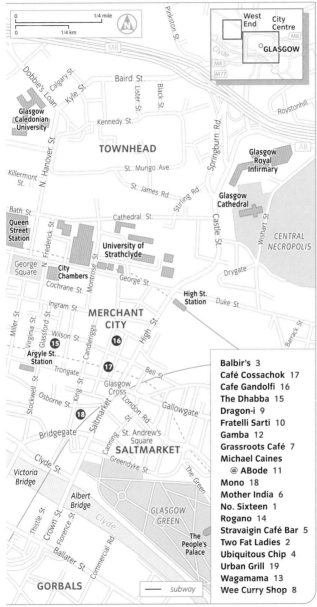

Balbir's 3
Café Cossachok 17
Cafe Gandolfi 16
The Dhabba 15
Dragon-i 9
Fratelli Sarti 10
Gamba 12
Grassroots Café 7
Michael Caines
  @ ABode 11
Mono 18
Mother India 6
No. Sixteen 1
Rogano 14
Stravaigin Café Bar 5
Two Fat Ladies 2
Ubiquitous Chip 4
Urban Grill 19
Wagamama 13
Wee Curry Shop 8

Dining **Best Bets**

Best Fish & Seafood
★★ Gamba $$$–$$$$ *225a W. George St. (p 132)*

Best Dining Entertainment
★ Café Cossachok $–$$ *38 Albion St. (p 131)*

Best Brasserie
Cafe Gandolfi $–$$ *64 Albion St. (p 131)*

Best Indian
★★ The Dhabba $$–$$$ *44 Candleriggs (p 131)*

Best Chinese
★ Dragon-i $$ *313 Hope St. (p 131)*

Best Pizza
★ Fratelli Sarti $$ *133 Wellington St. (p 131)*

Best Vegetarian
★ Grassroots Café $–$$ *93–97 St. Georges Rd. (p 132)*

Best Fancy French
★ Michael Caines @ ABode $$$–$$$$ *129 Bath St. (p 132)*

Best Neighborhood Restaurant
★ Two Fat Ladies $$ *88 Dumbarton Rd. (p 133)*

Best Art Deco Design
★ Rogano $$$–$$$$ *11 Exchange Place (p 133)*

Best Landmark Restaurant
★★ Ubiquitous Chip $$$$ *12 Ashton Lane (p 133)*

Best for Families
★ Wagamama $–$$ *97–103 W. George St. (p 133)*

Best Cheap Eats
★★ Wee Curry Shop $ *7 Buccleuch St. (p 133)*

Best Gastro-Pub
★ Stravaigin Café Bar $ *28 Gibson St. (p 133)*

Best Southside Brasserie
★ Urban Grill $$ *61 Kilmarnock Rd. (p 133)*

The brasserie cooking at Cafe Gandolfi is a favorite of local foodies.

Glasgow Restaurants A to Z

★ **Balbir's** WEST END *INDIAN* This sprawling place serves first-class Indian specialties, which are lighter than the norm. The tandoori oven is used to good effect, especially on the appetizer of barbecued salmon. *7 Church St.* ☎ *0141/339-7711. Entrees £6–£12. AE, MC, V. Dinner daily. Underground: Kelvinhall.*

★ **Café Cossachok** MERCHANT CITY *RUSSIAN* A restaurant that mixes a gallery and performance space with a menu that focuses on hearty Slavic/Russian fare. Come here for borscht soup or blinis, and then stick around for some live music. *38 Albion St.* ☎ *0141/553-0733. www. cossachok.com. Entrees £7–£14. MC, V. Lunch Tues–Thurs, dinner Tues–Sun. Underground: St. Enoch.*

★★ **Cafe Gandolfi** MERCHANT CITY *SCOTTISH/CONTINENTAL* This favorite of local foodies serves up solid cooking at the right price. Particularly recommended are the Stornoway black pudding and creamy Cullen skink (smoked haddock chowder). Bar Gandolfi is up the steel staircase. *64 Albion St.* ☎ *0141/552-6813. www.cafegandolfi.com. Entrees £6–£12. MC, V. Breakfast Mon–Sat, lunch & dinner daily. Underground: Buchanan St.*

Café Mao MERCHANT CITY *ASIAN* A lively place for an East Asian-influenced meal, with a night-time buzz that you would expect at a popular bar. *84 Brunswick St.* ☎ *0141/ 564-5161. www.cafemao.com. Entrees £8.50–£12. AE, MC, V. Lunch & dinner daily. Underground: St. Enoch.*

★★ **The Dhabba** MERCHANT CITY *INDIAN* This is not your stereotypical Glasgow curry house. Instead, it's a refined, slightly more expensive, and considerably more stylish restaurant that specializes in North Indian cuisine. *44 Candleriggs.* ☎ *0141/553-1249. www.thedhabba. com. Entrees £8–£18. AE, MC, V. Lunch & dinner daily. Underground: St. Enoch.*

★ **Dragon-i** COMMERCIAL CENTER *CHINESE* At the elegant Dragon-i, the cuisine never falls into the bland or typical chow mein and sweet-and-sour standards. Expect an excellent wine list and unusual dishes, such as tiger prawns with asparagus in a garlic chardonnay sauce. *313 Hope St.* ☎ *0141/332-7728. www.dragon-i. co.uk. Entrees £11–£16. AE, MC, V. Lunch Mon–Sat, dinner daily. Underground: Cowcaddens.*

★ **kids** **Fratelli Sarti** COMMERCIAL CENTER *ITALIAN* The pizza at this cafe/deli is excellent, with a thin, crispy crust and modest amounts of sauce, cheese, and toppings. Pasta dishes, such as "al

The modern, Asian-style bistro cooking at Café Mao makes it a popular nighttime hangout.

The pizza and authentic Italian coffee drinks are big hits at Fratelli Sarti. See p 131.

forno" with sausage, are filling. *133 Wellington St.* ☎ *0141-204-0440. www.sarti.co.uk. Reservations recommended. Entrees £7–£10. AE, MC, V. Breakfast, lunch & dinner Mon–Fri; lunch, dinner Sat–Sun. Underground: Buchanan St.*

★★ **Gamba** COMMERCIAL CENTER *FISH/SEAFOOD* This is *the* place for a first-rate fish dinner. The basement dining room is modern and stylish without feeling excessively fancy. Main courses may include whole lemon sole in browned butter or delicate pan-seared sea bream. *225a W. George St.* ☎ *0141-572-0899. www.gamba.co.uk. Entrees £19–£26. AE, MC, V. Lunch & dinner Mon–Sat. Underground: Buchanan St.*

★ **Grassroots Café** WEST END *VEGETARIAN* The atmosphere in the city's leading vegetarian restaurant is casual and relaxed. Try the risotto-style rice cakes with goat's cheese or a Middle Eastern tagine with couscous; you can wash down your meal with an organic wine. *93–97 St. Georges Rd. (near Woodlands Rd.).* ☎ *0141-333-0534. Entrees £5–£8. MC, V. Breakfast, lunch & dinner daily. Underground: St. George's Cross.*

★ **Michael Caines @ ABode** COMMERCIAL CENTER *FRENCH* It's hard to find fault with the cooking and presentation at this modern and stylish hotel restaurant. Chef/owner Michael Caines has earned Michelin stars elsewhere, and he and his staff are clearly aspiring to earn those plaudits here. *129 Bath St. (in the ABode hotel).* ☎ *0141-572-6011. www.abodehotels.co.uk. Entrees £18–£25; set dinner £60. AE, MC, V. Lunch & dinner Mon–Sat. Underground: Buchanan St.*

Mono MERCHANT CITY *VEGETARIAN/VEGAN* This hip and welcoming bar/diner does basic dairy- and meat-free meals in laid-back surroundings. Mono also houses a CD shop, literally next to the bar, with the latest in indie rock and the hippest nonmainstream music. *12 Kings Court.* ☎ *0141/553-2400. Entrees £5–£7. AE, MC, V. Lunch & dinner daily. Underground: St. Enoch.*

★ **Mother India** WEST END *INDIAN* In business for more than a decade, this is the most respected Indian restaurant in Glasgow. The menu is not overloaded with hundreds of different dishes, and the staff is professional and courteous. Down the road, a second branch—**Mother India's Café**—offers less expensive, tapas-style dishes. *28 Westminster Terrace (at Kelvingrove St.).* ☎ *0141/221-1663. www.motherindia.co.uk. Entrees £7.50–£12. MC, V. Dinner daily, lunch Wed–Sat. Bus: 16, 18, or 42.*

No. Sixteen WEST END *SCOTTISH* No. Sixteen has a neighborhood feel, but its appeal extends far beyond those who live in the area. This Scottish bistro offers inventive cooking of local ingredients, from braised pig's cheek to pan-fried mackerel. *16 Byres Rd.* ☎ *0141/339-2544. Entrees £12–£20. AE, MC, V. Lunch & dinner daily. Underground: Kelvinhall.*

★ **Rogano** COMMERCIAL CENTER *FISH/SEAFOOD* This landmark celebrity favorite has a well-preserved Art Deco interior patterned after the *Queen Mary* ocean liner. The look is sometimes more impressive than the traditional cuisine. *11 Exchange Place.* ☎ *0141/248-4055. www.rogano glasgow.com. Entrees £17–£34. AE, DC, MC, V. Lunch & dinner daily. Underground: Buchanan St.*

★ **Stravaigin Café Bar** WEST END *SCOTTISH/INTERNATIONAL* The motto is "think global, eat local" at this cordial pub/cafe, with a more expensive restaurant in the basement. Scottish produce gets international twists; cheese and herb fritters with sweet chili sauce is just one example. *28 Gibson St.* ☎ *0141/ 334-2665. www.stravaigin.com. Entrees £6–£10. AE, MC, V. Lunch & dinner daily. Underground: Kelvinbridge.*

★ **Two Fat Ladies** WEST END *SCOTTISH/FISH* A casual bistro whose specialties include pan-seared bream and balsamic roasted breast of chicken. The name of this local favorite refers to its street number— the number 88 is "two fat ladies" in bingo parlance. *88 Dumbarton Rd.* ☎ *0141/339-1944. Entrees £14–£18. MC, V. Lunch Mon–Sat, dinner daily. Underground: Kelvinhall.*

★★ **Ubiquitous Chip** WEST END *SCOTTISH* No restaurant has been more responsible for a culinary renaissance in Scotland than this place, set inside the walls of a former stable. The ever-changing menu might feature Aberdeen Angus beef, shellfish with crispy seaweed snaps, or wild rabbit. Upstairs, a friendly pub and small brasserie serves similar-quality fare at a fraction of the price. *12 Ashton Lane (near Byres Rd.).* ☎ *0141/ 334-5007. www.ubiquitouschip.co.uk. Reservations recommended. Set dinner £40. AE, DC, MC, V. Lunch & dinner daily. Underground: Hillhead.*

★ **Urban Grill** SOUTHSIDE *INTERNATIONAL* Set in the heart of the Southside, Urban Grill (owned by the same people behind Gamba; see above) mixes a bit of cosmopolitan sophistication with a diverse brasserie menu. *61 Kilmarnock Rd.* ☎ *0141/649-2745. www.urbangrill. co.uk. Entrees £8–£15. MC, V. Lunch & dinner daily. Bus: 22, 23, 29, or 38A.*

★ kids **Wagamama** COMMERCIAL CENTER *ASIAN/JAPANESE* This London-based chain of casual noodle bars has proved successful in Glasgow. Seating is at long tables and benches. It's one of the best places in town for a quick bite. *97–103 W. George St.* ☎ *0141/229-1468. www. wagamama.com. Entrees £6.50–£10. Lunch & dinner daily. Underground: Buchanan St.*

★★ **Wee Curry Shop** COMMERCIAL CENTER *INDIAN* This tiny place is hardly big enough to swing a cat in, but the aptly named Wee Curry Shop offers the best, low-cost Indian dishes in the city. *7 Buccleuch St. (near Cambridge St.).* ☎ *0141/ 353-0777. Entrees £5–£7. No credit cards. Lunch Mon–Sat, dinner daily. Underground: Cowcaddens.*

The Ubiquitous Chip, housed in a former stable, was the prime mover behind Scotland's culinary renaissance.

Hotels in Glasgow

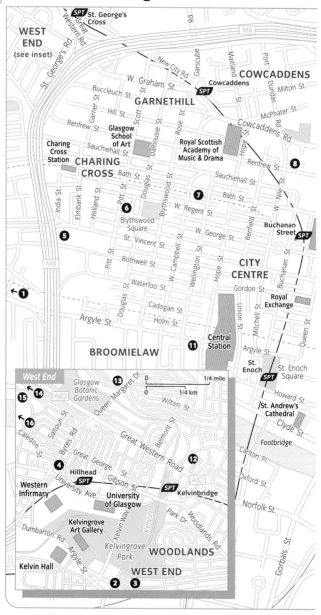

WEST END
(see inset)

St. George's
Cross

COWCADDENS

Cowcaddens

GARNETHILL

Glasgow School
of Art

Royal Scottish
Academy of
Music & Drama

Charing
Cross Station

CHARING CROSS

Buchanan
Street

Blythswood
Square

CITY CENTRE

BROOMIELAW

Central
Station

Royal
Exchange

St. Enoch

St. Enoch
Square

West End

Glasgow
Botanic
Gardens

Western
Infirmary

Hillhead

University
of Glasgow

Kelvinbridge

Kelvingrove
Art Gallery

Kelvin Hall

Kelvingrove
Park

WOODLANDS

WEST END

St. Andrew's
Cathedral

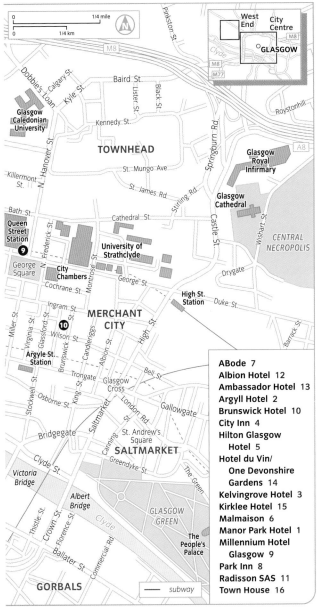

ABode **7**
Albion Hotel **12**
Ambassador Hotel **13**
Argyll Hotel **2**
Brunswick Hotel **10**
City Inn **4**
Hilton Glasgow
  Hotel **5**
Hotel du Vin/
  One Devonshire
  Gardens **14**
Kelvingrove Hotel **3**
Kirklee Hotel **15**
Malmaison **6**
Manor Park Hotel **1**
Millennium Hotel
  Glasgow **9**
Park Inn **8**
Radisson SAS **11**
Town House **16**

— subway

Hotel Best Bets

Most **Glamorous Hotel**
★★★ Hotel du Vin/One Devonshire Gardens $$$$ *1 Devonshire Gardens* *(p 138)*

Best **Small Hotel**
★ Ambassador Hotel $$ *7 Kelvin Dr.* *(p 137)*

Best **Hip Hotel**
★ Brunswick Hotel $$–$$$ *106–108 Brunswick St. (p 137)*

Best **Family Hotel**
Kirklee Hotel $$ *11 Kensington Gate* *(p 138)*

Best **Hotel Dining Experience**
ABode $$$ *129 Bath St. (p 137)*

Best **Boutique Hotel**
★ Malmaison $$$ *278 W. George St.* *(p 138)*

Best **B&B**
★★ Town House $$ *4 Hughenden Terrace (p 139)*

Best **Bargain Hotel**
Manor Park Hotel $–$$ *28 Balshagray Dr. (p 138)*

Best **Traditional Hotel**
★ Hilton Glasgow Hotel $$$–$$$$ *1 William St. (p 138)*

Most **Central Hotel**
Millennium Hotel Glasgow $$$ *George Sq. (p 139)*

Most **Like a Highland Lodge**
kids Argyll Hotel $$ *969-973 Sauchiehall St. (p 137)*

Best **River Views**
City Inn $$–$$$ *Finnieston Quay* *(p 138)*

Most **Friendly/Helpful Staff**
★ Kelvingrove Hotel $$ *944 Sauchiehall St. (p 138)*

Best **Hotel Spa Facilities**
Park Inn $$$ *2 Port Dundas Place* *(p 139)*

Best **Large Modern Hotel**
H Radisson SAS $$$ *301 Argyle St.* *(p 139)*

The Hilton Glasgow is the city's best traditional hotel.

Glasgow Hotels A to Z

The tartan-filled decor at The Argyll Hotel gives it a lodge-like feel.

ABode COMMERCIAL CENTER
Formerly the Arthouse, this handsome Edwardian building is a striking boutique hotel. Colors and textures blend in with the older structure while commissioned art and period pieces evoke some of the original splendor. *129 Bath St.* ☎ *0141/221-6789. www.abodehotels.co.uk/glasgow. 65 units. Doubles £125. AE, DC, MC, V. Underground: Buchanan St.*

Albion Hotel WEST END   This unpretentious and friendly small hotel occupies two nearly identical sandstone row houses in a convenient and leafy district of the West End. Its high-ceilinged units have modern furniture and shower-only bathrooms. *405–407 N. Woodside Rd.* ☎ *0141/339-8620. www.glasgow hotelsandapartments.co.uk. 20 units. Doubles £66. AE, DC, MC, V. Underground: Kelvin Bridge.*

★ **Ambassador Hotel** WEST END
Across from the Botanic Gardens, this small Edwardian town-house hotel offers individually decorated and attractively furnished bedrooms, each with well-maintained bathroom with tub and/or shower. *7 Kelvin Dr.* ☎ *0141/946-1018. www.glasgow hotelsandapartments.co.uk. 16 units. Doubles £66. AE, DC, MC, V. Underground: Hillhead.*

kids Argyll Hotel WEST END
Only a short walk from Kelvingrove Park, the Argyll lives up to its Scottish name—full of tartan and the like. The atmosphere here is more Highland lodge than urban inn. There is a clutch of spacious family rooms. *969–973 Sauchiehall St.* ☎ *0141/337-3313. www.argyllhotelglasgow.co.uk. 38 units. Doubles £78. AE, MC, V. Underground: Kelvin Hall.*

★ **Brunswick Hotel** MERCHANT CITY   One of the hippest hotels in town, though it's far from pretentious. The units are generally small but soothing and inviting, with neutral color schemes, comfortable mattresses, and adequate bathrooms

For a hip but unpretentious stay in Glasgow, the Brunswick Hotel is a good choice.

(several with both tub and shower). *106–108 Brunswick St. ☎ 0141/552-0001. www.brunswickhotel.co.uk. 18 units. Doubles £55–£100. AE, DC, MC, V. Underground: Buchanan St.*

City Inn WEST END   Right on the River Clyde, this smart hotel with a waterside terrace is part of a small chain with other branches in London, Bristol, and Manchester—all of them modern with good facilities (including power showers in the bathrooms). *Finnieston Quay. ☎ 0141/240-1002. www.cityinn.com. 164 units. Doubles £99. AE, DC, MC, V. Suburban train: Exhibition centre.*

★ **Hilton Glasgow Hotel** COMMERCIAL CENTER   Glasgow's first-class Hilton is perched over the M8 freeway that slashes through the city of Glasgow. Despite its odd location, it is a classy and modern hotel, with plush but conservative units that offer good city views. *1 William St. ☎ 800/445-8667 in the U.S. & Canada, or 0141/204-5555. www.hilton.co.uk/glasgow. 331 units. Doubles £100–£180. AE, DC, MC, V. Suburban train: Charing Cross.*

★★★ **Hotel du Vin/One Devonshire Gardens** WEST END   This luxurious boutique hotel, spread

Hotel du Vin/One Devonshire Gardens is the most glamorous place to stay in Glasgow.

over five town houses, is the most glamorous the city has to offer—the place where the rich and famous (George Clooney anyone?) traditionally stay. The guest rooms have all the necessary modern gadgets, and the hotel's Bistro offers first-class dining. *1 Devonshire Gardens. ☎ 0141/339-2001. www.onedevonshiregardens.com. 49 units. Doubles £155–£250. AE, DC, MC, V. Underground: Hillhead.*

★ **Kelvingrove Hotel** WEST END   At this friendly, family-run hotel, the comfortable rooms (most with modern furnishings) are set within converted flats on the ground and garden levels. *944 Sauchiehall St. ☎ 0141/339-5011. www.kelvingrove-hotel.co.uk. 22 units. Doubles £60. MC, V. Bus: 16, 18A, or 42A.*

kids **Kirklee Hotel** WEST END   A red-sandstone Edwardian terraced house, with elegant bay windows, overlooking a private garden. A few of the high-ceilinged units are large enough to accommodate families. *11 Kensington Gate. ☎ 0141/334-5555. www.kirkleehotel.co.uk. 9 units. Doubles £72. MC, V. Underground: Hillhead.*

★ **Malmaison** COMMERCIAL CENTER   The interior decor of this converted church, with its fine Greek-style exterior, is sleek and modern. Units vary in size from quite cozy to average, but all are chic and well-appointed with special extras such as CD players and top-of-the-line toiletries. *278 W. George St. ☎ 0141/572-1000. www.malmaison-glasgow.com. 72 units. Doubles £140. AE, DC, MC, V. Suburban train: Charing Cross.*

Manor Park Hotel WEST END   In the Broomhill district of the West End (off the beaten track), this impressive town house (built in 1895, but first used as a hotel in 1947) offers a

The chic rooms at Malmaison are sleek, modern, and very comfortable.

blend of modern and traditional furnishings. Each guest room (top units are the largest) comes with a neat little bathroom with either tub or shower. *28 Balshagray Dr.* ☎ *0141/ 339-2143. www.manorparkhotel.com. 9 units. Doubles £65. AE, DC, MC, V. Bus: 44 or 16.*

Millennium Hotel Glasgow

COMMERCIAL CENTER   This landmark hotel, once called the Copthorne and erected at the beginning of the 19th century, has been thoroughly modernized. It faces onto the city's central plaza, George Square, and rooms in the front offer views of the opulent Glasgow city chambers. *George Sq. (at George St.).* ☎ *0141/332-6711. www. millenniumhotels.com. 117 units. Doubles £185. AE, DC, MC, V. Underground: Buchanan St.*

Park Inn COMMERCIAL CENTER
Formerly Langs, this contemporary hotel has a medley of bedrooms in various shapes, sizes, and configurations—each attempting to offer a certain flair. The smallest units are

the studios, but guests can opt for a duplex, a theme room, or a large suite (all have great bathrooms with power showers). *2 Port Dundas Place.* ☎ *0141/333-1500. Fax 0141/ 333-5700. www.parkinn.co.uk. 100 units. Doubles £148. DC, MC, V. Underground: Buchanan St.*

★ Radisson SAS COMMERCIAL
CENTER   Still shiny since its November 2002 opening, the Radisson is just a stone's throw from Central Station. The contemporary guest rooms, with their blonde wood details and Scandinavian cool, have all the modern conveniences. *301 Argyle St.* ☎ *0141/204-3333. www.radissonsas. com. 250 units. Doubles £105. AE, DC, MC, V. Underground: St. Enoch.*

★★ Town House WEST END
This is one of the most charming of the city's B&Bs. The finely corniced entry hall and landings are decorated with original artwork. The sitting room features a coal fire, though the hotel is modern enough to provide a computer with high-speed Internet access. *4 Hughenden Terrace (near Great Western & Hyndland rds.).* ☎ *0141/357-0862. www.thetownhouseglasgow.com. 10 units. Doubles £72. MC, V. Free parking. Underground: Hillhead.*

The lobby bar at the ultramodern Radisson SAS.

Shopping in Glasgow

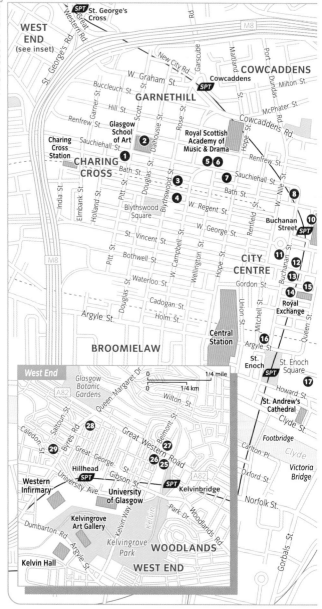

WEST END
(see inset)

St. George's Cross · SPT

COWCADDENS

Cowcaddens · SPT

GARNETHILL

Glasgow School of Art · ②

Charing Cross Station · ①

CHARING CROSS

Royal Scottish Academy of Music & Drama · ⑤ ⑥

⑦

③

④

Blythswood Square

⑧

Buchanan Street · SPT · ⑩

CITY CENTRE · ⑪

⑫

⑬

⑭ ⑮

Royal Exchange

⑯

Central Station

BROOMIELAW

St. Enoch · SPT · St. Enoch Square

⑰

St. Andrew's Cathedral

West End

Glasgow Botanic Gardens

0 — 1/4 mile
0 — 1/4 km

②⑧

②⑦

②⑥ ②⑤ · SPT

②⑨

Hillhead · SPT

Western Infirmary

University of Glasgow

Kelvingrove Art Gallery

Kelvingrove Park

Kelvin Hall

WOODLANDS

WEST END

Victoria Bridge

Footbridge

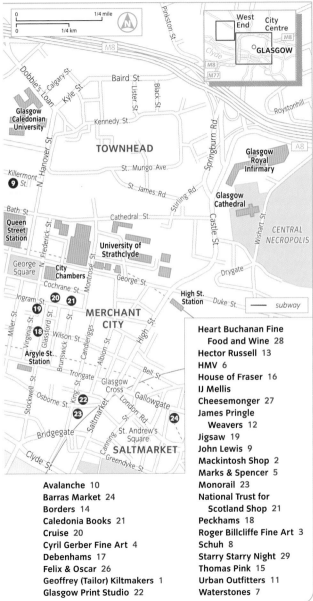

Avalanche 10
Barras Market 24
Borders 14
Caledonia Books 21
Cruise 20
Cyril Gerber Fine Art 4
Debenhams 17
Felix & Oscar 26
Geoffrey (Tailor) Kiltmakers 1
Glasgow Print Studio 22

Heart Buchanan Fine
   Food and Wine 28
Hector Russell 13
HMV 6
House of Fraser 16
IJ Mellis
   Cheesemonger 27
James Pringle
   Weavers 12
Jigsaw 19
John Lewis 9
Mackintosh Shop 2
Marks & Spencer 5
Monorail 23
National Trust for
   Scotland Shop 21
Peckhams 18
Roger Billcliffe Fine Art 3
Schuh 8
Starry Starry Night 29
Thomas Pink 15
Urban Outfitters 11
Waterstones 7

Shopping Best Bets

Best Art Shop
★ Roger Billcliffe Fine Art, *134 Blythswood St.* (p 143)

Best Secondhand Books
★ Caledonia Books, *483 Great Western Rd.* (p 143)

Best Designer Labels
★ Cruise, *180 Ingram St.* (p 143)

Best Shirts
Thomas Pink, *1 Royal Bank Place* (p 144)

Best Department Store
★ John Lewis, Buchanan Galleries, *220 Buchanan St.* (p 144)

Best Food Shop
★★ Heart Buchanan Fine Food and Wine, *380 Byres Rd.* (p 144)

Best for Quirky Gifts
★ Felix & Oscar, *459 Great Western Rd.* (p 145)

Best for Mackintosh Memorabilia
★ Mackintosh Shop, Glasgow School of Art, *167 Renfrew St.* (p 145)

If you need a well-made button-down shirt, Thomas Pink is the place to get it. See p 144.

Best Alternative CD Shop
★ Monorail, *10 King St.* (p 145)

Shopping Tips

Glasgow is a shopping mecca in Northern Britain, second apparently only to London in retail therapy. Shops keep similar hours to those in Edinburgh, generally 9am to 6pm except Thursday, when they're open until 8pm, and Sunday, when they may open later and close earlier. Unless otherwise stated, all shops in the Commercial Center are best reached by the Underground station at Buchanan Street, which is the city's foremost shopping avenue, and all shops take major credit cards.

Glasgow Shopping A to Z

Art

Cyril Gerber Fine Art COMMERI-CAL CENTER One of Glasgow's best small galleries, it veers away from the avant-garde, specializing in British paintings of the 19th and 20th centuries. *148 W. Regent St. ☎ 0141/221-3095. www.gerberfineart.co.uk.*

★ **Glasgow Print Studio** MER-CHANT CITY The shop of this prestigious collective of artists sells limited-edition etchings, wood blocks, aquatints, and screen prints by Print Studio members, as well as other notable artists. *25 King St. (just below the Trongate). ☎ 0141/552-0704. www.gpsart.co.uk. Underground: St. Enoch.*

★ **Roger Billcliffe Fine Art** COMMERCIAL CENTER Fine artwork, from original contemporary paintings by British artists to delicate ceramics, is exhibited across several floors. *134 Blythswood St. (at Sauchiehall St.). ☎ 0141/332-4027. www.billcliffegallery.com.*

Books

★ **Borders** COMMERICAL CENTER This multistory U.S.-based shop at the back of Royal Exchange Square sells books, periodicals, DVDs, and CDs. It has the best selection of international periodicals and newspapers in Scotland. *98 Buchanan St. (at Gordon St.). ☎ 0141/222-7700. www.borders.com.*

★ **Caledonia Books** WEST END One of few remaining secondhand and antiquarian shops in the city of Glasgow. Charming and well run. *483 Great Western Rd. ☎ 0141/334-9663. No credit cards. Underground: Kelvin Bridge.*

Waterstones COMMERCIAL CEN-TRE Like Borders, this giant Barnes & Noble–like operation has plenty of

stock, a cafe, and lots of soft seating. *174 Sauchiehall St. ☎ 0141/248-4814. www.waterstones.co.uk.*

Clothing & Fashions

★ **Cruise** MERCHANT CITY Bring your credit cards and prepare to spend big for the best selection of designer togs in town. Labels include Prada, Armani, and Dolce&Gabbana. *180 Ingram St. (at the Italian Centre), Merchant City. ☎ 0141/572-3232. Underground: Buchanan St.*

★ **Jigsaw** MERCHANT CITY Housed under the glorious dome of the baroque former Savings Bank of Glasgow, this branch of a fashionable U.K. chain sells stylish clothes for women and juniors, as well as accessories. *177 Ingram St. (at Glassford St.). ☎ 0141/552-7639. www.jigsaw-online.com. Underground: Buchanan St.*

★ **Starry Starry Night** WEST END This shop normally stocks a bunch of antique styles and clothing worth dusting off. Also available are secondhand kilts and matching

Roger Bilcliffe Fine Art sells quality pieces by British artists.

attire. *19 Dowanside Lane (off Ruthven Lane).* ☎ *0141/337-1837. Underground: Hillhead.*

Thomas Pink COMMERCIAL CENTER   The closest thing in Glasgow to that temple of preppy sensibilities: Brooks Brothers. This is the place for the finest button-down Oxford shirts. *1 Royal Bank Place (at Buchanan St.).* ☎ *0141/248-9661.*

Urban Outfitters COMMERCIAL CENTER   Those familiar with Manhattan will recognize the stock in this popular store for youth, which carries a balance of metro-retro, kitsch, and chic clothing. *157 Buchanan St. (at Nelson Mandela Sq.).* ☎ *0141/ 248-9203. www.urbn.com.*

Flea Market Extraordinaire

If you're in Glasgow over a weekend and love flea markets, then check out the stalls at the weekend ★ **Barras Market,** on London Road (www.glasgow-barrowland.com; bus: 40, 61, or 62) in the city's East End. You'll find loads of junk for certain, but you never know what bargain or collectible might be discovered.

Department Stores

Debenhams COMMERCIAL CENTER   Sturdy department store with midrange prices. *St. Enoch Shopping Centre, 97 Argyle St.* ☎ *0844/561-6161. www.debenhams.com. Underground: St. Enoch.*

★ **House of Fraser** COMMERCIAL CENTER   This is Glasgow's modest version of London's Harrods, with a Victorian-era glass arcade four stories tall and a wide assortment of goods. *45 Buchanan St. (at Argyle St.).* ☎ *0870/160-7243. www.houseof fraser.co.uk. Underground: St. Enoch.*

★ **John Lewis** COMMERCIAL CENTER   Scotland's closest equivalent of Macy's, with quality brand names, assured service, and a no-questions-asked return policy on damaged or faulty goods. *Buchanan Galleries, 220 Buchanan St.* ☎ *0141/353-6677. www.johnlewis.com.*

Marks & Spencer COMMERCIAL CENTER   This branch of the U.K.'s famous chain of department stores sells well-made clothing and has a very good food hall. *172 Sauchiehall St.* ☎ *0141/332-6097. www.marks andspencer.com.*

Food & Wine

★★ **Heart Buchanan Fine Food and Wine** WEST END   Perfect for picnic nosh to take to the nearby Botanic Gardens, this is Glasgow's premier fine food shop. It also has a small cafe. *380 Byres Rd.* ☎ *0141/ 334-7626. http://heartbuchanan. co.uk. Underground: Hillhead.*

★ **IJ Mellis Cheesemonger** WEST END   The Glasgow branch of this excellent Edinburgh-based cheese specialist offers an outstanding selection of British and Irish cheeses. *492 Great Western Rd.* ☎ *0141/339-8998. www.ijmellischeesemonger.com. Underground: Kelvin Bridge.*

Peckham's MERCHANT CITY   A full delicatessen with fresh bread and a good wine shop in the basement.

Heart Buchanan Fine Food and Wine is the best place in Glasgow for picnic fare.

61 Glassford St.
☎ 0141/553-
0666. www.
peckhams.co.uk.

Gifts

★ Felix &
Oscar WEST END
An offbeat, fun
shop for toys, kitschy
accessories, fuzzy bags,
and a selection of T-shirts
that you're not likely to
find anywhere else. 459
Great Western Rd. ☎ 0131/339-8585.
www.felixandoscar.co.uk. Underground: Kelvin Bridge.

★ Mackintosh Shop COMMER-
CIAL CENTER   This small gift shop in
the Glasgow School of Art prides
itself on its stock of books, stationery,
glassware, and jewelry created from
or inspired by the original designs
of Charles Rennie Mackintosh.
167 Renfrew St. ☎ 0141/353-4500.
www.gsa.ac.uk/shop. Underground:
Cowcaddens.

National Trust for Scotland
Shop MERCHANT CITY   "Glasgow
style" is celebrated on the ground
floor of Hutcheson Hall, a historic
landmark that dates to 1812. Drop
in here for contemporary arts and
crafts, pottery, furniture, or jewelry.
158 Ingram St. ☎ 0141/552-8391.
Underground: Buchanan St.

Kilts & Tartans

Geoffrey (Tailor) Kiltmakers
COMMERCIAL CENTER   Both a
retailer and a manufacturer of tartans, which means they have all the
clans and have also created their own
range of 21st-century–style kilts. 309
Sauchiehall St. ☎ 0141/331-2388.
www.geoffreykilts.co.uk. Underground: Cowcaddens.

Hector Russell COMMERCIAL
CENTER   Founded in 1881, this is

*Geoffrey (Tailor) Kiltmak-
ers sells both original
and historic tartans.*

one of Scotland's
long-established
kilt makers. Crys-
tal and gift items
are also sold. 110
Buchanan St.
☎ 0141/221-0217.
www.hector-
russell.com.

James Pringle
Weavers COMMER-
CIAL CENTER   In busi-
ness since 1780, this
shop is best known for
traditional clothing, such as bulky
wool sweaters, as well as some
unique items (need a tartan night-
shirt?). 130 Buchanan St. ☎ 0141/
221-3434.

Music

★ Avalanche COMMERCIAL CEN-
TER   Small and cramped, but possi-
bly the best for the latest releases by
everybody from the White Stripes to
Yo La Tengo. 34 Dundas St. (near
Queen St. Station). ☎ 0141/332-2099.

HMV COMMERCIAL CENTER   HMV
is Great Britain's largest purveyor
of mainstream music CDs, DVDs,
and videos. 154 Sauchiehall St.
☎ 0141/332-6631.

★ Monorail MERCHANT CITY
Located within the vegan restaurant
and bar, Mono (see p 132), this is
the most individual of the independent CD outlets in the city. 10 King St.
☎ 0141/553-2400. Underground:
St. Enoch.

Shoes

Schuh COMMERCIAL CENTER
Pronounced "shoe," this shop has
the biggest range of footwear in
town, from stilettos and sneakers
to Converse high-tops and Doc
Martens. 9 Sauchiehall St. (near
Buchanan Galleries). ☎ 0141/353-
1990. www.schuhstore.co.uk.

Nightlife and A&E in Glasgow

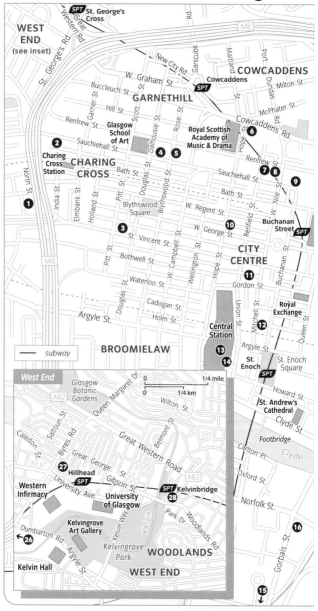

WEST END (see inset)

St. George's Cross · SPT

COWCADDENS

Cowcaddens · SPT

GARNETHILL

W. Graham St.

New City Rd

Buccleuch St.

Garnet St.

Hill St.

Renfrew St.

Scott St.

Dalhousie St.

Rose St.

Milton St.

McPhater St.

Cowcaddens Rd.

Hope St.

Dundas St.

Garscube Rd.

Maitland St.

Port

Glasgow School of Art

Royal Scottish Academy of Music & Drama **⑥**

④ **⑤**

Sauchiehall St.

Renfrew St. **⑦** **⑧**

② Charing Cross Station

Sauchiehall St.

CHARING CROSS

Bath St.

W. Nile St.

⑨

North St.

India St.

Elmbank St.

Holland St.

Pitt St.

Douglas St.

Blythswood St.

Bath St.

Renfield St.

Buchanan Street · SPT

Blythswood Square

③

St. Vincent St.

W. Regent St.

W. George St.

⑩

CITY CENTRE

Hope St.

Buchanan St.

Bothwell St.

W. Campbell St.

Wellington St.

Gordon St.

⑪

Royal Exchange

Queen St.

Waterloo St.

Cadogan St.

Mitchell St.

⑫

Pitt St.

Douglas St.

Argyle St.

Holm St.

Central Station

⑬

Argyle St.

St. Enoch Square

BROOMIELAW

Union St.

⑭

St. Enoch · SPT

Howard St.

St. Andrew's Cathedral

Clyde St.

Footbridge

Clyde

Carlton Pl.

Oxford St.

Norfolk St.

Gorbals St.

⑯

⑮ ↓

— subway

West End

Glasgow Botanic Gardens

Queen Margaret Dr.

Wilton St.

0   1/4 mile
0   1/4 km

A82

Caledon St.

Saltoun St.

Byres Rd

Great George St.

Great Western Road

Belmont St.

Gibson St.

Kelvinbridge · SPT **㉘**

㉗ Hillhead · SPT

University Ave.

University of Glasgow

A82

Park Dr.

Woodlands Rd

Western Infirmary

Kelvingrove Art Gallery

Kelvin Way

Kelvin

Kelvingrove Park

WOODLANDS

← Dumbarton Rd. **㉖**

Argyle St.

Kelvin Hall

WEST END

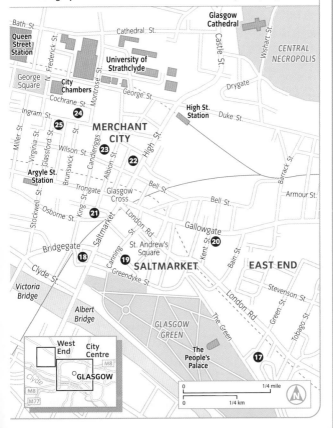

Nightlife/A&E **Best Bets**

Best for Real Ales
Bon Accord, *153 North St. (p 149)*

Best Pint of Guinness
★ Heraghty's Free House, *708 Pollokshaws Rd. (p 149)*

Best "Palace Pub"
★ The Horse Shoe, *17 Drury St. (p 149)*

Best Whisky Bar
★ The Pot Still, *154 Hope St. (p 149)*

Best Micro Brewery
★ West Brewing Company, *Binnie St., Glasgow Green (p 149)*

Best Dance Club
★ The Sub Club, *22 Jamaica St. (p 151)*

Best for Contemporary Drama
★★ Tron Theatre, *63 Trongate (p 152)*

Best Classic Theatre/Opera House
★★ Theatre Royal, *282 Hope St. (p 152)*

Best Independent Cinema
★★ Glasgow Film Theatre, *12 Rose St. (p 150)*

Best Concert Hall
★ The City Halls, *Candleriggs (p 150)*

Best Rock Venue
★★ Barrowland, *244 Gallowgate (p 151)*

Best Live Rock Bar
★ King Tut's Wah-Wah Hut, *272 St. Vincent St. (p 151)*

Best Juke Box
Nice 'n' Sleazy, *421 Sauchiehall St. (p 152)*

Best for Folk Jam Sessions
★ Babbity Bowster, *16 Blackfriars St. (p 149)*

Best Modern Gaelic Bar
Lismore Bar, *206 Dumbarton Rd. (p 149)*

Best Real Ale Pub
Bon Accord, *153 North St. (p 149)*

Best Bargain Tickets
★ Citizens Theatre, *119 Gorbals St. (p 152)*

Best Gay Dance Club
Bennets, *80 Glassford St. (p 151)*

Best Comedy Club
★ The Stand, *333 Woodlands Rd. (p 150)*

If you want a dram of whisky, the Pot Still is the best place in Glasgow to get it.

Glasgow Nightlife/A&E A to Z

Bars & Pubs

★ Babbity Bowster MERCHANT CITY   A civilized place for a pint, with no piped-in soundtrack of mindless pop (or indeed any music) to distract from the conversation. The wine selection is good, the food is worth sampling, and there's live folk music on Saturday. *16 Blackfriars St.* ☎ *0141/552-5055. Underground: Buchanan St. Suburban train: High St.*

Bar 10 COMMERCIAL CENTER   A good mix of folk come to this comfortable bar for a drink—and not only because of its convenient city center location, opposite the Lighthouse architecture center. *10 Mitchell Lane.* ☎ *0141/572-1448. Underground: St Enoch.*

Bon Accord WEST END   This amiable pub, just west of the city center, is the best in the city for hand-pulled cask-conditioned real ales from across Britain. *153 North St.* ☎ *0141/248-4427. Suburban train: Charing Cross.*

Brel WEST END   Ashton Lane is full of pubs and bars, but this one is possibly the best. It has a Belgian theme—serving up beers and cuisine from that country. *39–43 Ashton Lane.* ☎ *0141/342-4966. www.brel barrestaurant.com. Underground: Hillhead.*

★ Heraghty's Free House SOUTHSIDE   An authentic Irish pub that serves up perfect pints of Guinness, as well as lively craic (banter). No food, though. *708 Pollokshaws Rd.* ☎ *0141/423-0380. Bus: 38, 45, or 56.*

★ The Horse Shoe COMMERCIAL CENTER   If you visit only one pub in Glasgow, make it this one. It's the last remaining "Palace Pub," which opened around the turn of the 20th century. The circular bar is one of the longest in Europe. *17 Drury St. (between Renfield & W. Nile sts.).* ☎ *0141/229-5711. Underground: Buchanan St.*

Lismore Bar WEST END   Tastefully decorated in a modern manner that still recognizes traditional Highland culture, the Lismore's whisky selection is excellent. Scottish and Gaelic music is played Tuesday and Thursday nights. *206 Dumbarton Rd.* ☎ *0141/576-0103. Underground: Kelvinhall.*

★ The Pot Still COMMERCIAL CENTER   This traditional pub is the best place for sampling single malt whiskies—you can select from hundreds and hundreds of them. *154 Hope St.* ☎ *0141/333-0980. www. thepotstill.co.uk. Underground: Buchanan St.*

Revolver MERCHANT CITY   Gay-owned and -operated, this fun and friendly bar generally forgoes the more cheesy elements of the LGBT scene. *6A John St.* ☎ *0141/553-2456. Underground: Buchanan St.*

★ West Brewing Company EAST END   Opened in 2005, this Munich-style beer hall brews its own: the best, freshest lager in Glasgow—perhaps in all of Scotland. Food leans toward Bavarian dishes. *Binnie St., at Glasgow Green.* ☎ *0141/550-0135. www. westbeer.com. Bus: 16, 43, or 64.*

Cinema

Cineworld Renfrew Street COMMERCIAL CENTER   This multiplex's screens are dominated by blockbusters and big releases, but a couple are reserved for foreign and independent art house films. *7 Renfrew St.* ☎ *0871/200-2000.*

Annual International Events

Glasgow hosts some annual festivals that essentially hold their own against Edinburgh's better-known summer options. ★ **Celtic Connections** (☎ 0141/353-8000; www.celticconnections.com) is the best-attended annual festival in Glasgow, and the largest folk/traditional music festival of its kind in the world. It kicks off the year every January. The **Glasgow Film Festival** (☎ 0141/332-6535; www.glasgowfilmfestival.org.uk) gets better and better every year, screening more than 100 movies over 10 days in mid-February.

Finally, a lone piper can sound impressive; a band-full of bagpipes blown in unison, however, is one of the most stirring sounds on the planet. Every August, at **Piping Live!** (☎ 0141/353-8000; www.pipingfestival.co.uk), the cream of the crop of international piping ensembles congregate in Glasgow, competing to be acknowledged as the best bagpipe band in the world.

www.cineworld.co.uk. *Tickets £4.50– £6.50. Underground: Buchanan St.*

★★ **Glasgow Film Theatre** COMMERCIAL CENTER   Head here for a well-programmed daily output of independent, foreign, repertory, and art house films. *12 Rose St.* ☎ *0141/ 332-8128. www.gft.org.uk. Tickets £4–£6. Underground: Cowcaddens.*

Comedy

Jongleurs Comedy Club COMMERCIAL CENTER   A corporate-owned entity from England with acts

The City Halls are acoustically better than many other venues in Glasgow.

that tend to be mainstream. *11 Renfrew St.* ☎ *0870/787-0707. £12 cover. Underground: Buchanan St.*

★ **The Stand** WEST END   The city's only purpose-built comedy club, it helped to establish an annual International Comedy Festival in Glasgow every spring. *333 Woodlands Rd.* ☎ *0870/600-6055. www.thestand.co.uk. £2–£10 cover. Underground: Kelvin Bridge.*

Concert Halls

★ **The City Halls** MERCHANT CITY Emerging from £8 million in renovations in 2006, these small halls, which date to the 1840s and are the home of the BBC's Scottish Symphony Orchestra and many special events, are acoustically superior to the city's larger auditoriums. *Candleriggs.* ☎ *0141/353-8000. www.glasgow cityhalls.com. Ticket prices vary. Underground: Buchanan St.*

Glasgow Royal Concert Hall COMMERCIAL CENTER   Very little is subtle about this modern music hall, primarily home to the Royal Scottish National Orchestra, which plays its yearly Winter–Spring series and

Piping Live!, held every August in Glasgow, features performances by some of the best pipers in the world.

Pops seasons in the main auditorium. *2 Sauchiehall St.* ☎ *0141/353-8000. www.grch.com. Tickets £10–£35. Underground: Buchanan St.*

Dance Clubs

Bennets MERCHANT CITY   Self-described as the city's "premier gay and lesbian nightclub," this two-level club is the most consistently popular on the gay scene. *80 Glassford St.* ☎ *0141/552-5761. £3–£10 cover. Underground: Buchanan St.*

★ **The Sub Club** COMMERCIAL CENTER   The city's best-known "underground" club, with DJs such as the long-standing kings of house, Harri and Dom of Subculture. *22 Jamaica St.* ☎ *0141/248-4600. www. subclub.co.uk. £3–£10 cover. Underground: St. Enoch.*

Folk Music

St. Andrew's in the Square EAST END   This sympathetically converted early-18th-century church is the city's venue dedicated to folk, Celtic, and traditional Scottish music. *1 St. Andrews Sq. (off Saltmarket).* ☎ *0141/559-5902. www.standrews inthesquare.com. Tickets £4–£8. Bus: 16, 18, 64, or 263.*

The Scotia Bar MERCHANT CITY   Opened in 1792 (and arguably the oldest bar in Glasgow), The Scotia frequently has live music, which includes a good dose of folk. *112 Stockwell St.* ☎ *0141/552-8681. No cover. Underground: St. Enoch.*

Pop & Rock

★ **ABC** COMMERICAL CENTER   With room for a crowd of about 1,250, this hall is a good place to get a bit closer to the rock and pop bands that play here. *300 Sauchiehall St.* ☎ *0870/400-0818. www.abcglasgow. com. Underground: Cowcaddens.*

★★ **Barrowland** EAST END   There are no seats and it generally stinks of beer, but this former ballroom remains the most exciting place in the city to see touring bands. The hall rocks. *244 Gallowgate.* ☎ *0141/552-4601. Bus: 62.*

★ **King Tut's Wah-Wah Hut** COMMERCIAL CENTER   This sweaty, crowded rock bar is a good place to check out the Glasgow music and arts crowd, as well as local bands and the occasional international act. *272 St. Vincent St.*

St. Andrew's in the Square is Glasgow's top venue for Celtic and traditional Scottish music.

Barrowland is the best place in the city to see touring bands. See p 151.

☎ *0141/221-5279. www.kingtuts. co.uk. Bus: 40, 61, or 62.*

Nice 'n' Sleazy COMMERCIAL CENTER   This bar books live acts to perform in its dark basement space. The cover is quite reasonable. The ground-floor bar has the city's best jukebox. *421 Sauchiehall St.* ☎ *0141/333-9637. Suburban train: Charing Cross.*

Theater

★ **The Arches** COMMERCIAL CENTER   A contemporary arts complex that stages edgy new plays, as well as Shakespeare, at inexpensive prices. There's also a fairly full schedule of live music of all description, regular dance clubs, and visual art exhibits. *253 Argyle St.* ☎ *0870/240-7528. www.thearches.co.uk. Tickets £4–£10. Underground: St. Enoch.*

★ **Citizens Theatre** SOUTHSIDE   The "Citz," a symbol of the city's democratic approach to theater, is home to a repertory company and has three performance spaces. Prices are always reasonable. *119 Gorbals St. (at Ballater St.).* ☎ *0141/429-0022. www.citz.co.uk. Tickets £5–£15.*

Underground: Bridge St. Bus: 5, 12, 20, or 66.

★★ **Theatre Royal** COMMERCIAL CENTER   This Victorian-style theater is the home of the ambitious Scottish Opera, as well as the recently ascendant Scottish Ballet. London's *Daily Telegraph* has called it (with a trifle of exaggeration) "the most beautiful opera theatre in the kingdom." *282 Hope St.* ☎ *0870/060-6647. www.theatreroyalglasgow. com. Ticket prices vary. Underground: Cowcaddens.*

★★ **Tron Theatre** MERCHANT CITY   Housed in part of a 15th-century church, this is one of Scotland's leading venues for new drama. It's used often by local companies, such as the acclaimed Vanishing Point, to debut works that end up on the national and international circuit. *63 Trongate.* ☎ *0141/ 552-4267. www.tron.co.uk. Tickets £3–£20. Underground: St. Enoch.* ●

The Theatre Royal, home of the Scottish Opera.

The Best of the Central Belt

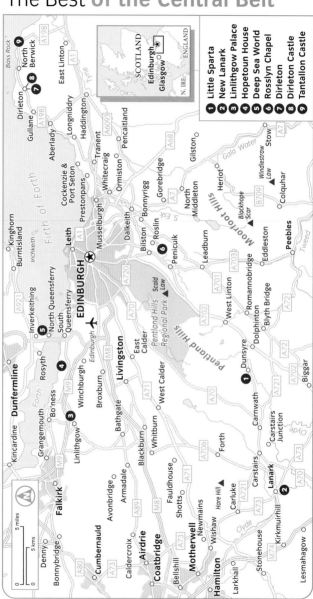

1. Little Sparta
2. New Lanark
3. Linlithgow Palace
4. Hopetoun House
5. Deep Sea World
6. Rosslyn Chapel
7. Dirleton
8. Dirleton Castle
9. Tantallon Castle

Previous Page: The towering sandstone ruins of Sweetheart Abbey in the Borders and Galloway.

There are some interesting sites and memorable places to visit in Scotland's central belt, a region that surrounds the country's two main cities. Indeed, the stops on this tour could be visited as excursions out of Edinburgh or Glasgow. I have organized them, however, in this chapter, so that you could see them all in 2 days.

START: **On the edge of the Pentland Hills, about 29km (18 miles) south-west of Edinburgh. Trip Length: About 161km (100 miles) over 2 days.**

① ★★ Little Sparta. Little Sparta, called the "only original garden" created in Great Britain since World War II, was devised by one of the most intriguing artists of the 20th century, the late Ian Hamilton Finlay (1925–2006). It is a surprisingly lush plot of land, given the harsh terrain surrounding it. Dotted throughout the garden are stone sculptures (many with Finlay's pithy sayings and poems) created in collaboration with master stonemasons and other artists. Unique. ⏱ 1½ hr. *Stonypath, near Dunsyre, off the A702.* ☎ *07758/812-263. www.little sparta.org. Admission £10. Jun 15–Oct 14 Fri & Sun 2:30–5pm.*

From Dunsyre, take Newbigging and Dunsyre roads, turning right on A721 to A70 (at Carnwath) and A743, finally following A743 to Lanark (total 22km/14 miles).

② kids New Lanark. A UNESCO World Heritage Site, New Lanark was a progressive industrial mill and village in the early19th century, offering its workers and families free education, a day-care nursery, a social club, and a co-operative store. Today, the attraction includes a chairlift ride that tells the story of what life here was like, as well as self-guided tours of the principal buildings. ⏱ 2 hr. *Braxfield Rd., outside Lanark.* ☎ *01555/661-345. www.newlanark.org. Admission £5.95 adults, £4.95 kids, £18 family. Daily 11am–5pm.*

The grounds of New Lanark World Heritage Site.

Take A706 out of Lanark heading north toward Whitburn, exiting on to the A801 after 27km (17 miles) and then taking the A706 to the A803 and Linlithgow (total 42km/26 miles).

③ ★ Linlithgow Palace. Birthplace of Mary Queen of Scots, this architectural landmark (built primarily between 1425 and 1437) was a favorite residence of Scottish royalty, and is now one of Scotland's most poignant ruins. Enough of the royal rooms are still intact that you

Coats of arms above the entrance to Linlithgow Palace.

can see how grand the palace once was. King James V (Mary's father) was born here in 1512, and when he wed, the palace's impressive fountain ran with wine. ⏱ *1½ hr. Linlithgow (A904).* ☎ *01506/842-896. www.historic-scotland.gov.uk. Admission £5 adults, £4 seniors, £2.50 kids. Daily Apr–Sept 9:30am–6:30pm; Oct–Mar 9:30am–4:30pm.*

From Linlithgow join M9 east (signposted Edinburgh) to the B8046 (exit junction 2), turning right on A904 through Newton Village, and follow signs bearing left toward South Queensferry (total 11km/6¾ miles).

❹ ★ **Hopetoun House.** Amid beautifully landscaped grounds, the home of the earls of Hopetoun is one of Scotland's best examples of 18th-century palatial Georgian architecture. You can wander through splendid reception rooms filled with Renaissance paintings, statuary, and other artwork. The views of the Firth of Forth are panoramic from the rooftop observation deck. ⏱ *1½ hr. South Queensferry (off the A904).* ☎ *0131/331-2451. www.hopetounhouse.com. Admission £8 adults, £4.25 kids, £22 family. Daily Apr–Sept 10:30am–4pm (last entry).*

Take A904 east to the Forth Road Bridge and A90, crossing north to the B981 and then driving back toward the sea and into North Queensferry (total 11km/6¾ miles).

❺ kids **Deep Sea World.** By Orlando standards, it may seem amateurish, but this is Scotland's most comprehensive aquarium. From a submerged 112m (367-ft.) poly-glass tunnel, you can view kelp forests, schools of stingrays, and murky caves favored by conger eels. Curiously, the curvature of the tunnel's thick clear plastic makes everything seem about 30% smaller. ⏱ *2 hr. Battery Quarry (below Forth Road Bridge).* ☎ *01383/411-880. www.deepseaworld.com. Admission £11 adults, £7.50 kids, £36 family. Mon–Fri 10am–5pm; Sat & Sun 10am–6pm.*

Hopetoun House is one of the country's best examples of Georgian architecture.

Return to Forth Road Bridge, taking A90 south to A902 and the A8 (signs for City Bypass) for less than a mile to A720. Exit on the A702 south to the A703, following signs to Roslin (total 32km/20 miles).

6 ★ **Rosslyn Chapel.** Thanks to the *Da Vinci Code*, the elaborately carved Rosslyn Chapel is now firmly entrenched on the tourist trail. Visitor numbers apparently doubled in the run-up to the release of the movie, part of which was filmed here. The chapel was founded in 1446 by Sir William St. Clair and has been long noted for its architectural and design idiosyncrasies. ⏲ *45 min. Roslin (off the A701).* ☎ *0131/440-2159. www.rosslynchapel.org.uk. Admission £7. Mon–Sat Apr–Sept 9:30am–6pm; Oct–Mar 9:30am–5pm; Sun noon–4:45pm, year-round.*

Scenic Rosslyn Chapel is renowned for its architectural details.

Return to City Bypass (A720) heading east toward Berwick upon Tweed and the A1. Exit A1 onto the A198, driving about 16km (10 miles) through Aberlady and Gullane to the B1345 into Dirleton (total 38km/24 miles).

7 ★ **Dirleton.** This village has been cited as the prettiest village in Scotland. I'm not entirely convinced, but it does have a picture-postcard perfection, as if created for a movie set. It does have one note of history: Back in the 1940s, FDR and Winston Churchill met here to plan the D-day landings. ⏲ *45 min.*

8 ★ **Dirleton Castle.** Dating to the 13th century, this castle was sacked by Oliver Cromwell's forces in 1650, leaving behind the romantic ruins you see today. The surrounding garden—with a flower bed that Guinness ranks as longest in the world—is the main attraction for some. Other highlights include the imposing gatehouse, vaulted arcades, and a 16th-century "beehive" dovecote. ⏲ *1 hr. Dirleton.* ☎ *01620/850-330.*

www.historic-scotland.gov.uk. Admission £4.50 adults, £3.25 seniors, £2.25 kids. Daily Apr–Sept 9:30am–6pm; Oct–Mar 9:30am–4:30pm.

Return to A198, heading east through North Berwick (total 9km/5⅔ miles).

9 ★ **Tantallon Castle.** After its construction on North Sea cliffs in the 14th century, this became the stronghold of the powerful Douglas family, who tended to side with England in its wars and disputes with Scotland. Like most castles in the region, Tantallon endured a fair number of attacks, but the Cromwellian troops truly sacked it in the mid-1600s. Nevertheless, the ruins remain formidable and include a square five-story central tower. ⏲ *1 hr. Off the A198.* ☎ *01620/892-727. www. historic-scotland.gov.uk. Admission £4.50 adults, £3.50 seniors, £2.25 kids. Daily Apr–Sept 9:30am–6:30pm; Sat–Wed Oct–Mar 9:30am–4:30pm.*

Where **to Stay**

A bedroom with fireplace at the Open Arms hotel.

Arden House LINLITHGOW   This award-winning Victorian B&B is set on the outskirts of town, amid a country retreat on the Belsyde Estate. Rooms are large and the beds are famously spacious and plush. *Off the A706 (2km/1¼ miles southwest of town).* ☎ *01506/670-172. www.ardencountryhouse.com. 3 units. Doubles from £70. AE, MC, V.*

Bonsyde House Hotel LINLITH-GOW   This historic 19th-century country mansion was once home to the man credited with mapping the seven seas: Professor Charles Thomson (1830–82). In addition to the regular guest rooms, there are cabins with their own screened rear patios. *Just northwest of Linlithgow, off the A706 on the edge of West Lothian Golf Club.* ☎ *01506/842-229. www.bonsydehouse.co.uk. 8 units. Doubles from £65. MC, V.*

The Open Arms DIRLETON   Just across the road from Dirleton Castle (see p 157, ⑧), this old stone hotel has some rooms that overlook the castle's romantic ruins, while others offer vistas of the town. It specializes in golfing packages, so links masters often stay here. *Main St.* ☎ *01620/850-241. www.openarmshotel.com. 12 units. Doubles £130. AE, MC, V.*

kids Peebles Hotel Hydro
PEEBLES   Once a Victorian hydro-pathic resort (it opened in 1881) that claimed to cure whatever ailed you, today its main features remain a whirlpool and sauna for adults, and a pool for kids. Outdoor recreational options for all ages are plentiful. One-fifth of the guest rooms are geared toward families. *Innerleithen Rd., off A72.* ☎ *01721/720-602. www. peebleshotelhydro.co.uk. 125 units. Doubles £214–£260. AE, DC, MC, V.*

Where to Dine

★ **The Boat House** SOUTH QUEENSFERRY *FISH/SEAFOOD* This restaurant is down a few steps from the main street, which means diners are closer to the sea, with views of the marvelous Forth bridges. The typical seafood dishes are creative but not overcomplicated. *19b High St.* ☎ *0131/331-5429. Entrees £12–£18. Lunch & dinner Tues–Sun.*

★ **Champany Inn** CHAMPANY CORNER *SCOTTISH* You'll find some of the best steaks in Britain and an award-winning wine list at this converted mill. The meat here is properly hung before butchering, adding to its flavor and texture. Next to the main dining room is the Chop House, offering less expensive cuts. *A904 (3km/1¾ miles northeast of Linlithgow).* ☎ *01506/834-532. www.champany.com. Entrees £18–£33. AE, DC, MC, V. Lunch Mon–Fri, dinner Mon–Sat.*

★ **La Potiniere** GULLANE *MODERN SCOTTISH/FRENCH* A local land-mark that, despite changes in owner-ship, continues to rank among the very best in East Lothian. The decor may be old-fashioned but the French-influenced cooking's up to date. *Main St.* ☎ *01620/843-214. Set dinner £40. AE, MC, V. Lunch & dinner Wed–Sun.*

★ **The Wee Restaurant** NORTH QUEENSFERRY *MODERN SCOTTISH* Tiny (just 24 seats), but its reputation in Central Scotland has been big since opening in 2006. Chef/owner Craig Wood offers innovative fare off a reg-ularly changing menu. Located under the famous Firth railway bridge. *17 Main St.* ☎ *01383/616-263. www.the weerestaurant.co.uk. Entrees £16. MC, V. Lunch & dinner Tues–Sat.*

The award-winning Champany Inn serves some of the best steaks in Scotland.

The Best of the **Borders & Galloway**

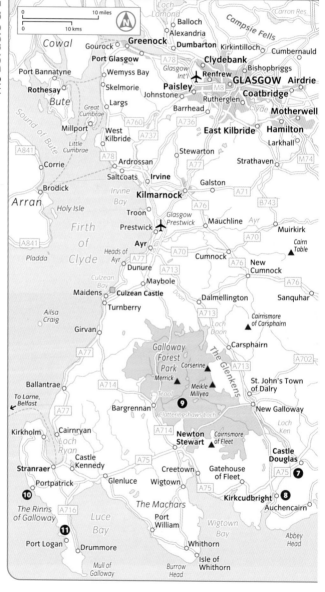

1 Jedburgh Abbey
2 Melrose Abbey
3 Abbotsford
4 Burns House
5 Caerlaverock Castle
6 Sweetheart Abbey
7 Threave Castle
8 Kirkcudbright
9 Loch Trool
10 Portpatrick
11 Logan Botanic Garden

The ancient abbeys and castles across these two regions remind one of Scotland's ecclesiastical past and turbulent history, as most of these places became ruins after battles with England. The Borders was favored territory of romantic historical author Sir Walter Scott (1771–1832), while Galloway stretches westward, with rolling hills to the blue Irish sea and some reasonably dramatic coastlines to explore. START: **In Jedburgh. Trip Length: Take 3 days as it's about 250km (155 miles) and some of the roads are, shall I say, scenic.**

❶ ★ Jedburgh Abbey. This ruined abbey, founded by King David I in 1138, is one of Scotland's finest. In the mid-1500s, the English sacked it repeatedly and few efforts to repair the abbey were made from 1560 until 1875, when teams of Victorian architects set about restoring the structure to its original medieval design. While it remains roofless, most of the exterior stonework is in place. ⏱ *1 hr. Jedburgh, on the A68.* ☎ *01835/863-925. www.historic-scotland.gov.uk. Admission £5 adults, £4 seniors, £2.50 kids. Daily Apr–Sept 9:30am–6:30pm; Oct–Mar 9:30am–4:30pm.*

Take the A68 northwest for about 15km (9⅓ miles) to the A6091 and Melrose (total 21km/13 miles).

❷ ★★ Melrose Abbey. These lichen-covered ruins, among the most evocative in Europe, are all that's left of an ecclesiastical community established in the 12th century. While the soaring remains follow the lines of the original abbey, these walls were largely constructed in the 15th century. The heart of the Scottish king, Robert the Bruce (1274–1329), is believed to be interred in the abbey, per his wishes. ⏱ *1 hr. Abbey St., Melrose.* ☎ *01896/822-562. www. historic-scotland.gov.uk. Admission £5 adults, £4 seniors, £2.50 kids. Daily Apr–Sept 9:30am–6:30pm; Oct–Mar 9:30am–4:30pm.*

A short drive, taking the A6091 west to the B6360 (total 4km/ 2½ miles).

Jedburgh Abbey, one of Scotland's finest, has an interesting mix of Gothic and Romanesque architectural elements.

The entrance hall at Abbotsford, the former home of Sir Walter Scott.

③ ★ Abbotsford. Sir Walter Scott's home from 1817 until his death, this Scots baronial style mansion is considered the author's most enduring monument. After his literary works, that is. The home contains many relics and mementos, from Rob Roy's sporran to a sword given to the Duke of Montrose by Charles I for his cooperation (some say collaboration). 🕐 *1 hr. B6360 (off the A6091). ☎ 01896/752-043. www.scottsabbotsford.co.uk. Admission £6 adults, £3 kids. Daily Apr–Oct 9:30am–5pm.*

Expect this leg to take nearly 2 hrs. Take the A7 south to Selkirk and the A708 for about 55km (34 miles) to Moffat. From there take the A701 south (crossing the M8 motorway) to the roundabouts outside Dumfries, following the signs to the town center (total 99km/62 miles).

④ Burns House. One of the attractions on the Burns Heritage Trail (see p 171), this modest house in the town of Dumfries is where the bard died in 1796. It's a tiny place filled with relics and items, such as some original manuscripts. The most impressive feature may be the poet's signature, scrawled with a diamond on an upstairs window of the sandstone cottage. 🕐 *45 min. Burns St. Dumfries. ☎ 01387/255-297. Free admission. Apr–Sept daily 10am–5pm (from 2pm Sun); Oct–Mar Tues–Sat 10am–1pm, 2–5pm.*

Take the B725 south out of central Dumfries (total 13km/8 miles).

⑤ ★★ kids Caerlaverock Castle. A favorite target of English armies, Caerlaverock (pronounced Ka-*lah*-ver-ick) is one of Scotland's most impressive medieval castles. There are a water-filled moat, a twin-towered gatehouse, some pretty serious battlements, and an example of the huge siege-engine or trebuchet that launched boulders at its fortifications. If the weather cooperates, take the woodland nature trail to see the foundations of the original castle, set nearer to the swampy banks of the Nith River estuary. *B725. ☎ 01387/770-224. www.historic-scotland.gov.uk. Admission £5 adults, £4 seniors & students, £2.50 kids. Daily Apr–Sept 9:30am–6:30pm; Oct–Mar 9:30am–4:30pm.*

Take the B725 back to Dumfries, cross the River Nith, joining the A710 south to New Abbey (total 12km/7½ miles).

⑥ ★ Sweetheart Abbey. An unusual story explains the name of this towering red sandstone ruin. In 1273 Lady Devorgilla of Galloway founded the abbey in memory of her husband, John de Balliol (the man behind Balliol College at Oxford University). So attached was she to her husband that she apparently carried his embalmed heart around with her for 22 years until she died in 1290. When she was buried here, in front of the altar, the heart went with her. 🕐 *45 min. A710, at New Abbey village. ☎ 01387/850-397. www.historic-scotland.gov.uk.*

Admission £3 adults, £2.50 seniors & students, £1.50 kids. Daily Apr–Sept 9:30am–6:30pm; Sat–Wed Oct–Mar 9:30am–4:30pm.

There some winding alternative roads, but the simplest route is to return toward Dumfries and take the A75 southwest toward Castle Douglas (total 44km/27 miles).

7 Threave Castle. One of the best things about this massive 14th-century tower house (last used as a 19th-c. prison for Napoleonic soldiers) is getting there. Ring a bell to call a boatman, who ferries you to the island in the River Dee on which the castle sits. *Note:* Leave your best shoes behind; the path from the parking area can get muddy. *Off the A75 (5km/3 miles west of Castle Douglas).* ☎ *07711/223-101. www.historic-scotland.gov.uk. Admission £4 adults, £3 seniors & students, £2 kids under 16. Daily Apr–Sept 9:30am–4:30pm (last sailing); Sat–Wed Oct 9.30am–3:30pm (last sailing).Closed Nov–Mar.*

Return to A75, taking it west (signs to Stranraer), then turn left

Charming Kircudbright was a thriving artist colony in the late 19th and early 20th centuries.

Caerlaverock Castle, off the Nith River, is one of Scotland's most impressive medieval castles. See p 163.

on A711 and head south (total 13km/8 miles).

8 ★★ Kirkcudbright. My favorite southern Scottish town, Kirkcudbright (pronounced Kerr-*coo*-bree) was a thriving artist colony in the late 19th and early 20th centuries, drawing many notable artists, such as leading "Glasgow Boy" E. A. Hornel and genius graphic artist Jessie M. King. The appeal of this adorable village remains, although the colony is more of a heritage spot these days, with galleries keeping the artistic history alive. The center of town is full of small, colorful cottages, many with charming wee lanes. From April to September you can visit Hornel's home, Broughton House, High Street (☎ 01557/330-437; www.nts.org.), a Georgian-era mansion that the artist adapted. ⏱ *2½ hr. Tourist information, Harbour Sq.* ☎ *01557/330-494. Admission to Broughton House £8 adults, £20 family.*

Take A755 across the River Dee to the A75, heading west for about 30km (19 miles) through Creetown to the A714, turning right and heading north 15km

(9⅓ miles). Just past Bargrennan, turn right to Glen Trool Village (total 60km/37 miles).

⑨ ★ Loch Trool. My tour doesn't offer too much of the great outdoors, but this stop's an exception. The trail around Loch Trool (moderate to easy) is one of the best short walks in Dumfries and Galloway. On one side of the loch, the army of Robert the Bruce is believed to have defeated a much stronger English force in 1307. Bruce's Stone is a granite monument commemorating the victory. ⏲ *2–3 hr. Off the A714 (13km/8 miles north of Newton Stewart). Free admission. Daily dawn–dusk.*

Take A714 back to A75, turn right, and go west to Stranraer (about 55km/34 miles). Turn left at Station St., following the signs to Portpatrick, and using the A77 south out of Stranraer, turn right at the 3km junction, heading west though Lochans (total 73km/45 miles).

⑩ ★ Portpatrick. The site of a natural harbor that has been improved over the years, Portpatrick is one of the most picturesque towns in southwest Scotland. There are a few cute shops, a small beach in the harbor, and hiking/walking trails that lead away from the village, both up

and down the coast. Just south of town, one well-marked path leads to the ruins of 15th-century Dunskey Castle, perched on the edge of a cliff above the sea. ⏲ *2 hr. A77 (10km/6¼ miles southwest of Stranraer).*

Take the A77 back out of town, turning right onto the B7042 to Sandhead and then turn onto the A716 south, turning right onto the B7065 toward Port Logan (total 24km/15 miles).

⑪ ★★★ Logan Botanic Garden. Here, in part thanks to the Gulf Stream, a microclimate allows the successful cultivation of palms, tree ferns, and other exotic plants—including towering, flowering columns of *Echium pininanas,* which are native to the Canary Islands. In addition to a more formal walled garden, Logan also has wilder plantings, such as the *Gunnera manicata,* whose leaves are larger than an elephant's ears. Affiliated with Edinburgh's Royal Botanic Garden, this garden is worth the trip if you fancy plants at all. ⏲ *1¾ hr. B7065, near Port Logan.* ☎ *01776/860-231. www. rbge.org.uk. Admission £3.50 adults, £3 seniors & students, £1 kids under 16, £9 family. Daily Apr–Sept 10am–6pm, Mar & Oct 10am–5pm.*

Set on the site of a natural, Portpatrick is one of the most picture-perfect towns in southwest Scotland.

Where to Stay

★ **Burt's Hotel** MELROSE   This family-run inn dates to 1722, offering a taste of small-town Scotland, although much of the decor is modern. All guest rooms are well furnished. If it's busy, alternative accommodations are offered across the street at its sister, the Townhouse Hotel, where double rooms start at £96. *Market Sq.* ☎ *01896/ 822-285. Fax 01896/822-870. www. burtshotel.co.uk. 20 units. Doubles £106. AE, DC, MC, V.*

kids Cairndale Hotel & Leisure Club DUMFRIES   This early-20th-century resort with a stone facade offers comfortable rooms, but its best features are in the Barracuda Club (spa, steam room, gym, indoor

The tranquil and remote Knockinaam Lodge has beautiful gardens and its own private beach.

pool). Twenty-two rooms are suitable for families. *132–136 English St., just off High St.* ☎ *01387/254-111. www.cairndalehotel.co.uk. 91 units. Doubles £109. AE, DC, MC, V.*

Crown Hotel PORTPATRICK   It doesn't offer luxury accommodations, but the unpretentious Crown is right on the harbor and its guest rooms, with big old-fashioned bathtubs, overlook the sea. You may, however, prefer a unit in the back to avoid noise from the popular hotel pub below. *9 N. Crescent.* ☎ *01766/ 810-261. www.crownportpatrick. com. Doubles £72–£78. MC, V.*

★★ **Knockinaam Lodge** PORT-PATRICK   Built in 1869, this small luxury hotel a few miles south of Portpatrick resembles a country manor, with well-manicured gardens and its own private beach. In this tranquil and remote setting, Churchill, Eisenhower, and their staff met during World War II. *Portpatrick* ☎ *01776/ 810-471. www.knockinaamlodge.com. 9 units. Doubles £270–£400 (includes breakfast, dinner). AE, MC, V.*

Moffat House Hotel MOFFAT   It's hard to miss this 18th-century stone mansion (a smaller version of Hopetoun House; see p 156, ❹), set in the center of this former spa town. The guest rooms are individually decorated. A literary footnote: Author James Macpherson (who invented the works of a mythical ancient poet, Ossian) wrote the forgeries here in 1759. *High St.* ☎ *01683/220-039. www.moffat house.co.uk. 21 units. Doubles £106. AE, MC, V.*

Where **to Dine**

★ **Campbells** PORTPATRICK *FISH/ SEAFOOD* Facing the harbor, this welcoming family-run restaurant is almost old-fashioned in its unpretentious manner, the decor mixing rustic seaport with modernity. The fresh fish is excellent. *1 S. Crescent.* ☎ *01776/810-314. Entrees £12–£20. DC, MC, V. Lunch & dinner Tues–Sun.*

Chapters Bistro GATTONSIDE *SCOTTISH/GLOBAL* This unassuming bistro just across the Rivet Tweed from Melrose has a menu that ranges from scallops St. Jacques to venison with juniper berries. The wine list is pretty extensive, too. *Main St., Gattonside by Melrose.* ☎ *01896/823-217. Entrees £10–£16. MC, V. Lunch & dinner Tues–Sat.*

Halcyon PEEBLES *MODERN SCOTTISH* Stylish and contemporary in decor and cuisine, Halcyon uses local suppliers (and organic fruits and vegetables) for ingredients in its modern Scottish dishes, which might include rabbit rillettes or a rump of lamb with aubergine pickle.

39 Eastgate. ☎ *01721/725-100. www.halcyonrestaurant.com. Entrees £11–£20. MC, V. Lunch & dinner Tues–Sat.*

★★ **Knockinaam** PORTPATRICK *SCOTTISH/FRENCH* Even if you don't stay at this lodge overnight, you can still enjoy its outstanding meals, which earned the kitchen a vaunted Michelin star. The bar has an excellent whisky selection. *Portpatrick.* ☎ *01776/810-471. www.knockinaamlodge.com. Set dinner £50. AE, MC, V. Lunch & dinner daily.*

Wheatsheaf Restaurant SWINTON *MODERN BRITISH* Located between Melrose and Eyemouth, from whose harbor the kitchen secures fresh seafood, the Wheatsheaf is an award-winning restaurant that pops up on many "best of" lists. Leave the kids at home at dinnertime. *Main St.* ☎ *01890/860-257. www.wheatsheaf-swinton.co.uk. Entrees £13–£18. MC, V. Lunch & dinner daily.*

One of many upscale modern British dishes at the award-winning Wheatsheaf Restaurant.

The Best of **Ayrshire & Southern Argyll**

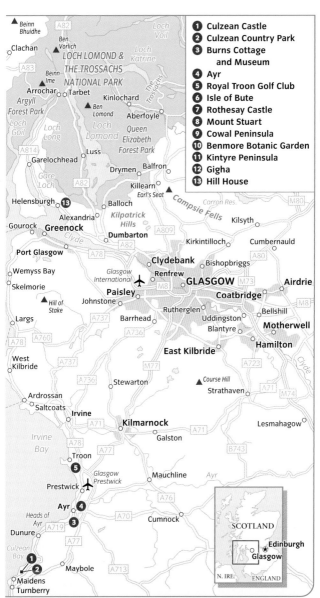

1 Culzean Castle
2 Culzean Country Park
3 Burns Cottage and Museum
4 Ayr
5 Royal Troon Golf Club
6 Isle of Bute
7 Rothesay Castle
8 Mount Stuart
9 Cowal Peninsula
10 Benmore Botanic Garden
11 Kintyre Peninsula
12 Gigha
13 Hill House

Ayrshire stretches north from Galloway nearly to Glasgow, and its attractions include various landmarks associated with the life of the great poet Robert Burns—and the country's highest concentration of links-style golf courses. My tour of the region also includes the southern fringes of Argyll because it's among my favorite parts of Scotland, with peninsulas and islands—and fun ferry trips connecting them all. Argyll, which means the "coast of the Gaels," was part of the kingdom of Dalriada, an ancient dynasty that began in the 5th century. START: **South Ayrshire coast. Trip Length: Take 3 days for this 288km (179-mile) journey.**

❶ ★ Culzean Castle. In addition to the architectural attributes of this 18th-century "castellated" mansion—such as turrets and ramparts—it is of special interest to many Americans because General Eisenhower was given an apartment for life here. Fans of the Scottish cult 1973 horror film *The Wicker Man* may recognize the place: Scenes at the home of the devilish character played by Christopher Lee were filmed at Culzean (pronounced *Cull*-ane). ⏱ 1¼ hr. *A719 (7km/4⅓ miles west of Maybole).* ☎ *01655/884-455. www.culzean experience.org. Admission (including country park) £12 adults, £8 seniors & kids, £30 family. Daily Apr–Oct 10:30am–4pm (last entry).*

❷ ★★ kids Culzean Country Park. However grand the house may be, I think the grounds of Culzean are better. The 228-hectare (563-acre) grounds contain a formal walled garden, aviary, swan pond, camellia house, orangery, adventure playground, and a restored 19th-century pagoda. The country park—Scotland's first, opened in 1969—is a real highlight on a fine Ayrshire day. ⏱ *2–3 hr. Culzean Castle.* ☎ *01655/ 884-400. Admission (park only) £8 adults, £5 seniors & kids, £20 family. Daily Apr–Oct 9am–dusk; Thurs–Sun Nov–Mar 11am–4pm.*

Take the scenic coastal route up the A719 for 19km (12 miles), turning right on Greenfield Ave. and right again on Alloway St. in the town of Alloway (total 20km/ 12 miles).

The grandeur of Culzean Castle is only magnified by its beautiful grounds.

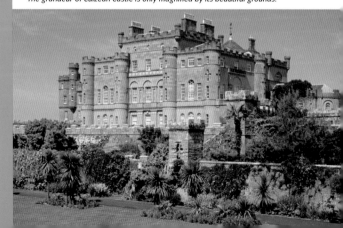

③ ★ Burns Cottage and Museum.

Although its perennially underfunded, I have a soft spot for this attraction, which remains a must visit for even the casual Robert Burns fan. A self-guided tour of the cottage shows the kitchen box bed where the poet was born on January 25, 1759, as well as the room that his family *and livestock* shared. The museum, while rather modestly housed, is a treasure-trove of Burnsiana, displaying the best collection of Burns's manuscripts, and original letters that Burns wrote and received. ⏱ *1½ hr. B7024, in Alloway (3km/1¾ miles south of Ayr).* ☎ *01292/443-700. www.burnsheritagepark.com. Admission £4 adults, £2.50 kids & seniors, £10 family. Daily Apr–Sept 10am–5:30pm; Oct–Mar 10am–5pm.*

The ground-floor kitchen at Burns Cottage and Museum.

Head 3km (1¾ miles) north up the B7024.

④ Ayr.

This is another key place in Burns Country, although 20th-century construction has left little sense of Ayr's history. One exception is the 15th-century Auld Brig (old bridge), which, according to Burns, would still be standing when the "New Brig" (built in his lifetime) was reduced to a "shapeless cairn." Burns was correct. Ayr's Auld Kirk, where Burns was baptized, and which dates to 1655, replaced a 12th-century church dismantled by the invading forces of Oliver Cromwell. The church's greatest curiosity is a macabre series of "mort safes," metal grates protecting the dead from robbers or body snatchers. ⏱ *1½ hr. Tourist information, 22 Sandgate.* ☎ *01292/290-300.*

Take the A79 through Prestwick, turning left after about 8km (5 miles) onto Monktonhill Rd. (B749) into Troon (total 13km/8 miles).

Scotland's National Bard: Robert Burns

Two key destinations on the Burns Heritage Trail are the national poet's places of birth in Alloway (see above) and death in Dumfries (see p 163). Born in Alloway on a night so gusty that part of the cottage came down, Burns was the son of a simple and pious gardener who encouraged the boy to read and seek an education. Burns was, by trade, a hardworking though largely unsuccessful farmer who became a tax collector later in his life. But the world knows him as the author of poetry, often set to song, such as *Auld Lang Syne,* or narrative masterpieces, such as *Tam O'Shanter.* Other works, such *as A Man's a Man for a' That,* show Burns's humanitarian leanings. In his short life, he wrote hundreds of poems and songs. Burns was also a prodigious pursuer of women who fathered numerous children, legitimate and otherwise. He died at 37 of heart disease, distinguished but destitute.

❺ ★ Royal Troon Golf Club.

Ayrshire is home to links-style golf, with dune-covered courses set all along the coast. This one is arguably the best: a 7,150-yard seaside course that hosts the prestigious Open Championship. The 8th "Postage Stamp" hole is particularly famous. A much less expensive but still gratifying golf option is to play one of the municipal courses run by the South Ayrshire Council (golf hot line ☎ 01292/616-255), such as Darnley or Lochgreen, which runs parallel to Royal Troon. *Craigend Rd., Troon.* ☎ *01292/311-555. www.royal troon.co.uk. Greens fee £220.*

The Royal Troon Golf Club is home to one of the most prestigious links courses in Scotland.

Take Dundonald Rd. (A759) east to the A78, heading north past Irvine and Saltcoats, and continue through Largs to Wemyss Bay and the ferry terminal. Ferry to Bute (total 61km/38 miles).

❻ ★ Isle of Bute.

One of the easiest Scottish islands to reach, Bute officially calls itself Scotland's "unexplored" isle—but "underappreciated" is a more accurate description. Roam a bit and find the ruins of an ancient Christian settlement at St. Blane's near the southern tip of the island. Walk out to the more meager remains of a chapel at St. Ninan's point on the west coast, and you'll be treated to the company of dozens of seabirds along the wind-swept shoreline. ⏱ *6–24 hr. Tourist information, Winter Garden, Victoria St., Rothesay.* ☎ *08707/200-619. Ferries to Rothesay on Bute depart every 45 min. from Wemyss Bay (about 54km/34 miles southwest of Glasgow). One-way ticket £4; cars £15.* ☎ *08705/650-000. www.calmac. co.uk.*

❼ Rothesay Castle.

Located in Bute's principal port, Rothesay, this castle (some of whose ruins date to the 13th c.) is unusual for its circular plan. Interestingly, part of the exhibit here emphasizes the links

Arran: Scotland in Miniature

The Isle of Arran in the Firth of Clyde is often called Scotland in miniature because it combines pasture-filled lowlands with some reasonably mountainous highland scenery. Arran also offers a castle, half a dozen golf courses (including one with 12 holes), and a whisky distillery. It's a popular camping and cycling destination, with a growing reputation for producing excellent food, whether harvested from the sea or grown on the land. **Caledonian Macbrayne Ferries** (☎ 01294/463-470; www.calmac.co.uk) to Brodick on the Isle of Arran leave regularly from Ardrossan near Saltcoats. For more information on the island, check out **www.ayrshire-arran.com**.

Island "Hopscotch" Passes

If you want the freedom to hop around a bit from mainland to island and from island to peninsulas west of Glasgow, it may be worth buying an "Island Hopscotch" ticket from the ferry operator, **Caledonian MacBrayne** (☎ 08705/650-000; www.calmac.co.uk). For example, you can hop from Wymess Bay to the Isle of Bute, from there to Cowal peninsula, and then onward to Kintyre. In summer, the cost for that excursion is £7.30 per passenger and £29 for a car.

that ancient Scotland had to Norse rulers—King Haakon IV (1204–63) in particular. If you dare (and if you're thin enough), you can descend from the gatehouse into a small dungeon once reserved for prisoners. ⏱ *1 hr. Rothesay, Isle of Bute.* ☎ *01700/ 502-691. www.historic-scotland.gov. uk. Admission £4 adults, £3 seniors, £2 kids. Daily April–Sept 9:30am– 5:30pm; Oct–Mar 9:30am–4:30pm.*

Take the A844 south out of Rothesay for 8.5km (5¼ miles).

8 ★ Mount Stuart. This neo-Gothic mansion (built in the 1870s) belongs to the Marquess of Bute's family (descendants of the Stuart royal line). The interiors reveal the particular interests of John Crichton-Stuart, the Third Marquess (1847–1900), such as a ceiling covered in constellations, reflecting his interest in astrology. The garden dates back to the early decades of the 18th century. The extensive grounds have a woodlands park, a huge walled area—called the "wee garden"—and a working vegetable plot, too. ⏱ *2 hr. A844 near Soulag.* ☎ *01700/503-877. www.mount stuart.com. Admission (house & grounds) £7.50 adults, £3.50 kids. House May–Sept Sun–Fri 11am–5pm, Sat 10am–2:30pm; Gardens May–Sept daily 10am–6pm.*

Drive about 4.5km/2¾ miles north of Rothesay to catch a 5-min. ferry from Rhubodach to Colintraive.

9 Cowal Peninsula. For many years a huge U.S. naval base kept Cowal in business, and when the end of the cold war terminated the Yankee presence, a large gap in the economy was created. Only now is tourism beginning to fill it. Cowal is easily reached, and has nice forested glens and plenty of sea coast to explore. The principal town of Dunoon is ordinary, but coastal villages such as Tighnabruaich are charming. *Tourist information, 7 Alexandra Parade, Dunoon.* ☎ *08452/255-121.*

From Dunoon take the A815 north 11km (6¾ miles).

10 Benmore Botanic Garden. Part of Scotland's national botanic gardens, Benmore specializes in forest planting, including an impressive row of Pacific redwoods (some over 150 years old) and a cluster of towering monkey puzzle trees. ⏱ *1½ hr. A815.* ☎ *01396/706-261. Admission £3.50 adults, £1 kids, £8 family. Daily Mar–Oct 10am–5pm.*

From Dunoon, take the B836 west some 24km (15 miles), turning right onto the A886 and then left heading south on the A8003 past Tighnabruaich. Follow sign to ferry terminal at Portavadie and take the 25-min. ferry to Tarbert (total 42km/26 miles).

⓫ ★ **Kintyre Peninsula.** The westernmost mainland in central Scotland, Kintyre feels as remote as the Highlands. The pretty harbor of Tarbert on Loch Fyne is where many local fishing boats land. Indeed, you can purchase fresh scallops, as well as live crabs and lobsters, at the ferry slip. Bird populations abound in this region, too. There is an observatory on the island of Sanda, just off the tip (or mull) of Kintyre. On the peninsula itself, however, a blind is situated near the west-coast village of Machrihanish. *Tourist Information, Harbour St., Tarbert.* ☎ *08452/255-121. Closed in winter.*

From Tarbert take the A83 south (32km/20 miles) to basic ferry terminal at Tayinloan, boarding 20-min. ferry (total 37km/23 miles).

⓬ ★★ **Isle of Gigha.** Pronounced *Gee*-a, with a hard "g" (as in gear), this small island gets its name (meaning the good isle) from the ancient Norse ruler King Haakon. Small and placid, Gigha is best known for its Achamore Gardens (opened in 1944), with their exceptional springtime display of rhododendrons and azaleas. But it's also a quiet place where you

can escape and relax. There are plenty of rural and coastal walks. *Hourly ferry service from Tayinloan. Tickets £3 per passenger, £9 car.*

Retrace your journey to Dunoon and take the ferry across to Gourock. Take the A770 east, joining the A8 in Greenock. Continue about 19km (12 miles) to the Erskine Bridge, crossing north to the A82 west (signposted Crianlarich), turning left on the A814 to Helensburgh (total from Tarbert 107km/66 miles).

⓭ ★★★ **Hill House.** Designed by Charles Rennie Mackintosh, this timeless house in Helensburgh has been lovingly restored. Inspired by Scottish baronial style, Hill House is still pure Mackintosh, from the asymmetrical juxtaposition of its windows to the sumptuous but uncluttered interior with bespoke details by both the architect and his artist wife, Margaret Macdonald. Though it was completed in 1904, it still looks modern today. *Upper Colquhoun St., Helensburgh (48km/30 miles west of Glasgow).* ☎ *01436/673-900. www.nts.org.uk. Admission £8 adults, £5 seniors & kids, £20 family. Daily Apr–Oct 1:30–5:30pm.*

The Isle of Gigha is well known for its spring flowers.

Where to Stay

A suite at the Piersland House Hotel.

★ **Abbotsford Hotel** AYR A small hotel with a popular, civilized pub in a quiet residential neighborhood—less than a 10-minute walk from the shoreline. Most of the guest rooms are stylish and comfortable, with flatscreen TVs and modern bathrooms. *14 Corsehill Rd.* ☎ *01292/261-506. www.abbotsfordhotel.co.uk. 12 units. Doubles £85. AE, MC, V.*

★★ **An Lochan** TIGHNABRUAICH Formerly the Royal, this hotel overlooking the sea in Tighnabruaich offers some luxurious rooms, but not a hint of pretension or attitude from the staff. The "superior sea view" rooms fit the bill, offering super king-size beds and ample bathrooms (with tubs and showers), comfy leather-upholstered furnishings, and little goodies such as fresh fruit on arrival. ☎ *01700/811-236. www.anlochan.co.uk. 11 units. Doubles £100–£180. AE, MC, V.*

★ **Hunters Quay Hotel** DUNOON Right on the water, north of the village center, this up-to-date whitewashed mansion is a very welcoming and comfortable hotel. Guest rooms are individually sized and decorated. Your best option in the immediate vicinity. *Hunters Quay, Marine Parade.* ☎ *01369/707-070. www.huntersquayhotel.co.uk. 10 units. Doubles £90–£100. AE, MC, V.*

Hunting Lodge Hotel KINTYRE The name might lead you to expect a 17th-century inn, but some 20th-century renovations have rather masked most of its historic charms. Forgive the redesign and just enjoy the views, such as languid summer sunsets over the sea. The whisky bar offers the character that the hotel's name promises. *A83 (just south of Bellchantuy).* ☎ *01583/421-323. www.thehuntinglodgehotel.com. Doubles £90. MC, V.*

★ **Piersland House Hotel** TROON Opposite Royal Troon Golf Club, this hotel was originally built in 1899 for a member of the Johnnie Walker whisky family. The moderately sized guest rooms have traditional country-house styling; a row of cottages offer more privacy and space. *15 Craigend Rd.* ☎ *01292/314-747. www.piersland.co.uk. 30 units. Doubles £136. AE, MC, V.*

The Borders & Lowlands

Where to Dine

★ **An Lochan** TIGHNABRUAICH
SEAFOOD   Meals in these two hotel conservatory dining rooms highlight locally landed seafood and fish (they even tell you the names of the scallop divers), as well as Argyllshire venison and beef. Expect good sea views and unpretentious cooking that empha-sizes natural flavors. ☎ *01700/811-236. www.anlochan.co.uk. Entrees £18–£20. Lunch & dinner daily.*

★★ **Braidwoods** DALRY
FRENCH/SCOTTISH   One of the standout restaurants in Scotland, the exclusive but not overly formal Braidwoods is housed in a tiny con-verted cottage. Holder of a Michelin star and other accolades, it's expen-sive but worth the price for such dishes as roast quail with black pud-ding, and baked turbot on a smoked salmon risotto. Very busy on week-ends. *Saltcoats Rd., off the A737.* ☎ *01294/833-544. www.braidwoods. co.uk. Set dinner £34. AE, MC, V. Lunch Wed–Sun, dinner Tues–Sat.*

MacCallums of Troon TROON
FISH/SEAFOOD   At the harbor, this seaside bistro is adjacent to a fresh fish market. Oysters, whole sardines, sole, and combination platters are frequently on the menu. *The Harbour.* ☎ *01292/319-339. Entrees £15. AE, MC, V. Lunch Tues–Sun, dinner Tues–Sat.*

★ **Seafood Cabin** SKIPNESS
FISH/SEAFOOD   This summer-only operation (also called the Crab Shack) is worth a detour if you love seafood. Cooked in a converted 1950s-style minitrailer, the meals feature langoustines, queen scal-lops, mussels, smoked salmon, and more. It is completely unassuming, and there's no better place to eat on a sunny day. *B8001 off the A83 (at Skipness Castle, 20km/12 miles south of Tarbert).* ☎ *01880/760-207. Entrees £6–£14. No credit cards. Lunch Sun–Fri.* ●

A highlight of the dining room at An Lochan is the Argyllshire beef.

The Best of Perthshire to Fife

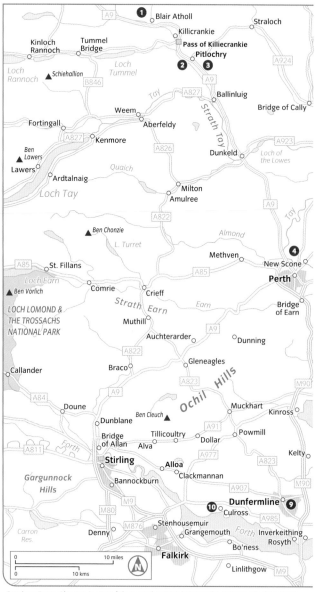

1 Blair Atholl

Straloch

Killicrankie

Pass of Killiecrankie

2 **3** **Pitlochry**

Kinloch Rannoch

Tummel Bridge

Loch Rannoch

▲ Schiehallion

Loch Tummel

B846

A924

Ballinluig

Strath Tay

Bridge of Cally

Weem

Fortingall

Aberfeldy

A827

Kenmore

Ben Lawers

Lawers

Ardtalnaig

A826

Dunkeld

Loch of the Lowes

A923

Quaich

Milton

Amulree

Loch Tay

A822

A9

Tay

▲ Ben Chonzie

L. Turret

Almond

Methven

4

New Scone

A85

St. Fillans

Loch Earn

▲ Ben Vorlich

Comrie

Crieff

Strath Earn

Earn

Perth

Bridge of Earn

LOCH LOMOND & THE TROSSACHS NATIONAL PARK

Muthill

Auchterarder

A9

Dunning

Callander

A84

Braco

A822

Gleneagles

A823

Ochil Hills

M90

Doune

Ben Cleuch ▲

Muckhart

Kinross

Dunblane

Tillicoultry

A91

Dollar

Powmill

Bridge of Allan

Alva

A977

Kelty

A811

Forth

Stirling

Alloa

Clackmannan

A907

M90

Gargunnock Hills

Bannockburn

A985

10 Culross

Dunfermline **9**

Carron Res.

M80

M9

Stenhousemuir

Grangemouth

Forth

Inverkeithing

Denny

M876

Bo'ness

Rosyth

Falkirk

Linlithgow

M9

0   10 miles
0   10 kms

Previous Page: Glencoe is one of the most hauntingly beautiful spots in all of Scotland.

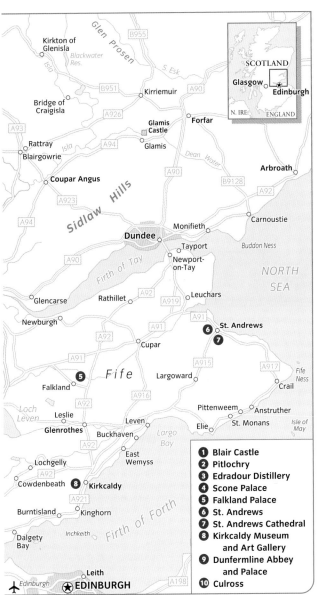

Kirkton of Glenisla
Blackwater Res.
Glen Prosen
B955
S Esk
Isla
B951
Kirriemuir
A90
Bridge of Craigisla
A926
Glamis Castle
Forfar
Rattray
Isla
A94
Glamis
Dean Water
Arbroath
Blairgowrie
A93
Coupar Angus
A923
B9128
A92
A94
Sidlaw Hills
Monifieth
Carnoustie
A90
Dundee
Tayport
Buddon Ness
Firth of Tay
Newport-on-Tay
NORTH SEA
Glencarse
Rathillet
A92
A919
Leuchars
Newburgh
A91
A91
St. Andrews
A92
Cupar
❻
❼
Fife
A915
A917
Fife Ness
Falkland
❺
Largoward
Crail
Loch Leven
A92
A916
Pittenweem
Anstruther
Leslie
Leven
St. Monans
Isle of May
Glenrothes
Buckhaven
Elie
A92
Largo Bay
Lochgelly
East Wemyss
A92
Cowdenbeath
❽
Kirkcaldy
A921
Burntisland
Kinghorn
Dalgety Bay
Inchkeith
Firth of Forth
Leith
Edinburgh ✈
A198
★ EDINBURGH

Inset map:
SCOTLAND
Glasgow
★ Edinburgh
N. IRE.
ENGLAND

❶ Blair Castle
❷ Pitlochry
❸ Edradour Distillery
❹ Scone Palace
❺ Falkland Palace
❻ St. Andrews
❼ St. Andrews Cathedral
❽ Kirkcaldy Museum and Art Gallery
❾ Dunfermline Abbey and Palace
❿ Culross

From the Highland gateway town of Pitlochry to the self-proclaimed Kingdom of Fire, this tour covers the rural territory north of Edinburgh, including world-famous St. Andrews, golf's most hallowed ground. You could see some of the attractions in the area on single-day excursions out of the capital. But if you want to see the region properly, you'll need more time. START: **On the A9 at Blair Atholl. Trip length: 2 days covering about 192km (119 miles).**

The armor- and antler-laden halls of Blair Castle make it popular with kids.

1 ★ **kids Blair Castle.** This fairy tale white castle (begun in 1269) is the home of the Dukes of Atholl and chock-full of antlers and armor. Deer horns decorate one long hall and a ballroom; the weaponry collection spans hundreds of years. But this attraction has something (including pony trekking) for nearly everyone. ⏱ *2 hr. Blair Atholl, off the A9 (10km/ 6¼ miles northwest of Pitlochry).* ☎ *01796/481-207. www.blair-castle. co.uk. Admission £8 adults, £5 kids, £21 family. Daily Apr–Oct 9:30am– 4:30pm; Nov–Mar Tues, Sat 9:30am– 12:30pm.*

Take the A9 south to the Pitlochry exit (12km/7½ miles).

2 **Pitlochry.** The common expression used to describe places on the routes up north is "Highland gateway town." Pitlochry is a classic one: Lots of shops with woolen goods—and a parking area full of tour buses. Check it out, stroll the River Tummel, and move on. ⏱ *1 hr. Tourist information, 22 Atholl Rd.* ☎ *01796/472-215.*

Take the A924 1.6km (1 mile).

3 **Edradour Distillery.** One of Scotland's littlest distilleries (using the smallest legal spirit stills), Edradour offers visitors a good primer on the whisky-making process. It's a cute place, with whitewashed buildings and friendly staff. And you get a free dram to sample. ⏱ *about 1½ hr. Off the A924 (just outside Pitlochry).* ☎ *01796/472-095. www.edradour.co. uk. Free admission. Mar–Oct Mon– Sat 9:30am–5pm, Sun noon–4pm; Nov–Feb Mon–Sat 10am–4pm, Sun noon–4pm.*

Stone of Scone: A Long, Strange Trip

The Stone of Destiny—aka the Stone of Scone—on which monarchs were enthroned dates to Biblical times, according to myth. It reputedly traveled through Egypt and Italy before coming to Scotland with Celtic pilgrims in the 9th century. The lure of the stone was so powerful that English King Edward I stole it in 1296 and the stone remained in London until Christmas 1950, when Scottish nationalists briefly purloined it. In 1996, the stone was officially returned amid plenty of manufactured fanfare and is on display in Edinburgh Castle. Presumably, that's where it will stay—at least until the next king gets crowned.

From Pitlochry, take the A9 south to Perth, crossing the River Tay, joining the A93 north (signposted Blairgowrie) for 1.6km (1 mile; total 46km/29 miles).

❹ ★ Scone Palace.

Scotland's early kings were enthroned at this hallowed place (pronounced "scoon"). The castellated palace dates only to the early 1800s, though parts of much earlier buildings (some dating as far

The coat of arms on the entrance gate to Scone Palace.

back as the 12th c.) are incorporated. A replica Stone of Scone (where royalty once sat) marks its historical location by a little chapel. Today the palace is loaded with fine furniture, ivory, and a particularly noteworthy porcelain collection. ⏲ 2 hr. ☎ 01738/552-300. www.scone-palace. net. Admission £7.50 adults, £4.50 kids, £23 family. Daily Apr–Oct 9:30am–5pm; Nov–Mar arranged group tours only.

The castellated Scone Palace is home to a noteworthy collection of decorative arts and furniture.

From Perth, take the M90 south to exit junction 9, joining the A912 (which merges with A91 from Gateside to Srathmiglo), continuing to Falkland (total 27km/17 miles).

⑤ Falkland Palace. This royal hunting lodge and country home was constructed for the Stuart monarchs between 1450 and 1541. The highlights are the ornate Chapel Royal, King's Bedchamber, and Queen's Room. On the grounds is a royal tennis court, one of only two to survive since the 1500s. ⏱ *2 hr. High St.* ☎ *01337/857-397. Admission £10 adults, £7 kids, £25 family. Mar–Oct Mon–Sat 10am–5pm, Sun 1–5pm; Nov–Feb Mon–Sat 11am–4pm, Sun 1–4pm.*

Take Newton Rd. (B936) east through Newton of Falkland, turning left onto the A92, heading north; turn right onto the A91, heading east through Cupar (total 33km/21 miles).

⑥ ★★ St. Andrews. It's one of golf's meccas (golf was played here at least as early as the 1600s), but this medieval royal burgh was also a revered place of Christian pilgrimage, filled with monasteries and ancient buildings. Only a few of the structures

The ornate King's Bedchamber at Falkland Palace.

It was sacked in 1559, but the ruins of St. Andrew's Cathedral still evoke images of its former glory.

survive today. The city's university is Scotland's first and the third oldest in the U.K. ⏱ *2 hr. Tourist information, 70 Market St.* ☎ *01334/472-021.*

⑦ ★ St. Andrews Cathedral. Founded in 1161 and once the largest in Scotland, this cathedral certified the town as an ecclesiastical capital. But the ruins (it was sacked in 1559, a victim of the Reformation) only suggest former glory. Admission allows entry to nearby St. Andrews Castle, where the medieval clergy lived. ⏱ *1½ hr. A91, off Pends Rd.* ☎ *01334/472-563. www.historic-scotland.gov.uk. Admission £7 adults, £3.50 kids. Daily Apr–Sept 9:30am–5:30pm; Oct–Mar 9:30am–4:30pm.*

Take the A915 southwest from St. Andrews into Kirkcaldy and the town center via Nether St. (A921), following signs to the railway station (38km/24 miles).

⑧ ★ Kirkcaldy Museum and Art Gallery. This is the most underrated public art collection in Scotland. One room is devoted to the brightly hued paintings of Colourist S. J. Peploe (1871–1935). There are more masterpieces by Scottish luminaries such as Eardley, Hornel, and McTaggart. The unassuming and humble

gallery is arguably the best provincial art museum in Great Britain. *War Memorial Gardens, next to the train station.* ☎ *01592/412-860. Free admission. Mon–Sat 10:30am–5pm, Sun 2–5pm.*

Take the A910 out of Kirkcaldy to the A92 southwest, exiting onto the A907 (signposted Dunfermline) into town and the roundabout onto East Port (24km/15 miles).

❾ Dunfermline Abbey and Palace. Construction on the "new" abbey, built on the site of an older 11th-century church, began in 1120—the Romanesque medieval nave you see today is what remains of it. A host of royalty, beginning with David I, has been buried here; Robert the Bruce is buried here, minus his heart, which is reportedly interred at Melrose Abbey (p 162, ❷). The palace, now in ruins, dates to the 1660s; Charles I, the last British monarch born in Scotland, made his arrival here in 1600. ⏱ *1½ hr. St. Margaret's St.* ☎ *01383/739-026. www.historic-scotland.gov.uk. Admission £3.50 adults, £1.75 kids. Daily Apr–Sept 9:30am–5:30pm; Oct–Mar daily 9:30am–4:30pm.*

Take Pittencrief St. (A907) west out of Dunfermline, joining the

The charming and well-preserved town of Culross is allegedly the birthplace of St. Mungo, patron saint of Glasgow.

A994 through Crossford to the A985 (signposted Kincardine Bridge), turning left on the B9037 (total 12km/7½ miles)

❿ ★★ Culross. With cobbled streets lined by stout cottages featuring crow-stepped gables, this well-preserved town shows what life was like in a typical village from the 16th to the 18th century. Culross may also have been the birthplace of St. Mungo, who established Glasgow Cathedral (p 112, ❻). ⏱ *1½ hr. Tourist information, tours* ☎ *01383/880-359. www.nts.org.uk.*

Dunfermline Abbery and Palace is the final resting place of many Scottish kings, including King Robert the Bruce.

Where to Stay

A suite at the world-class Old Course Hotel in St. Andrews.

★★ Gleneagles AUCHTERARDER
Scotland's most famous luxury hotel and golf resort, Gleneagles was built in 1924 in the style of a French château. At the top end, the Whisky Suites have separate sitting rooms and dining spaces for relaxed breakfasts. *A823, off A9 (25km/16 miles southwest of Perth).* ☎ *01764/662-231, in the U.S.* ☎ *866/881-9525. www.gleneagles.com. 250 units. Doubles £295–£520. AE, DC, MC, V.*

Keavil House Hotel CROSSFORD
This tranquil country hotel is set on acres of forested land and gardens near Dunfermline. The spacious guest rooms are well equipped, and the hotel facilities include a gym, a spa, and an indoor pool. *Main St., A994 (3km/1¾ miles west of Dunfermline).* ☎ *01383/736-258. www.keavilhouse.co.uk. 47 units. Doubles £99–£120. AE, DC, MC, V.*

Macdonald's Restaurant & Guest House PITLOCHRY   This popular inn and restaurant has a deserved loyal following. The rooms are well decorated, the hospitality is generous, and the price is unbeatable. *140 Atholl Rd.* ☎ *01796/472-170. www.macdonalds-pitlochry.co.uk. 10 units. Doubles £60. AE, MC, V.*

★ Old Course Hotel ST. ANDREWS
It overlooks the 17th fairway of St. Andrew's Old Course (to which the hotel has no formal connection), offering world-class accommodations (with full spa facilities) and a price tag to match. *Old Station Rd.* ☎ *0133/447-4371. www.oldcoursehotel.co.uk. 144 units. Doubles from £220. AE, DC, MC, V.*

Parklands Hotel PERTH   This award-winning small hotel occupies a stylish Georgian town house once owned by a lord provost (mayor). The spacious rooms at this peaceful oasis are nicely decorated. *2 St. Leonard's Bank.* ☎ *01738/622-451. www.theparklandshotel.com. 14 units. Doubles £100–£155. AE, DC, MC, V.*

The suites at the Gleneagles Hotel come with a host of luxury amenities.

Where to Dine

Meals at Andrew Fairlie at Gleneagles are the finest in all of Scotland.

★★★ Andrew Fairlie at Gleneagles AUCHTERARDER *FRENCH*
Scotland's only two-Michelin-star restaurant, this may be the finest dining experience in the country. Meals here are seamless but not stuffy. If you have the money, go for the six-course "degustation" tasting menu. *Gleneagles Hotel.* ☎ *01764/694-267. www.gleneagles.com. Set dinner £65; tasting menu £85. AE, MC, V. Dinner Mon–Sat.*

★ Deans @ Let's Eat PERTH *SCOTTISH/FRENCH*
In 2005, chef Willie Deans, a member of the Master Chefs of Great Britain, took over this well-established venture. His dishes (most made from local ingredients) include a warm salad of Scottish lobster and prawns. *77–79 Kinnoull St.* ☎ *01738/643-377. Entrees £11–£19. MC, V. Lunch & dinner Tues–Sat.*

★★ Peat Inn NEAR LATHONES *MODERN SCOTTISH/FRENCH*
Meals at this inn (which dates back to 1760) highlight local, seasonal ingredients, such as seared scallops with fennel purée or roast filet of beef with chanterelle mushrooms. *B940 (off A915, 12km/7½ miles southwest of St. Andrews).* ☎ *01334/840-206. Set dinner £32. MC, V. Lunch & dinner Tues–Sat.*

The Seafood Restaurant
ST. ANDREWS *FISH/SEAFOOD* The seafront location, combined with a glass-enclosed dining room offering excellent views, makes for a special meal. Dishes range from crab risotto to pan-seared scallops, all of them served with fancy accompaniments. *The Scores.* ☎ *01334/479-475. www.theseafoodrestaurant.com. Set dinner £30. AE, MC, V. Lunch & dinner daily.*

63 Tay Street PERTH *MODERN SCOTTISH*
Owned by the same team as the Parklands Hotel, this contemporary dining space enlivens a historic building overlooking the River Tay. The modern Scottish dishes feature local produce whenever possible. *63 Tay St.* ☎ *01738/441-451. www.63taystreet.com. Set dinner £28. AE, MC, V. Lunch & dinner Tues–Sat.*

Head to 63 Tay Street if you want fresh and contemporary Scottish cuisine.

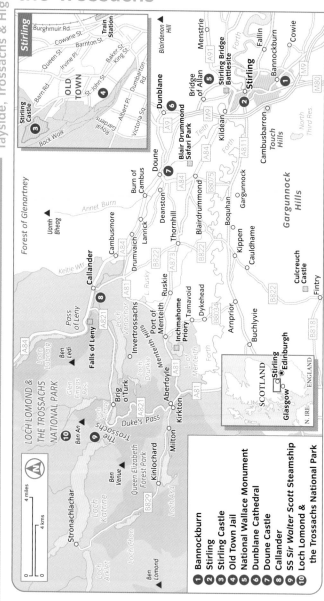

The Best of Stirlingshire & the Trossachs

Stirling

Burghmuir Rd.
Cowane St.
Barnton St.
Train Station
Queen St.
Irvine Pl.
Baker St.
King St.
Barn Rd.
St. John St.
Dumbarton Rd.

OLD TOWN

❹

Stirling Castle ❸

Albert Pl.
Victoria Sq.
Royal Gardens

Back Walk

Blairdenon Hill

Menstrie
Forth
Fallin
Cowie

Stirling Bridge Battlesite ❺

Bridge of Allan

Stirling ❷

Bannockburn ❶

M9
M80

Dunblane ❻

A9

Blair Drummond Safari Park

Doune

Burn of Cambus

❼

Deanston

A84
A820

Kildean

Cambusbarron
Touch Hills

North Third Res.

A811

Gargunnock Hills

Gargunnock

B8075

Blairdrummond

Forest of Glenartney

Uamh Bheag

Annet Burn

Keltie Wtr.

Cambusmore

A84

Drumvaich

L. Ruskie

B822

Callander ❽

Pass of Leny

Loch Lubnaig Res.

Ben Ledi

Falls of Leny

Lanrick

Thornhill

Ruskie

Port of Menteith

Inchmahome Priory

Tamavoid

Dykehead

B8034

Boquhan
Kippen

Cauldhame

Arnprior

Buchlyvie

Culcreuch Castle

Fintry

B818

B822

LOCH LOMOND & THE TROSSACHS NATIONAL PARK

Glen Finglas Res.

Ben A'n ❿

❾

The Trossachs

Duke's Pass

Brig o'Turk

A821

Aberfoyle

Menteith Hills

Loch Drunkie

Kirkton

Milton

A81

Ben Venue

Queen Elizabeth Forest Park

Kinlochard

Loch Ard

B829

Stronachlachar

Loch Katrine

Loch Chon

Loch Arklet

Ben Lomond

SCOTLAND
Stirling ★Edinburgh
Glasgow
N. IRE. ENGLAND

4 miles
4 kms

Once the de facto capital of Scotland, Stirling is an ancient royal burgh with a magnificent castle. Northwest of the area are the Trossachs, a mountain range smaller than the Highlands but almost as appealing for its wooded forests. Key attractions in this region are Loch Katrine, originally popularized by Sir Walter Scott, and Loch Lomond. START: **Just outside of Stirling. Trip Length: Take 2 days and expect to travel some 84km (52 miles).**

① Bannockburn. In a country full of famous battlegrounds, this boggy land is perhaps the best known. It's certainly one where events turned decisively in Scotland's favor: King Robert the Bruce defeated the English troops of Edward II here in 1314, ensuring Scottish independence. The heritage center will tell you everything you need to know about the famous battle. ⏱ *2 hr. A872, Glasgow Rd. (3km/1¾ miles south of Stirling).* ☎ *0844/493-2139. www.nts.org.uk. Admission £5 adults, £4 kids, £14 family. Daily Mar–Oct 10am–5:30pm (only 4pm in Mar).*

Take the A9 north.

② ★ Stirling. Stirling, assigned royal status by David I in 1124, was preferred as a base by the royal Stuarts over Edinburgh in the 16th century. The Old Town merits a stroll. Stirling Bridge is believed to be the crucial site of a 13th-century battle between English invaders and the ragtag band of Scots led by William "Braveheart" Wallace. ⏱ *2 hr. Tourist information, 41 Dumbarton Rd.* ☎ *08452/255-121.*

③ ★ Stirling Castle. This historic and architectural landmark was the site of Mary Queen of Scots' coronation in 1543, and the home of several Stuart monarchs. Even if you don't tour the impressive castle (you should!), its ramparts and surrounding grounds are good fun—particularly the cemetery and the "Back Walk" along a wall that once protected Stirling.

⏱ *2–3 hr. Castle Wynd.* ☎ *01786/450-000. www.historic-scotland.gov.uk. Admission £8.50 adults, £4.25 kids. Daily Apr–Sept 9:30am–5:15pm; Oct–Mar 9:30am–4:15pm.*

④ kids Old Town Jail. On some tours of this old prison, guides don historic garb, taking you through the paces of penal life here as actors roleplay as wardens and inmates. This "gaol" replaced a less humane one (it was condemned as the worst in Britain) across the street in 1847. ⏱ *1½ hr. Stirling. St. John St.* ☎ *01786/450-050. www.oldtownjail.com. Tours (with actor) £6 adults, £3.80 kids, £16 family. Daily tours Apr–May 9:30am–4:30pm; June–Sept 9:30am–5pm; Oct 9:30am–4pm; Nov–Mar 10am–3pm.*

It was at Stirling Bridge that William Wallace and the Scots battled the English in the 13th century.

A statue of famed freedom fighter William "Braveheart" Wallace at the National Wallace Monument. No, he doesn't look like Mel Gibson.

⑤ National Wallace Monument.

You'll be able to see this 66m (217-ft.) sandstone tower, completed in 1869, from any location close to Stirling. Dedicated to the 13th-century Scottish freedom fighter William Wallace (1272?–1305), the monument's popularity soared after the release of the movie *Braveheart*. Climb to the top—the view's the real highlight. ⏱ *1 hr. Alloa Rd., Abbey Craig.* ☎ *01786/472-140. www. nationalwallacemonument.com. Admission £6.50 adults, £4 kids, £17 family. Daily Mar–May, Oct 10am–5pm; June 10am–6pm; July–Aug 9am–6pm; Sept 9:30am–5:30pm; Nov–Feb 10:30am–4pm.*

Take the A84 north from the city to the M9 (signposted Perth), exiting on the B8033 to Dunblane (total 10km/6¼ miles).

⑥ Dunblane Cathedral.

St. Blane brought Christianity to this region in A.D. 602, and this intact church (one of the few medieval churches to survive the Reformation) dates to the 12th and 13th centuries. The bell tower's 5-foot-thick walls represent the oldest part (though its top floors are from around the 1500s and the roof above the nave dates to a late-19th-century restoration). ⏱ *45 min. Dunblane, B8033.* ☎ *01786/823-388. www.dunblanecathedral. org.uk. Free admission. Apr–Sept Mon–Sat 9:30am–5:30pm, Sun 2–5:30pm; Oct–Mar Mon–Sat 9:30am–4:30pm, Sun 2–4:30pm.*

Take B8033 south, turning right on to the A820 to Doune (total 7km/4½ miles).

⑦ ★★ Doune Castle.

Because its ongoing restoration mainly ensures that this medieval castle doesn't fall down, visitors with fit imaginations will get a good notion of 14th-century life: low doors, narrow spiral stairs, and pervasive damp. Fans of the 1974 film *Monty Python and the Holy Grail* should note that the exterior was a location for scenes in the movie. ⏱ *1½ hr. Doune, near the A84.* ☎ *01786/841-742. www.historic-scotland.gov.uk. Admission £4 adults, £2 kids. Daily Apr–Sept 9:30am–5:30pm; Oct–Mar (Sat–Wed only) 9:30am–4:30pm.*

Dunblane Cathedral is one of the few medieval churches in Scotland to survive the Reformation.

The SS Sir Walter Scott has been operating on Loch Katrine for over a century.

Take the A84 northwest 13km (8miles).

8 Callander. Another "gateway" town, though this time to the Trossachs, the foothills of the Highlands. It's not a bad place for a quick rest, Trossach and regional tourist information, shopping, and a bite to eat. ⏱ *45 min. Rob Roy & Trossachs Visitor Centre, Ancaster Sq.* ☎ *08707/200-628.*

Take the A84 northwest out of town, turning left on the A821 for about 15km (9½ miles) past Brig o' Turk.

9 SS *Sir Walter Scott* Steamship. For more than 100 years, this white ship—the last screw-driven steamship to sail in Scotland—has ferried passengers on Loch Katrine (popularized in Walter Scott's poem *The Lady of the Lake*). The views from the ship are stunning. This popular trip can get crowded in summer, so try for a weekday. ⏱ *45 min. (scenic cruise); 1¾ hr. (sailing to Stronachlachar). Off A821.* ☎ *01877/376-316. www.lochkatrine.com. Tickets £7 adults, £5 kids. Daily sailings Apr–Oct (weather permitting)*

10:30am, 1:15pm, 2:30pm, 3:45pm (on selected weekdays), 5pm.

Take the A81 south through Aberfoyle, turning right and southwest on the A811 through Drymen to Balloch (43km/27 miles).

❿ ★ Loch Lomond & the Trossachs National Park. Loch Lomond is Great Britain's largest inland body of water. Its national park—Scotland's first, established in 2002—comprises some 1,865 sq. km (720 sq. miles). If you're hiking, the trails up the eastern shoreline are preferable. If you kayak, the Lomond Shores' visitor center has rentals (☎ 01389/602-576; www.canyouexperience.com). Up the western banks, visitors can take loch cruises. ⏱ *1–8 hr. National Park Gateway Centre, Lomond Shores, Balloch.* ☎ *01389/722-199. www.lochlomond-trossachs.org. Daily 10am–5pm.*

A view from the Balmaha boatyard, located in the Loch Lomond & the Trossachs National Park.

Where to Stay

★ **Creagan House** STRATHYRE
There is a clutch of individually decorated rooms at this charming and
hospitable inn, including one with a
four-poster bed. Dinners here are
great, but the baronial dining room
is a recent addition to this restored
17th-century farmhouse. *A84
(14km/8⅔ miles north of Callander).*
☎ *01877/384-638. www.creagan
house.co.uk. 5 units. Doubles £110.
AE, MC, V. Closed Feb.*

★ **De Vere Cameron House**
LOCH LOMOND   Posh, plush, and
perched on the shores of Loch
Lomond, this luxury hotel offers premier lodgings, some of which are
located in an 18th-century baronial
mansion. Facilities include a range
of outdoor activities, a spa, and a
swimming pool. *A82 (just north of
Balloch).* ☎ *01389/755-565. www.
cameronhouse.co.uk. 95 units. Doubles £255–£300. AE, DC, MC, V.*

The Portcullis STIRLING   This fun
little family-run hotel, in the shadow
of Stirling Castle, has been here for
hundreds of years (it was built in
1787) and has the feel of an old
coach inn and tavern. The down-
stairs bar is great for a nightcap,
but not such good news for the
early-to-bed crowd. *Next to Stirling
Castle.* ☎ *01786/472-290. www.the
portcullishotel.com. Doubles £82–
£87. AE, MC, V.*

★ **Roman Camp Country
House & Restaurant** CALLANDER
This country house hotel, set near
Roman ruins on 20 secluded acres
(8.1 hectares) of gardens, is the most
historic place to stay locally. Built in
1625 as a hunting lodge (it became a
hotel in 1939), it retains charming low
ceilings, creaking corridors, and snug
furniture. *Off the A84.* ☎ *01877/330-
003. www.romancamphotel.co.uk.
Doubles £135–£175. AE, DC, MC, V.*

The Lady Esher bedroom in the Roman Camp Country House & Restaurant.

Where to Dine

The contemporary interior dining room at Monachyle Mhor, which serves tasty modern Scottish cuisine.

Barnton Bar & Bistro STIRLING
CAFE/PUB FOOD   Stirling isn't
exactly overloaded with great dining
options, but this casual place is
welcoming and convenient, with
burgers, sandwiches, and a decent
vegetarian selection on the menu.
3 Barnton St. ☎ *01786-461-698.
Entrees £6–£10. MC, V. Lunch &
dinner daily.*

★ **Clive Ramsay Cafe and
Restaurant** BRIDGE OF ALLAN
CAFE/BRASSERIE   Adjacent to a
sister deli (if you're planning a picnic,
this is the place to stock up) and specializing in quality Scottish produce,
this bistro offers a plethora of dining
options, ranging from a simple scone
to hearty entrees such as pot roast.
*28 Henderson St. (3 miles north of
Stirling).* ☎ *01786/833-903. Entrees
£6–£10. MC, V. Breakfast, lunch &
dinner daily.*

★ **The Inn at Kippen** KIPPEN
MODERN SCOTTISH   Kippen is a
classic country village, and this pub/
restaurant/guest house is a modernized version of the archetypal rural
tavern. The menu focuses on Scottish
fare (most of it locally sourced) with
contemporary twists. *Fore Rd. (off the
A811, west of Stirling).* ☎ *01786/871-
010. www.theinnatkippen.co.uk.
Entrees £8–£16. AE, MC, V. Lunch &
dinner daily.*

★★ **Monachyle Mhor** BALQUHID-
DER SCOTTISH   Up the highway
from Creagan House (p 190), this gem
serves wonderful food in an 18th-
century farmhouse overlooking Loch
Voil. The conservatory dining room is
modern and so is the cooking. *Off the
A84 (turn at Kingshouse Hotel, 9.5km/
6 miles).* ☎ *01877/384-622. www.
monachylemhor.com. Set dinner £46.
AE, MC, V. Lunch & dinner daily.*

Mid-Argyll & the Highlands

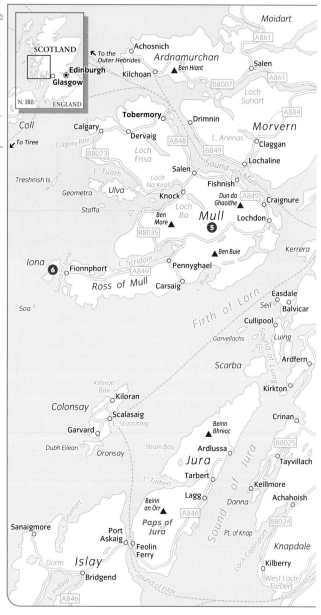

SCOTLAND

☒ Edinburgh
Glasgow

N. IRE.

ENGLAND

Moidart

↖ To the
Outer Hebrides

Achosnich

Ardnamurchan

Kilchoan

▲ Ben Hiant

Salen

A861

A861

B8007

Loch
Sunart

A884

Coll

↙ To Tiree

Calgary

Tobermory

Drimnin

Morvern

Calgary Bay

Dervaig

A848

B849

L. Arienas

Claggan

B8073

Loch
Frisa

Lochaline

Treshnish Is.

L. Tuath

Loch
Na Keal

Salen

Sound of Mull

Geometra

Ulva

Fishnish

Dun da
Ghaoithe ▲

A849

Craignure

Staffa

Knock

Loch
Ba

Mull ⑤

Lochdon

Iona ⑥

Ben
More ▲

B8035

Kerrera

Fionnphort

L. Scridain

A849

Ben Buie ▲

Soa

Ross of Mull

Pennyghael

Carsaig

L. Buie

Firth of Lorn

Easdale

Seil

Balvicar

Cullipool

Garvellachs

Luing

Scarba

Sound of Luing

Ardfern

Colonsay

Kiloran
Bay

Kiloran

Kirkton

Scalasaig

L. Staosnaig

Beinn
Bhreac ▲

Crinan

Garvard

Shain Bay

Ardlussa

B8025

Dubh Eilean

Oronsay

Jura

Tayvillach

L. Tarbert

Tarbert

Sound of Jura

Keillmore

Achahoish

Lagg

Danna

Sanaigmore

L. Gruinart

Beinn
an Orr ▲

Paps of
Jura

A846

Pt. of Knap

B8024

Knapdale

Port
Askaig

Feolin
Ferry

Islay

L. Gorm

Bridgend

Sound of Islay

A846

L. Indaal

Kilberry

West Loch
Tarbert

Loch Caolisport

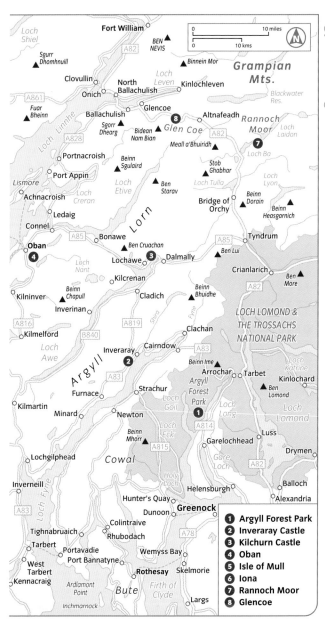

1	**Argyll Forest Park**
2	**Inveraray Castle**
3	**Kilchurn Castle**
4	**Oban**
5	**Isle of Mull**
6	**Iona**
7	**Rannoch Moor**
8	**Glencoe**

Your Scotland adventures take you north into Argyll on this tour, to the place where the historic Dalriada kingdom overlaps with the scenic wonderland of the Scottish Highlands. (See p 170 for a tour focusing on the southern reaches of this region.) Highlights include a couple of castles, a foray to the isles of Mull and Iona, and a stop in beautiful, haunting Glencoe. START: **A83 Near Arrochar. Trip Length: Take 3 days, traveling at least about 340km (211 miles).**

1 ★ Argyll Forest Park. Its 24,000 hectares (about 60,000 acres) are filled with flowers, birds, and even sea lions. The park also is home to one of my favorite hikes: up the Cobbler into the "Arrochar Alps." If you want some reasonably strenuous hill walking, try reaching its craggy peak, which looks down on Loch Long near Succoth. ⏱ *4 hr. A83 at Loch Long. Ardgartan Visitor Center* ☎ *01301/702-432. www. forestry.gov.uk. Free admission. Daily dawn–dusk.*

From Ardgartan, take the A83 up and over the mountains to Loch Fyne and around its head to Inveraray (total 32km/20 miles).

2 Inveraray Castle. An almost picture-perfect pile (completed in 1789) with fairy tale spires belonging to the clan Campbell, whose current 13th Duke (a champion elephant polo player) still lives here. The highlights open to visitors are the armory hall and an elaborately decorated state dining room. ⏱ *1½ hr. Off the A83 (1km/⅔ mile northeast of Inveraray).* ☎ *01499/302-203. www.inveraray-castle.com. Admission £6.80 adults, £4.60 kids, £19 family. Apr–Oct Mon–Sat 10am–5pm, Sun noon–5pm.*

Take the A819 north, joining the A85 west at Loch Awe (26km/16 miles).

3 ★ Kilchurn Castle. Part of what I call the tea towel tour of Scottish castles, as its image is usually found on souvenir castle kitchen towels. Still, it is quite a sight, with well-preserved ruins (it was damaged in 1760 by lightning and subsequently abandoned) dating to the 15th century. ⏱ *1½ hr. Off the A85 (northeast end of Loch Awe). Summer boat from Loch Awe pier* ☎ *01866/833-333.*

Follow the A85 west 35km (22 miles).

4 ★ Oban. I was never a big fan of this port town (pronounced *Oh-binn*), but it has (1) improved and (2)

The fairy-tale-style exterior of Inveraray Castle makes it a photographer's dream.

A cross at the Iona Abbey Cloisters on Iona, an important pilgrimage site for Christians.

grown on me. Today the "gateway to the isles" is more than a place to catch the ferry. Try fresh shellfish sold on the pier, take a stroll along the waterfront, or watch anglers reel in silvery mackerel. ⏱ *1½ hr. Tourist information, Albany St.* ☎ *01631/563-122.*

Take 45-min. ferry ride to Mull.

⑤ ★★★ Isle of Mull. One of my favorite places in the world, Mull (one of the Hebridean Islands off the west coast of Scotland) has easily a day's worth of exploration to keep you busy. The cute town of Tobermory is set on a crescent harbor, its buildings painted in pastels. For wildlife, there are sea eagles and whales. If you want, you can rent a bike in Salen, in the middle of the island, and ride to the west coast. If you prefer castles, visit Duart and Torosay. ⏱ *1 day. Tourist information, Craignure ferry pier* ☎ *01680/302-058 or* ☎ *08452/255-121. 7 ferries daily in summer from Oban.*

www.calmac.co.uk. Passenger tickets £4.25; car £38.

Take the A849 (56km/35 miles from Craignure ferry port) to Fionnphort, 10-min. ferry ride.

Island Excursions

To see Mull and Iona in a single day, **Bowman's Tours** (☎ 01631/566-809; www.bowmanstours.co.uk) depart out of Oban from April to October. Fares cost around £30.

⑥ ★★ Iona. This tiny Hebridean island was settled by Christian pilgrims from Ireland, beginning with St. Columba in the 6th century. It eventually evolved into a very important Christian pilgrimage site (rumored to be the place where Ireland's famed *Book of Kells* was at least partially produced). Certainly visit Iona Abbey (burial site of many Scottish, Norwegian, and Irish kings), but Iona is also great for just getting away from it all. ⏱ *3 hr.–1 day. Frequent ferries (no cars) from Fionnphort. www.calmac.co.uk. Ferry tickets £4.*

The Hebridean Isle of Mull is one of the most beautiful in Scotland.

Rannoch Moor might be desolate, but its beauty is undeniable.

Return to Oban, taking the A85 east, turning left onto the A82, north through Bridge of Orchy (69km/43 miles).

7 ★ **Rannoch Moor.** When it comes to beauty defined by desolate wilderness, Rannoch Moor is tops. The 130-sq.-km (50-sq.-mile) expanse resembles a prehistoric world: vast stretches of rocky outcrops, scrub heather, streams, peat bogs, and small lochs—often wind- and rain-blasted some 305m (1,000 ft.) above sea level. Fantastic. ⏱ *30 min. A82, north of Bridge of Orchy.*

Continue on the A82 north and west (24km/15 miles).

8 ★★★ **kids** **Glencoe.** Whoa, what a sight. But this gorgeous gorge has a bloody event tied to it: the massacre of 40 members of Clan MacDonald in 1692 by the Earl of Argyle's regiment. Set aside its grim past, however, as this valley, which extends about 16km (10 miles), is spectacular. The eco- and family-friendly visitor center at the western end has trail maps and interesting audiovisual presentations that explain the area's social history and geography. ⏱ *2–4 hr. A82 (visitor center 1 mile east of Glencoe Village).* ☎ *01855/811-307. www.glencoe-nts.org.uk. Visitor center admission £5 adults, £4 kids, £14 family. Daily Apr–Aug 9:30am–5:30pm; Sept–Oct 10am–5pm; Nov–Mar 10am–4pm.*

Hiking the West Highland Way

Scotland's best-known long-distance footpath is the West Highland Way, completed in 1980. It begins rather uneventfully in the Glasgow suburb of Milngavie (pronounced "*Mill*-guy"). But as the trail winds its way 152km (94 miles) north, it gets better and better: running along the eastern shore of Loch Lomond, through desolate Rannoch Moor, and along breathtaking and historic Glencoe, before ending finally in Fort William. For information on hiking the West Highland Way, head online to **www.west-highland-way.co.uk**.

Where to Stay

★★ **Ardanaiseig Hotel** KILCHRE-NAN   If you seek a bit of luxury in an out-of-the-way corner, this baronial hotel (pronounced *Ard*-na-sag) is a romantic retreat on the shores of Loch Awe. Some of the individually decorated rooms (most with antiques) overlook the gardens; others have views of the loch. A full slate of recreational activities, from tennis to boating, can be arranged. *B845 (5km/3 miles north of Kilchrenan) off the A85.* ☎ *01866/833-333. www.ardanaiseig.com. 16 units. Doubles £100–£300. AE, MC, V. Closed Jan to mid-Feb.*

★ **Argyll Hotel** IONA   Outstanding and obliging hospitality more than compensates for some smallish guest rooms at this hotel, built in 1868 as the village inn. It has an impressive environmental ethos, striving to maintain Iona's fragile ecology. Minimum 2-night stays.

Near Iona pier. ☎ *01681/700-334. www.argyllhoteliona.co.uk. 10 units. Doubles £140. MC, V.*

Greencourt Guest House OBAN   Among the B&Bs in Oban, this guesthouse stands out for its warm reception and the western views over Oban's bowling green. The breakfasts feature local produce and homemade preserves. *Benvoullin Rd.* ☎ *01631/563-987. www.greencourt-oban.co.uk. 6 units. Doubles £50–£68. MC, V. Closed Dec–Jan.*

Loch Fyne Hotel & Spa INVER-ARAY   This friendly hotel has a pool, sauna, steam room, full-service spa, and outdoor hot tub (which is rare in Scotland). Some of the clean and attractively furnished rooms have lovely loch views. *On the A83 (just outside Inveraray).* ☎ *01499/302-980. www.crerarhotels.com. 71 units. Doubles £125–£145. MC, V.*

A suite at the baronial-style Ardanaiseig Hotel.

Where to Dine

Clachaig Inn GLENCOE *PUB FOOD* Wood-burning stoves and the staff's sunny disposition warm the woody lounges and bars at this rustic inn. The traditional Scottish menu is popular with visitors and locals alike. *Near Glencoe Village, off the A82.* ☎ *01855/811-252. www. clachaig.com. Entrees £10. AE, MC, V. Lunch & dinner daily.*

Ee-usk OBAN *FISH/SEAFOOD* This modern restaurant's name, the phonetic pronunciation of the Gaelic for "fish," sums up the place quite well. It serves a host of simple seafood dishes. In addition to a good wine list, there's a selection of rare Scottish ales. On nice days, you can dine on the bayside deck. *North Pier.* ☎ *01631/565-666. www.eeusk.com. Entrees £13–£17. MC, V. Lunch & dinner daily.*

Gruline Home Farm MULL *SCOTTISH* Meals (made from local produce) at this small but highly rated B&B have an excellent reputation, and you can eat dinner here even if you aren't a guest (though you must arrange that in advance—no drop-ins!). Alcohol isn't served, but you can bring your own with no problem. No kids. *Gruline, off the B8035 (5km/3 miles southwest of Salen).* ☎ *01680/300-581. www.gruline.com. Set dinner £33. Call for times.*

★ **Loch Fyne Restaurant and Oyster Bar** CAIRNDOW *FISH/ SEAFOOD* At the head of Loch Fyne, this well-known casual spot serves oysters and mussels fresh from the clear, cool waters of the loch nearby. Few things are finer than the fish dishes and platters here. Be sure to browse the nice gift shop next door. *A83.* ☎ *01499/600-263. www.lochfyne.com. Entrees £11–£16. AE, MC, V. Lunch & dinner daily.*

★ **Real Food Cafe** TYNDRUM *FISH AND CHIPS* Opened in 2006, this casual roadside stop has laid claim to the best fish and chips in Scotland. Plus, the place is eco-friendly. *A82.* ☎ *01838/400-235. www.therealfoodcafe.com. Entrees £6. MC, V. Lunch & dinner daily (closed Tues–Wed Nov–Dec).* ●

Few things are finer than the seafood, such as this squid dish, at Loch Fyne Restaurant and Oyster Bar.

The Savvy Traveler

Before You Go

Government Tourist Offices

You can get tourist information on Scotland from **British Tourist Authority** offices (www.visitbritain.com), but the country does have its own dedicated website at **www.visitscotland.com**.

In the U.S.: 551 Fifth Ave., Suite 701, New York, NY 10176-0799 (☎ 800/462-2748 or 212/986-2200); 625 N. Michigan Ave., Suite 1001, Chicago, IL 60611-1977 (☎ 800/462-2748); 10880 Wilshire Blvd., Suite 570, Los Angeles, CA 90024 (☎ 310/470-2782). **In Canada:** 5915 Airport Rd., Suite 120, Mississauga, ON L4V 1T1 (☎ 888/VISIT-UK). **In Australia:** Level 2, 15 Blue St., North Sydney NSW 2060 (☎ 02/9021-4400). **In New Zealand:** c/o British Consulate General Office, Level 17, IAG House, 151 Queen St., Auckland 1 (☎ 09/303-1446).

The Best Time to Go

You've probably already heard about Scottish weather. Scots like to joke about getting "four seasons in 1 day." But weather (see below) isn't the only consideration to make when planning your trip to Scotland. The high summer season brings crowds and higher hotel rates, especially in Edinburgh, while the low season carries the possibility that some historic attractions and rural hotels will be closed during your visit (although it's quieter and cheaper).

The best time to see Scotland is between May and September, when the country's geared to receive tourists and the weather's generally warmer (and sometimes drier). All attractions, information centers, hotels, and restaurants—no matter how remote—are open to visitors. The days are longest during this time of year. In Edinburgh, fading sunlight lasts well into the evening, and on the west coast, you can discern a glimmer as late as 11pm or even midnight. Of course, the sun rises at about 4:30 in the morning, too. If you don't mind facing a little less heat and daylight (and the company of other tourists), consider visiting in April or

Festival of Films

The Edinburgh International Film Festival is actually one of the oldest film festivals in the world, beginning as an adjunct to the Edinburgh Festival and Fringe when they were launched in the late 1940s. Until 2007, the film fest coincided with the big August extravaganza of culture. But beginning in 2008, a new creative director decided—daringly—to move it to June. Whatever the date, it traditionally has attracted a mix of big Hollywood stars and films, as well as interesting independent cinema, and, usually, a set of films devoted to a classic golden-age actor or director. For information, contact the **Edinburgh International Film Festival office,** 88 Lothian Rd. (☎ 0131/228-4051; www.edfilmfest.org.uk).

Previous Page: A bus tour is a great way to get an overview of Edinburgh (p 13, ❶).

AVERAGE TEMPERATURE & RAINFALL IN EDINBURGH & GLASGOW

	JAN	FEB	MAR	APR	MAY	JUNE
Temp. (°F)	38	38	42	44	50	55
Temp. (°C)	3	3	6	7	10	13
Rainfall (in./mm)	2.2/56	1.6/41	1.9/48	1.5/38	2.0/51	2.0/51

	JULY	AUG	SEPT	OCT	NOV	DEC
Temp. (°F)	59	58	54	48	43	40
Temp. (°C)	15	14	12	9	6	4
Rainfall (in./mm)	2.5/64	2.7/69	2.5/64	2.4/61	2.5/64	2.4/61

October. If your visit will focus only on the country's major cities, you can come practically any time of the year.

Festivals & Special Events

JAN. Glasgow's **Celtic Connections** (☎ 0141/353-8080; www.celtic connections.com) folk and traditional music festival is the largest of its kind in the world. On **Burns Night,** the anniversary of poet Robert Burns's January 25 birth, special suppers (the serving of the haggis is heralded with a bagpipe) are held across Scotland.

MAR. The **Glasgow Comedy Festival** (☎ 0141/552-2070) brings a diverse range of funny men and women to stages around the city.

APR. Edinburgh's **Beltane Fire Festival** (☎ 0131/228-5353; www. beltane.org) celebrates paganism and the arrival of summer on Calton Hill with drums and dancing. A spot of nudity is almost guaranteed. Also in Edinburgh (and more family-friendly) is the **Edinburgh International Science Festival** (0131/557-5588; www.sciencefestival.co.uk), where adults and kids can take in some 250 workshops, exhibitions, and lectures that are both fun and entertaining.

MAY. In Ayr, **Burns and A' That** (☎ 01292/290-300; www.burns festival.com) celebrates the life of Robert Burns with performances by contemporary musicians.

JUNE. Glasgow's **West End Festival** includes lots of music concerts and a street parade. The **Royal Highland Show** (☎ 0131/335-6200; www. royalhighlandshow.org) in Ingliston, near Edinburgh, is Scotland's premier agriculture and food fair. The **Edinburgh International Film Festival** (www.edinburghfestivals.co.uk) moved from its traditional time in August to June in 2008.

JULY. The **Edinburgh International Jazz & Blues Festival** (☎ 0131/667-7776; www.jazzmusic.co.uk) is the longest-running jazz festival in the U.K. and draws musicians from all over the world.

AUG. The **Edinburgh Festival** (www. edinburghfestivals.co.uk), which began in 1947, actually encompasses several festivals at once nowadays. The **International Festival** attracts classical music and opera. The **Fringe** encompasses more than 1,800 performances—particularly comedy. The city also hosts the **Edinburgh International Book Festival** and the **Edinburgh International Television Festival.** Also in Edinburgh is the world-famous **Military Tattoo** (p 92), featuring music and marching at Edinburgh Castle. In Glasgow, the **World Pipe Championships** (☎ 0141/241-4400) draws some 200 bagpipe bands.

SEPT. The **Doors Open Days** (www. doorsopendays.org.uk) event allows you inside historic and architecturally significant buildings throughout Scotland—some of which are normally closed to the public. The **Taste of Mull & Iona Food Festival** (www.mi-food.co.uk) is a weeklong food festival that celebrates local produce and includes farm tours, wildlife walks, and special feasts.

OCT. The **International Story Telling Festival** (☎ 0131/556-9579) in Edinburgh celebrates the oral traditions of Scotland and other countries.

NOV. **St. Andrew's Day,** November 30, celebrates Scotland's patron saint with fireworks, concerts, and exhibitions. The best place to experience is (shock of shocks), St. Andrews, where the party lasts a week.

DEC. In Scotland, New Year's Eve is called **Hogmanay,** and it's traditionally bigger than Christmas. Outdoor concerts are held all over the country, and in Edinburgh (www.edinburghs hogmanay.org) a week of partying and events (many of them free) culminates in a fireworks display.

The Weather

No matter the time of year you visit, chances are slim that you'll make it back home without some Scottish raindrops falling on your head (this goes double if you're planning on touring Mull). Have a waterproof coat handy. As far as temperatures go—those don't vary radically. Scotland is reasonably cool year-round, although climate change is raising the average temps in the country. While a few summer weeks can see temperatures occasionally rise above 80°F (27°C), it's typically no hotter than 72°F (22°C), and not atypically around 55°F (13°C). In the coldest months, some subfreezing days can be expected, but you won't encounter the bitter cold of the American Midwest, for example, except in the Highlands.

Useful Websites

Surf the web and you'll find a host of sites aimed at Scottish visitors, which vary in usefulness. With some, I'm never quite convinced they're updated regularly. For official tourist information on Scotland, go directly to **www.visitscotland.com**, although it is arguably most helpful as a hotel reservation service. Here are some others to look at.

- **www.edinburgh.org**: Information specifically on Edinburgh and the surrounding region.

- **www.seeglasgow.com**: Data on Glasgow and the greater Clyde Valley region.

- **www.historic-scotland.gov.uk**: Information on the historical sites operated by the quasi-governmental organization Historic Scotland.

- **www.nts.org.uk**: Data on the historical sites operated by the voluntary charity the National Trust of Scotland.

- **www.scotland-info.co.uk**: Information particularly focused on the Highlands and Hebridean Islands.

- **www.undiscoveredscotland. co.uk**: Data on attractions, hotels, and businesses; it seems to be kept up-to-date.

- **www.rampantscotland.com**: Information on Scottish destinations and history, with lots of links to relevant websites.

- **www.nationalrail.co.uk**: Data on travel by train in Scotland.

Cellphones

First of all, they're called mobile phones in the U.K. The three letters that define much of the world's wireless capabilities are GSM (Global System for Mobiles), a big, seamless network that makes for easy cross-border cellphone use throughout Europe and dozens of other countries worldwide. You can make and receive calls in Scotland, though you will accrue whopping roaming charges. In some isolated areas, getting a signal can be difficult, though network coverage is good.

International visitors can buy a pay-as-you-go mobile phone at any phone store in Scotland. This gives you a local number and minutes that can be topped up with phone cards that can be purchased at newsagents. O2 and Vodaphone are among the best service networks.

The top hotels may be able to rent you a cellphone, though it won't be cheap; inquire before you arrive. North Americans can rent one before leaving home from **InTouch USA** (📞 800/872-7626; www.intouch global.com) or **RoadPost** (📞 888/290-1606 or 905/272-5665; www.roadpost.com).

Car Rentals

If you are going to Edinburgh and Glasgow, don't bother renting (or as the Brits say, "hiring") a car. I don't recommend it. You can get around quite a bit more easily using your feet, buses, trains, and taxis. If you plan on traveling outside those cities and into the countryside on regional tours, a car is a must. All major car-rental agencies are located at Scotland's major airports.

Most rental companies will accept your foreign driver's license, provided you've held it for more than a year and are over 21. Insurance will be included in your rental costs (the deductible, which is called "the excess," can vary). Finding a rental with automatic transmission is difficult. Finally, gasoline or petrol is expensive and you will be expected to return the vehicle with the same amount in the tank as when you took it out. Alas, rental agencies often don't make this easy by giving out vehicles with less than a full tank. It is always cheaper to buy petrol at a station rather than paying the rental company to refill the tank.

In Edinburgh, Avis is on West Park Place. near Haymarket Station (📞 **0870/153-9103**), Hertz is on Picardy Place. (📞 **0870/864-0013**), and Thrifty is at 42 Haymarket Terrace (📞 **0131/337-1319**). In Glasgow, Avis is at 70 Lancefield St. (📞 **0870/608-6339**); Budget is at 101 Waterloo St. (📞 **0800/212-636**); and the leading local company, Arnold Clark, has multiple locations (📞 **0845/607-4500**).

Getting **There**

By Plane

You're most likely to fly into a Scottish airport directly, or arrive via England (Heathrow, most likely). It's also possible to transfer from some other European hub, such as Amsterdam, which has several flights a day to Scotland. From North America, only a few carriers fly straight to Scotland. Often the service is seasonal (May–Sept) and it seems to change every year. Long-distance carriers don't appear convinced that the market is solid enough to make a commitment to direct flights to Scotland. Most visitors transit through London first. The trip by air from London to either Edinburgh or Glasgow airport takes only an hour. Remember that the two cities are separated by less than 80km (50 miles), so once you're on the ground, you don't have too far to go from either airport.

Edinburgh International Airport (EDI; ☎ 0870/040-0007) is about 10km (6¼ miles) west of the city's center and has become a growing hub of flights within the British Isles, as well as Continental Europe. From Edinburgh Airport, an **Airlink bus** (www.flybybus.com) makes the 30-minute trip to the city center about every 10 minutes during peak times. The one-way fare is £3. A taxi will run you at least £12.

Glasgow International Airport (GLA; ☎ 0870/040-0008) gets more intercontinental flights. It is located at Abbotsinch, near Paisley, about 16km (10 miles) west of the city via the M8. Bus services run to and from the city center frequently. The ride takes about 20 minutes (longer at rush hour) and costs £5. A taxi into the city will cost you about £17.

Another option is **Prestwick International Airport** (PRA; ☎ 0871/223-0700), which is favored by some of the low-budget airlines such as RyanAir. Prestwick's on the railway line to Ayr, and about a 45-minute ride from Glasgow's Central Station. The train fare to Glasgow costs around £5.

By Car

If you're driving north to Scotland from England, there are a couple of options. Take the **M1** motorway north from London. Near Newcastle-upon-Tyne, join the **A696,** which becomes **A68** for a final run north into Edinburgh. Alternatively, take the M1 to the **M6** near Coventry. Continue north on M6 to Carlisle. After crossing into Scotland, it becomes the **M74** heading toward Glasgow. The **M8** freeway links Glasgow and Edinburgh.

By Train

From England, two main rail lines link London and Scotland. The faster route is from **King's Cross Station** to Edinburgh, going by way of Newcastle. If you're going via the west coast (far less reliable), trains leave **Euston Station** in London for Glasgow, passing through Carlisle. Expect the trip to take at least 4½ hours. Fares can vary rather wildly. Call ☎ 0845/748-4950 or head online to www.nationalrail.co.uk for timetable and fare information.

By Bus

The journey from London (coaches depart from Victoria Coach Station) to Edinburgh or Glasgow can take 8 to 10 hours. Scottish **Citylink** (☎ 0870/550-5050; www.citylink.co.uk) has regular service to Edinburgh. **National Express** (☎ 0870/580-8080; www.nationalexpress.com) runs buses to Glasgow. Fares vary considerably depending on the route you choose, when you buy your ticket, and when you're traveling.

Getting **Around**

By Public Transportation

Edinburgh has an extensive bus network with a fare system that is fairly straightforward. Bus drivers will sell tickets but not make change. Prices depend on the distance traveled, with the adult one-way (single) fare of £1.10 covering the central Edinburgh districts. If you plan multiple trips in 1 day, purchase a Dayticket that allows unlimited travel on city buses for £2.50. For transport information, contact **Lothian Buses** (☎ 0131/555-6363; www.lothianbuses.co.uk).

In contrast, Glasgow's bus routes, run by **Strathclyde Passenger Transport** (☎ 0141/332-6811; www.spt.co.uk) can be quite confusing, and it feels as if the drivers often make up the price as they go along. Luckily, for most destinations, Glasgow's circular Underground (called "the subway" in American fashion) works out best. The one-way subway fare is £1. Additionally, there is a reliable suburban train service that crosses the city in several directions (£2–£3.50 round-trip).

If you plan on traveling between cities by bus, **Scottish Citylink** (☎ 0870/550-5050; www.citylink. co.uk) is the largest cross-country bus service and offers service between 200 cities and towns in Scotland. The buses are comfortable and relatively inexpensive, but they can be slow and will limit your itinerary options.

By Train

Train service around Scotland is adequate, but not up to the standards found elsewhere in Western Europe. Plus, it's more expensive. Trains between Edinburgh and Glasgow are frequent, but often crowded. Annoyingly, trains to other Scottish destinations have little space for luggage. The best way to check on fares and timetables is the website for Scotland's train company at **www.firstgroup.com/scotrail**. For general train inquiries call the Traveline at ☎ **0871/200-2233.**

By Taxi

Metered taxis are the so-called Fast Black, just like in London, which you can hail or pick up at taxi ranks in the major city centers. Expect to pay at least £5 for a trip across Edinburgh or Glasgow. Surcharges are often imposed for early-morning and late-night runs. Taxis are too expensive to be used for city-to-city travel within Scotland; renting a car or taking the train or bus is cheaper.

On Foot

If you are in shape, this is the best way to get around central Edinburgh, most of Glasgow, and most Scottish towns and villages. Drivers in the major cities can be a bit aggressive, however, so exercise caution before crossing any street. Remember, in Scotland you drive on the left, so you generally must look to your right first before crossing. Even so, I suggest looking both ways—twice.

By Car

Within Edinburgh or Glasgow, don't bother with a car. It's just a headache. Parking is expensive, and restricted to residents in some neighborhoods. There are lots of one-way boulevards, and streets change their names without warning. And the (large) expense of gas (petrol) must be factored into the driving equation as well.

If traveling outside the big cities, you will need a car. The big rule that you need to know is that you must drive on the left side of the road. The roads in Scotland are fine, though often congested around cities at peak times. Road signs are generally adequate. Remember, at roundabouts you must yield to traffic approaching from the right.

Fast **Facts**

ATMS/CASHPOINTS   The easiest and arguably the best way to get cash away from home is from an ATM (automated teller machine), or *cashpoint* as they are commonly called in Scotland. I recommend only using those at banks, however, and not any independent cashpoints that you might find in shops or in shopping malls. Expect your bank back home to extract a nominal charge for using overseas ATMs.

The **Cirrus** (☎ 800/424-7787; www.mastercard.com) and **PLUS** (☎ 800/843-7587; www.visa.com) networks span the globe; look at the back of your bank card to see which network you're on, then call or check online for ATM locations in Scotland.

BANKS Banks are normally open from 9 or 10am until about 5pm on weekdays.

BUSINESS HOURS Most businesses are open Monday through Saturday from 9 or 9:30am to 5 or 5:30pm, with some exceptions. Some businesses and shops are closed Sunday, although many shops in the major cities open on Sunday. Most cities also have extended shopping hours on Thursday until 8pm. Outside of Edinburgh and Glasgow, businesses may close for lunch, generally from 12:30 to 1:30pm.

Restaurants and pubs have different restrictions on hours of operation depending upon their licensing, which is controlled by local councils. Although some bars may not open until late afternoon, most serve drinks from noon to midnight and maybe later on weekends. Some pubs in residential and rural areas, however, close at 11pm. Many restaurants stop serving food at 2:30pm and resume at 5:30 or 6pm. Nightclubs in cities and larger towns have late-night hours, staying open until between 1 and 3am—but doors may not open until 10pm.

CONSULATES & EMBASSIES Embassies in the U.K. are located in London, England. Edinburgh is home to **consulates** for **Australia,** 69 George St. (☎ 0131/624-3700); **Canada,** 30 Lothian Rd. (☎ 0131/245-6013); and the **U.S.,** 3 Regents Terrace (☎ 0131/556-8315).

CURRENCY EXCHANGE You can exchange money anywhere you see a BUREAU DE CHANGE sign: mainly travel agencies, banks, post offices, and tourist information offices. All will charge some type of commission. Many hotels also offer currency exchange, but their rates are likely to be unfavorable. Your best bet is to withdraw cash from ATMs.

CUSTOMS The same rules for travel to any part of the U.K. apply to Scotland. Visitors from outside the European Union can bring in for their own use, without paying tax or duty, 200 cigarettes, 100 cigarillos, 50 cigars, or 250 grams of smoking tobacco; 60cc of perfume; 2 liters of still table wine; 250cc eau de toilette; 1 liter of spirits or strong liqueurs or 2 liters of fortified wine; and £145 worth of all other goods, including gifts and souvenirs. Any amounts over these limits should be declared.

For up-to-date information on customs, see **www.hmrc.gov.uk** and search for "information for travelers."

DENTISTS & DOCTORS See "Emergencies," below.

DINING It never hurts to make a reservation at local restaurants, as many people do as a matter of habit. It is positively a requirement at the best restaurants on weekends. In general, people don't eat out as late as you will find in Southern European countries. By 10pm many restaurants will no longer be taking orders. Exceptionally few restaurants, if any these days, have dress codes (although shirts and shoes tend to be basic requirements).

DRUGSTORES Drugstores are called pharmacies or chemists in Scotland. If you're visiting from North America, the rules for over-the-counter and prescription drugs will be different and you may not find your preferred brands. Consider bringing what you need with you. Call the NHS (see "Emergencies," below) in emergencies. In cities and towns, Boots is probably the most reliable chemist.

ELECTRICITY The electric current in Scotland is 240 volts AC, which is different from the U.S. current, so small appliances brought from the U.S., such as hair dryers and shavers, may not work (and the current will cause damage). If you're considering bringing your laptop, check the voltage first to see if it has a range between 110v and 240v. If the voltage doesn't have a range, the only option is to purchase an expensive converter. If the voltage falls within the range, then you still need to buy an outlet adapter because your prongs won't fit in Scottish sockets.

EMERGENCIES For any emergency, contact the police or an ambulance by calling ☎ **999** from any phone. You can also call the **National Health Service Helpline,** ☎ **0800/ 224-488,** which offers health-related advice and assistance from 8am to 10pm daily. If you must seek emergency help at a local hospital, the treatment will be free, although you will be billed for long stays.

EVENT LISTINGS The best source of event listings is a magazine called, appropriately, *The List.* Similar in format to London's *Time Out,* it is published every other Wednesday and is available at major newsstands in Edinburgh and Glasgow.

FAMILY TRAVEL Scotland could be more family-friendly. Some pubs cannot, by law, allow kids; some restaurants, by choice, limit how late in the day families are welcomed. But most historical attractions do offer discount family tickets. When booking hotel rooms, ask whether family suites are available.

Look for items tagged with a "kids" icon in this book.

GAY & LESBIAN TRAVELERS Bars, clubs, and hotels catering exclusively to gay and lesbian travelers do exist in Edinburgh and Glasgow, though the country doesn't boast much of a gay scene outside those cities. For advice, call the Lothian Gay and Lesbian Switchboard (☎ **0131/ 556-4049**) or the Strathclyde Gay and Lesbian Switchboard (☎ **0141/847-0447**). Scotland allows for civil partnerships; but gay-bashing does occasionally happen and open displays of affection in rural areas may not be warmly received.

HOLIDAYS There are several "bank holidays" in Scotland. In addition to national ones—primarily Christmas, Boxing Day (Dec 26), New Year's Day, Good Friday, Easter Monday, the first and last Mondays in May, and the first Monday in August—some local areas observe their own holidays as well.

INTERNET ACCESS Scottish cities and large towns have Internet cafes, while public libraries have terminals, too. **Easyinternet** (www.easyinternet cafe.com) operates cybercafes in Edinburgh and Glasgow, although their reputation has fallen. Fees vary, but expect to pay £1 for a half-hour. Increasingly, hotels and guesthouses have computer terminals that offer Internet access. If you're in remote parts of Scotland, public access to the Internet is rare (so are libraries, for that matter).

LIQUOR LAWS The legal drinking age in Scotland is 18. Liquor stores, called off-licenses (or off-sales) sell spirits, beer, and wine; they are generally open from 11am to 10pm.

MAIL & POSTAGE Most post office branches are open Monday through Friday from 9am to 5pm and Saturday from 9am to noon. Smaller and rural branches may be open weekdays from 9am to 1pm and 2:15 to 5pm, as well as on Saturday from 9am to 1pm. Many post offices close early on 1 day of the week, but how early and what day depends on the office.

Sending a postcard from Scotland to North America or Australia and New Zealand costs 54p. Letters (under 20 grams) cost 48p to 78p. Mail usually takes 1 week (sometimes less) to get to the United States. For information on mail services in Scotland and the U.K., call ☎ **08457/740-740** or visit **www. royalmail.com**.

MONEY   Europe's common currency, the euro, isn't used in Scotland. A huge debate once raged among U.K. politicians over trading the British pound sterling in for the euro—and the pound won. An independent Scotland would probably accept the euro more quickly than the U.K. as a whole, but nobody expects full Scottish autonomy anytime soon. Though the currency in Scotland is the pound, the notes are different than in England, featuring Scottish historical figures rather than Queen Elizabeth II. Be careful if you travel to England with Scottish bank notes. They're often not accepted by shops and restaurants, where employees are unaccustomed to seeing Scottish bank names on the paper currency.

The pound hit a 26-year peak against the U.S. dollar in 2007, trading at a whopping $2.10. By 2008, it had fallen back to around $1.98 per £1—still high by recent standards. All rates in this book were calculated at £1 = $2.

NEWSPAPERS & MAGAZINES
Published in Glasgow since 1783, the *Herald* is one of two major morning newspapers with local news, some international coverage, business reports, comment, sports, and cultural reviews; *The Scotsman* of Edinburgh, published since 1817, is the other. The Scottish *Daily Record* is for tabloid enthusiasts only. To get a less provincial view, buy one of the quality London papers, such as *The Guardian,* although they have limited coverage of Scottish events.

PASSPORTS   All U.S. citizens, Canadians, Australians, New Zealanders, and South Africans must have a valid passport to enter Scotland. No visa is required. An immigration officer may also want proof of your intention to return to your point of origin (usually a round-trip ticket) and visible means of support while you're in Scotland. For those who will require a visa: At press time, the U.K. was considering granting only 3-month automatic visas (replacing 6-month visas).

SAFETY   Like most big cities in the Western world, Edinburgh and Glasgow have their share of crime. Handguns are banned by law, however, and shootings are exceedingly rare. Knives present a problem but one largely confined to youth gangs. Fights occasionally flare up in either city center—and in Glasgow particularly when the city's two big soccer teams (Celtic and Rangers) play. In general, avoid conversations regarding those two football clubs and if pressed to give a preference, defer to the city's smaller teams, Partick Thistle or Queens Park.

Most rural areas in Scotland are safe. As a tourist, the most important thing you can do is guard yourself against theft. Pickpockets look for people who seem to have the most money on them and who appear to know the least about where they are. Be extra careful on crowded trains in the big cities and when taking money from ATMs.

SENIOR TRAVELERS   Many discounts, called concession rates, are available to seniors, generally those over 65. Even if "concessions" aren't posted, ask if they're available. Elderly travelers should always exercise caution in historic sites, where the ground can be uneven, and on cobbled streets in Edinburgh.

SMOKING   Smoking in all enclosed indoor public spaces is prohibited, including all bars and restaurants, which may have designated smoking areas outdoors only.

TAXES See "VAT," p 210.

TELEPHONES The country code for Scotland (like all of Great Britain) is **44.** The Edinburgh city code is **0131** (or just 131 if you're dialing from outside the country). Glasgow's city code is **0141.** To make international calls from Scotland, dial 00 and then the country code, local code, and telephone number. The U.S. and Canadian country code is **1,** Australia is **61,** and New Zealand is **63.** To make a collect call overseas, contact an international operator at ☎ **155.**

If you can't find a local number, directory assistance is available from various services (due to privatization), including ☎ **118-811** or ☎ **118-800** for domestic numbers and ☎ **118-505** for international numbers.

Scotland has pay phones that accept coins and credit cards, although the use of cellphones (called *mobiles*) means you see fewer pay phones. For information on cellphones in Scotland, see p 202.

TIME ZONE Scotland follows Greenwich Mean Time, which is five time zones ahead of Eastern Standard Time in the United States (8 hr. ahead of the Pacific Coast). So, when it's noon in New York, it's 5pm in Glasgow. The clocks are set forward by 1 hour for British *summer time* in late March, which expires at the end of October. The high latitude blesses the country with long days in the summer, with sunset as late as 10 or even 11pm. But the opposite is true in winter, when the sun sets as early as 3:30 or 4pm.

TIPPING Don't tip in bars or pubs. For sit-down meals, a 10% tip is standard; give more if the service is outstanding. A few restaurants automatically include a service charge, so check the bill. A reasonable range of gratuities for hotel services (from the maid to porters) is £1 to £5. For taxi drivers, round

the fare up to the nearest 50p or £1. Hairdressers should get 15%.

TOILETS Public toilets are not quite extinct, but the pattern across the country, in order for councils to save money, is their closure. In the cities, public toilets are usually manned and cost 20p. In country towns and villages they may not have any attendants. Generally speaking, the facilities are clean, but as with so many things, vandalism is not uncommon. Generally, all visitor information centers and tourist attractions have free restrooms.

TOURIST OFFICES In Edinburgh, the **Information Centre** is on Princes Street atop the Princes Mall near Waverley Station (☎ **0131/473-3800** or ☎ **0845/225-5121;** www.edinburgh.org). It can give you sightseeing information and also arrange lodgings. The center sells bus tours, theater tickets, and souvenirs of Edinburgh. It also has racks and racks of free brochures. It's open year-round, and hours vary from month to month. In summer you'll find the office open Monday through Saturday from 9am to 7pm and Sunday from 10am to 7pm.

In Glasgow, the **Greater Glasgow and Clyde Valley Tourist Board** (☎ **0141/204-4400;** www.see glasgow.com) is at 11 George Sq. in the heart of the city. In addition to piles of brochures, there are a small book shop, *bureau de change,* and hotel reservation service. During peak season it is open Monday to Saturday from 9am to 7pm and Sunday from 10am to 6pm. Hours are more limited during winter months.

See individual regional tours for information about tourist information offices in the countryside. Some of them are only open seasonally.

TOURS **CIE Tours International** (☎ 800/243-8687; www.cietours.com) offers escorted trips around Scotland and into the Highlands. Expect to pay around £440 per person for a 6-day tour (which includes accommodations but not all meals). If time is tight, a better option might be **Scottish Tours** (☎ 0131/557-8008; www. scottishtours.co.uk). It does minitours in air-conditioned buses departing from Edinburgh. Per-person rates start at around £30 for 1-day trips and go up to £225 for 2 nights (including breakfast and accommodation).

TRAVELERS WITH DISABILITIES Many Scottish hotels, museums, restaurants, and sightseeing attractions have wheelchair ramps and toilets that are accessible. Recent changes in Scottish law have also put the onus on all new premises to have wheelchair accessibility. At historical sites, however, and in older buildings, access can be limited. Also, not all public transport is accessible for travelers with disabilities.

For assistance and advice, contact **Capability Scotland** (☎ 0131/ 313-5510; www. capability-scotland. org.uk).

VAT A consumption tax of 17.5% is assessed on pretty much all goods and services. It's called the VAT (value-added tax), and it is calculated like local sales taxes are in the United States, although it is always included in the sticker price. Non-EU tourists are entitled to a refund, which may be significant on large buys. When you make your purchase at a participating retailer (look for signs saying TAX FREE SHOPPING), show your passport and ask for a tax refund form. Fill out the form and keep any receipts. When you leave the U.K., submit the form to Customs for approval.

Once Customs has stamped it, there are various ways to recover the tax. You can mail the form back to the shop and arrange repayment by mail. Some shops are part of networks run by commercial refund companies, whom you later contact for a refund, although an administration fee may be charged. *Note:* If you are going on to another E.U. country, the scheme doesn't work; you must be leaving the E.U. zone.

VAT is nonrefundable for services such as hotels, meals, and car rentals.

WEATHER For weather forecasts and severe weather warnings, contact the Met Office (☎ **0870/ 900-0100;** www.metoffice.gov.uk).

A Brief **History**

6000 B.C. Earliest known residents of Scotland establish settlements on the Argyll peninsulas.

3000 B.C. First Celtic tribes invade, making the use of Gaelic widespread.

90 A.D. Romans abandon any hope of conquering Scotland, retreating to England, behind the relative safety of Hadrian's Wall.

400–600 Celtic "Scots" from Ireland introduce Christianity; the Dalriadic kingdom in Western Scotland begins.

563 St. Columba establishes a mission on Iona.

1100s King David I's rule establishes royal burghs and abbeys, consolidating royal power and importing Norman values.

1270 Birth of William Wallace, key patriot in deflecting the forces of Edward I of England, who wishes to conquer Scotland.

1295 The "Auld Alliance" between Scotland and France begins.

1306–28 King Robert the Bruce leads an open rebellion against England, which is forced to recognize Scotland's sovereignty at the Treaty of Northampton.

1413 University of St. Andrews founded.

1424 James I is crowned, starting the royal Stuart line in Scotland.

1560–80s The Reformation establishes a new national religion and the Catholic Mary Queen of Scots is executed in 1587 on orders of her cousin, Queen Elizabeth I of England.

1603 Mary's son, King James VI of Scotland, also accedes to the throne of England as James I, unifying the crowns.

1707 The political and economic union of England and Scotland occurs; the Scottish Parliament is dissolved.

1745 Bonnie Prince Charlie leads a Jacobite rebellion, ending in defeat at the Battle of Culloden (1746).

1750–1850 The Scottish Enlightenment and rapid industrialization transform urban Scotland, while the Clearances strip many of their farms, fomenting bitterness.

LATE 1800s Astonishing success in the sciences propels Scotland into the role of international arbiter of industrial know-how.

MID-1900s The decline of traditional industries (especially shipbuilding) intensifies—redefining the Scottish economy.

1970 The discovery of oil and natural gas in the North Sea brings new vitality to Scotland.

1973 Scotland, as part of the United Kingdom, becomes part of the Common Market.

1997 Scotland passes a referendum to form a new Parliament and create greater self-rule.

1999 Elections for the first Scottish Parliament in almost 300 years are held.

2004 The expensive and much delayed new Parliament building opens in Edinburgh.

2007 The Scottish Nationalist Party, which favors complete independence from England, forms its first government in Scotland.

Useful Phrases

Yes, English is spoken in Scotland, but between the local expressions, heavy accents, and thick burr (trilling of the letter "r"), it can occasionally sound like a foreign language. Don't worry; at times even Scots from one region don't know what someone from another area is saying. Here is a glossary of some more common words and expressions.

auld	old
aye	yes
bonnie	pretty
boot	car trunk
burn	creek
cairn	stone landmark
ceilidh	social dance

cheers	thanks
dinnae	don't or didn't
dram	a shot of liquor
glen	valley
hen	woman
howff	meeting place or pub
ken	know or known
kipper	smoked herring
kirk	church
lad	boy
lassie	girl
lift	elevator
loch	freshwater lake or large sea inlet
pavement	sidewalk
petrol	gasoline
messages	groceries or the shopping
neep	turnip
quid	pound sterling
stramash	disturbance
stushie	fuss
take-away	to-go
tattie	potato
till	cash register
tins	canned goods
torch	flashlight
wee	little

Toll-Free Numbers & Websites

Airlines

AMERICAN AIRLINES
☎ *800/433-7300 (in U.S. and Canada)*
☎ *020/7365-0777 (in U.K.)*
www.aa.com

BMI BABY
☎ *087/1224-0224 (in U.K.)*
☎ *870/126-6726 (in U.S.)*
www.bmibaby.com

BRITISH AIRWAYS
☎ *800/247-9297 (in U.S. and Canada)*
☎ *087/0850-9850 (in U.K.)*
www.british-airways.com

CONTINENTAL AIRLINES
☎ *800/523-3273 (in U.S. and Canada)*
☎ *084/5607-6760 (in U.K.)*
www.continental.com

DELTA AIR LINES
☎ *800/221-1212 (in U.S. and Canada)*
☎ *084/5600-0950 (in U.K.)*
www.delta.com

EASYJET
☎ *870/600-0000 (in U.S.)*
☎ *090/5560-7777 (in U.K.)*
www.easyjet.com

NORTHWEST AIRLINES
☎ *800/225-2525 (in U.S.)*
☎ *870/0507-4074 (in U.K.)*
www.flynaa.com

UNITED AIRLINES
☎ *800/864-8331 (in U.S. and Canada)*
☎ *084/5844-4777 (in U.K.)*
www.united.com

VIRGIN ATLANTIC AIRWAYS
☎ *800/821-5438 (in U.S. and Canada)*
☎ *087/0574-7747 (in U.K.)*
www.virgin-atlantic.com

Car-Rental Agencies

ALAMO
☎ *800/GO-ALAMO (800/462-5266)*
www.alamo.com

AUTO EUROPE
📞 *888/223-5555 (in U.S. and Canada)*
📞 *0800/2235-5555 (in U.K.)*
www.autoeurope.com

AVIS
📞 *800/331-1212 (in U.S. and Canada)*
📞 *084/4581-8181 (in U.K.)*
www.avis.com

BUDGET
📞 *800/527-0700 (in U.S.)*
📞 *087/0156-5656 (in U.K.)*
📞 *800/268-8900 (in Canada)*
www.budget.com

DOLLAR
📞 *800/800-4000 (in U.S.)*
📞 *800/848-8268 (in Canada)*
📞 *080/8234-7524 (in U.K.)*
www.dollar.com

ENTERPRISE
📞 *800/261-7331 (in U.S.)*
📞 *514/355-4028 (in Canada)*
📞 *012/9360-9090 (in U.K.)*
www.enterprise.com

HERTZ
📞 *800/645-3131*
📞 *800/654-3001 (for international reservations)*
www.hertz.com

NATIONAL
📞 *800/CAR-RENT (800/227-7368)*
www.nationalcar.com

PAYLESS
📞 *800/PAYLESS (800/729-5377)*
www.paylesscarrental.com

THRIFTY
📞 *800/367-2277*
📞 *918/669-2168 (international)*
www.thrifty.com

Major Hotel & Motel Chains

BEST WESTERN INTERNATIONAL
📞 *800/780-7234 (in U.S. and Canada)*
📞 *0800/393-130 (in U.K.)*
www.bestwestern.com

COMFORT INNS
📞 *800/228-5150*
📞 *0800/444-444 (in U.K.)*
www. ChoiceHotels.com

CROWNE PLAZA HOTELS
📞 *888/303-1746*
www.ichotelsgroup.com/crowneplaza

DAYS INN
📞 *800/329-7466 (in U.S.)*
📞 *0800/280-400 (in U.K.)*
www.daysinn.com

HILTON HOTELS
📞 *800/HILTONS (800/445-8667 in U.S. and Canada)*
📞 *087/0590-9090 (in U.K.)*
www.hilton.com

HOLIDAY INN
📞 *800/315-2621 (in U.S. and Canada)*
📞 *0800/405-060 (in U.K.)*
www.holidayinn.com

HYATT
📞 *888/591-1234 (in U.S. and Canada)*
📞 *084/5888-1234 (in U.K.)*
www.hyatt.com

INTERCONTINENTAL HOTELS & RESORTS
📞 *800/424-6835 (in U.S. and Canada)*
📞 *0800/1800-1800 (in U.K.)*
www.ichotelsgroup.com

MARRIOTT
📞 *877/236-2427 (in U.S. and Canada)*
📞 *0800/221-222 (in U.K.)*
www.marriott.com

QUALITY
📞 *877/424-6423 (in U.S. and Canada)*
📞 *0800/444-444 (in U.K.)*
www.QualityInn.ChoiceHotels.com

RADISSON HOTELS & RESORTS
📞 *888/201-1718 (in U.S. and Canada)*
📞 *0800/374-411 (in U.K.)*
www.radisson.com

RAMADA WORLDWIDE
📞 *888/2-RAMADA (888/272-6232 in U.S. and Canada)*
📞 *080/8100-0783 (in U.K.)*
www.ramada.com

SHERATON HOTELS & RESORTS
📞 *800/325-3535 (in U.S.)*
📞 *800/543-4300 (in Canada)*
📞 *0800/3253-5353 (in U.K.)*
www.starwoodhotels.com/sheraton

THISTLE HOTELS
📞 *0870/333-9292*
www.thistlehotels.com

WESTIN HOTELS & RESORTS
📞 *800/937-8461 (in U.S. and Canada)*
📞 *0800/3259-5959 (in U.K.)*
www.starwoodhotels.com/westin

Index

Photo **Credits**

p viii: © David Robertson; p 4, bottom: © Jonathan Smith; p 5, top: © David Robertson/Digital Railroad; p 5, bottom: © Scottish Viewpoint; p 6, top: © Jonathan Smith; p 6, bottom: © Jonathan Smith; p 7: © Neil Setchfield; p 9, top: © Ed O'Keefe; p 10, top: © Neil Setchfield; p 10, bottom: © Jonathan Smith; p 11, bottom: © Neil Setchfield; p 13, bottom: Royal Collection © 2008, Her Majesty Queen Elizabeth II; p 14, top: © Adam Elder/Scottish Parliament; p 14, bottom: © Dynamic Earth; p 15, top: © Scottish Viewpoint; p 18, top: © Neil Setchfield; p 18, bottom: © Wojtek Buss—www.agefotostock.com; p 19, top: © Scottish Viewpoint; p 19, bottom: © Neil Setchfield; p 20, top: © Scottish Viewpoint; p 21: Courtesy John Freeman/Royal Collection © 2008, Her Majesty Queen Elizabeth II; p 23, top: © www.undiscoveredscotland.co.uk; p 23, bottom: © Angus Bremner 2003/National Trust for Scotland; p 24, top: © Jonathan Smith; p 24, bottom: © Jonathan Smith; p 25, top: © Neil Setchfield; p 27, top: © Erich Lessing/Art Resource, NY; p 27, bottom: © Fruitmarket Gallery; p 28, top: © Neil Setchfield; p 28, bottom: © Iain Masterton/Alamy; p 30, top: © Ruth Clark ; p 30, bottom: © Iain Masterton/Alamy; p 31, top: © Neil Setchfield; p 31, bottom: © Neil Setchfield; p 32, top: © Neil Setchfield; p 33: © Jones Huw/SIME/eStock Photo; p 35, top: © Jonathan Smith; p 35, bottom: © Neil Setchfield; p 36, top: © www.undiscoveredscotland.co.uk; p 37, top: © Chad Ehlers/Digital Railroad; p 37, bottom: © Neil Setchfield; p 39, top: © www.undiscoveredscotland.co.uk; p 40, top: © Neil Setchfield; p 41, top: © Jonathan Smith; p 41, bottom: © Doug Houghton; p 43, top: © Neil Setchfield; p 43, bottom: © Scottish Viewpoint; p 44, bottom: © The Vaults; p 45: © Neil Setchfield; p 48, bottom: © Neil Setchfield; p 49, top: © Neil Setchfield; p 49, bottom: © Neil Setchfield; p 50, top: © Neil Setchfield; p 51, top: © Scottish Viewpoint; p 51, bottom: © Neil Setchfield; p 52, bottom: © Neil Setchfield; p 53, top: © Neil Setchfield; p 53, bottom: © Sandy Young/Alamy; p 54, top: © Neil Setchfield; p 54, bottom: © Jonathan Smith; p 55: © Jonathan Smith; p 57, top: © David Robertson; p 57, bottom: © Neil Setchfield; p 58, bottom: © Jonathan Smith; p 59, top: © Jonathan Smith; p 61, bottom: © Scottish Viewpoint/Alamy; p 62, top: © Scottish Viewpoint; p 62, bottom: © Keith Hunter/Arcaid/Corbis; p 63: © Jonathan Smith/Lonely Planet Images; p 67, bottom: © Neil Setchfield; p 68, top: © Atrium; p 68, bottom: © Blue Bar; p 69, bottom: © Café Royal; p 70, top: © Scottish Viewpoint; p 70, bottom: © Neil Setchfield; p 71, bottom: © Neil Setchfield; p 72, bottom: © Rough Guides/Alamy; p 72, bottom: © Neil Setchfield; p 73, top: © Neil Setchfield; p 73, bottom: © Scottish Viewpoint; p 74, bottom: © Neil Setchfield; p 75: © Neil Setchfield; p 79, bottom: © Neil Setchfield; p 80, top: © Neil Setchfield; p 80, bottom: © www.undiscoveredscotland.co.uk; p 81, top: © Neil Setchfield; p 81, bottom: © www.undiscoveredscotland. co.uk; p 82, top: © Will Slater/Lonely Planet Images; p 83, bottom: © Neil Setchfield; p 84, bottom: © Trashed Management/eyevine; p 85: © Robbie Jack/Corbis; p 88, bottom: Courtesy The Stand, Edinburgh ; p 89, top: © Scottish Viewpoint; p 90, top: © Scottish Viewpoint; p 90, bottom: © Neil Setchfield; p 91, bottom: © Colin McPherson/drr.net; p 92, bottom: © Edinburgh Military Tattoo; p 93: © Neil Setchfield; p 98, bottom: © The Bonham, Edinburgh; p 99, top: © Neil Setchfield; p 100, top: © Neil Setchfield;